THIS WORK IS MOST RESPECTFULLY DEDICATED
TO SPORT LOVERS THE WORLD OVER, AND ALL
LOVERS OF CLEAN HONEST SPORTS AND PAS-
TIMES FOR BOTH THE OLD AND THE YOUNG,
WHOM SIR THOMAS J. LIPTON, LOVED TO
THE LAST, AND BY WHOM HE WAS
BELOVED.

To make the reading of this work easier and more understandable, the author found it necessary to insert several of the many letters received among the first pages of the book.

THE
LIFE AND TIMES

OF THE LATE

SIR THOMAS J. LIPTON

FROM THE CRADLE TO THE GRAVE

International Sportsman and Dean of the Yachting World

BY

CAPTAIN JOHN J. HICKEY

OFFICER "787"

1932

THE HICKEY PUBLISHING COMPANY

NEW YORK

Printing Statement:

Due to the very old age and scarcity of this book,
many of the pages may be hard to read due to the
blurring of the original text, possible missing pages,
missing text and other issues beyond our control.

Because this is such an important and rare work, we
believe it is best to reproduce this book regardless of
its original condition.

Thank you for your understanding.

CONTENTS

CONTENTS

FOREWORD

The writer of this work, a personal friend of Sir Thomas Lipton for more than thirty years, one that was always the first to greet this grand old dean of the yachting world and the last to say goodbye, year after year, in all of that time.

Dear friends and readers, it is my purpose in compiling this work from the lips and most cherished possessions of our late great friend, the world's greatest sportsman and friend, who loaned me his memorandums to copy from, as most of my writing is from the very lips of this great man. Peace be to him.

Sir Thomas said that he was glad to help me in any way in this tremendous work, and when leaving our shores Sir Thomas called upon me to have our photograph taken together, for the new book, on the deck of the steamer before sailing, and I have produced same in this book, as per promise.

This work is going to be the real truth, and I care not whose feelings I may hurt, I am writing my book to the lasting and fond loving memory of a dear good friend. Who could do more?

I am going to speak my mind on certain things, and every word of same will be gospel truth, as it will be before my God in Heaven at some time sooner or later—we know not the hour or place and it behooves us all to be ready for the bugle call, for there will not be any postponements allowed, but stand your ground.

For me, I have no regrets, when my time comes, if I am prepared, and I try hard to be, for the villainy of the people of the present day I mortally detest, and I am going to write as I feel, and that will be very distasteful to many of my former so-called friends, no doubt.

I feel from the bottom of my heart that Sir Thomas' death was hastened, and brought about by his trusted ones, whom he relied on to keep him rightly informed of all that he was concerned in, and I will, to the best of my ability, quote from some of the many letters received and the expert writings of our great newspaper men, and have you, with all my heart, be the sole judges of these facts, or, as I believe them to be, for if I am wrong, then I ask God to forgive me.

Respectfully,

JOHN J. HICKEY, *Author.*

"THE KING IS DEAD, LONG LIVE THE KING"

PART I—CHAPTER I

The hearts of the world were deeply affected when on September 29th, 1931, the sad news was flashed across the ocean, that the sands of life, were fast ebbing, and the last moments on earth was, so soon to follow.

For our grand old friend and famous sportsman and world traveler passed away, October 2nd, 1931, three days later, and this in spite of the fact that I, the writer, was in receipt of a letter from John Westwood, Secretary to Sir Thomas, stating that they were to leave for New York, on board the American "Queen" of the ocean, the Leviathan, commanded by his old friend and fellow sportsman, Commodore Harold Cunningham, whom Sir Thomas loved to travel with both going and coming to and from New York yearly.

The letter spoken of, with others of this same nature, you will read on the next page or pages, for I am publishing a copy of more than one hundred letters received by the writer, for I want my friends to read them so that you might read them over to your satisfaction, and pass upon them all for you are to be the judge, I am simply the Barrister presenting to you all of the evidence obtained, and many strange things that have happened, in the last ten years, since this grand old sportsman commenced to lose his sight and hearing, and the many inferences presented to this jury.

It was given out supposedly by the four doctors attending Sir Thomas, at "Osidge," his beautiful London home, that Sir Thomas died of chills, and this I don't believe, for if Sir Thomas was sick on September 29th, then he was not in a fit condition to sail the ocean blue on the day of his death, October 2nd, 1931, and again if Sir Thomas was then sick, one would think in all proper decency, that John Westwood would have mentioned something of it in this same letter to look out for them on the pier in New York October 9th, 1931, oh yes, there is something wrong there, that needs much explaining.

And to think of it, this grand old man that always loved plenty of company should be forced to die alone, not even his boyhood chum whom he thought the world of, and confided in all through life and no doubt he dearly wanted to see and speak with Sir Harry Lauder, but even this was denied him, and he passed onward and upward, but not of chills, but of a broken heart, that had been brought about by the members of the Invisible government that had been introduced to govern the Sir Thomas Lipton Corporation.

Yes, and I will swear before God that many things had been done that was not intended to aid and assist Sir Thomas, and his great industries, that is why I am asking Mr. John Westwood, Chairman of this ungodly invisible committee, to please explain. Will he?

The idea, to think of it, that a man of his, Sir Thomas', character so fond of pleasure, with his world-renowned charming personality, honesty and love of fair play, and charity, should die alone, and of a broken heart, I am, as were all that knew Sir Thomas Lipton, deeply amazed for those responsible have no excuse, to offer whatever.

I regret very much my not availing myself of the request of Sir Thomas to come over to Osidge and live with him, and keep his company for all time for he would then be kept informed of the activities, and the health of his many American friends.

Those were about the last words spoken of to me, in the presence of John Westwood, in Room 618 of the Hotel Biltmore, just as he was leaving for the steamer to take him back home to London, after having received the loving Cup, in 1930.

But alas, that request could not be complied with, for in the first place I knew that John Westwood, and his invisible committee did not want me near Sir Thomas, and I might be given another pill as I was in 1928.

Secondly, I could not think of separating myself from my family and my many goods friends that it has taken more than fifty years to make, but I did say, Sir Thomas, I will run over to London to see you, but under no conditions will I be your guest again in Osidge.

Sir Thomas asked me why, but what was the use in adding more worry on our dear old friend. I told him that I loved to live in the bright lights of New York or London, but not in the country of either place unless on vacation in the good old summertime.

"OSIDGE, SOUTHGATE, MIDDLESEX, LONDON, E. C.

"Mr. J. J. Hickey,   "17th September, 1931.
"Hotel Elton,
"365 Fourth Avenue,
"New York City.
"Dear Mr. Hickey:

"Very many thanks for your kind letter of the 8th inst., with interesting enclosures, all of which I am going to mail to Sir Thomas, whom I am sure will be very much pleased.

"I am glad to report that the Chief is getting along well, and so, too, is Mr. Westwood, and that's a pleasure, to me at least.

"They both want to be remembered to you, and they ask that you excuse them, so much business with yacht racing every day, they cannot do justice to you, but will explain all when next we meet, and it won't be long, now.

"I am also glad to say that my thumb is healing up good, and I can get around much better to my own and everyone here's satisfaction, I guess and calculate, as the Yankee says.

"Yes, Mr. Hickey, Sir Thomas is as fine as a fiddle, and working just as hard as ever, but he looks forward to the sea trip over to your side to fit him up again.

"Hoping this will find you well and happy, and with all good wishes. I am,
"Yours sincerely,
"H. C. WAGHORN, *Assistant Secretary.*"

"OSIDGE, SOUTHGATE, MIDDLESEX, LONDON, E. C.

"29th September, 1931.

"Mr. J. J. Hickey,
"Hotel Elton, 4th Avenue,
"New York City.
"Dear Mr. Hickey:
"Very many thanks for yours of the 16th inst., with the enclosed cuttings, which I have read with great pleasure and much interest.

"I am hoping to be on your side before many days elapse. This is strictly private, but you had better look for any stray passengers on the Leviathan arriving about October 9, next, 1931.

"Looking forward to the pleasure of meeting you again soon and with all kind wishes.

"Yours sincerely,
"JOHN WESTWOOD, *Secretary*."

Dear Readers, I would advise that you put on your thinking cap after reading these letters, and ask yourself the question, was Sir Thomas, at the time ill abed with four doctors attending him in Osidge, or were the newspapers publishing false reports, about his dying with chills?

If Sir Thomas was confined to his bed September 29th, 1931, then he could not be in a fit condition to sail for New York on October 2nd, 1931. There lies the mystery, for if Sir Thomas was ill abed, Westwood would have told me of it in his letter to me of September 29th, 1931.

No doubt, you, my readers, agree with me, that there was something strange and mysterious about these two letters, that is that of Mr. Waghorn, of September 17th, and that of Mr. Westwood, dated London, September 29th, 1931, sent to me with not a word in either of them about the illness of Sir Thomas.

Here we wake up with the papers of every known and unknown country printing in large headlines the following, Sir Thomas Lipton dying from the chill contracted by him two weeks ago, with four doctors in attendance but they see no hope, this was on or about the time that John Westwood had written to me to say, we leave for New York on Saturday, October 2nd, look for us in New York on the 9th of October, 1931. It seems to me that there was a monkey in the woodpile somewhere.

I hold the principal or original letters but will publish a copy of each for your information and guidance, for as stated before, you are the judges, I am simply the Attorney presenting my case. You are welcome to look over the original letters of both Sir Thomas, and his secretaries when at any time that you will drop me a line at the Hotel Grand Union, 34 E. 32nd Street, New York City, or any other matter that is printed in this book.

It is mighty hard to believe that such a world-wide popular man like Sir Thomas Lipton, would be allowed to die alone, with his many thousands of kind loving friends, and his secretaries, and if we must believe it, four highly paid physicians, that could not find time to send for the only real friend that Sir Thomas had in this world, Sir Harry Lauder. No, even this, his last request, was denied him.

Heavenly Father, how happy I would be if Sir Thomas had married and no doubt raised a family, or even if he had died in New York, the city that he loved so well, he would not die alone, no Sir, with a kind loving wife and sons and daughters, or his thousands of friends, would have cheered the poor old man's last moments, and send him on his way happy.

The more I think of this sad case, the more I am convinced that there was something wrong, for if the facts were as stated, as I believe they were, and that is that Sir Thomas died of a broken heart, thinking of his coming back to New York, to mingle with his friends, knowing that he was treated in a shameful manner, in September of 1930, but by persons at present unknown

Why, if this grand old Gentleman was the least bit sick, nothing in God's world would keep Duncan Neill, Doctor Goodheart, or Colonel Arthur Lynch and wife, from his bedside, and it goes without saying Sir Harry Lauder, who at the time, was resting up in Scotland, would be present to cheer him on his long, long route.

"Faithful until death." It is given out that the grand old Chieftain in his last moments willed that the Loving Cup, that was presented to him by his good friend, Mayor James J. Walker, bought by popular subscriptions of his American friends, should be returned to New York.

Why, I don't think that the poor man had a chance to will this cup or anything else to New York, or any where else, not that he would not will the cup to his American friends, but no, he did not, for God called him to him taking him away from the grafters of this sad world, and that is all there was to it, to the contrary notwithstanding. Sudden death, that's my verdict.

You have been taken from us Sir Thomas, whatever the cause, or by whom responsible, but your memory will always be kept green, and if necessary and God spares me, your untimely end will be avenged, sooner or later, and may you forever rest in peace, while these vagabonds will live to sup sorrow.

FAREWELL DEAR FRIEND, FAREWELL.

"OSIDGE, SOUTHGATE, LONDON
"July 19th, 1931.
"Mr. John J. Hickey,
"Hotel Elton, New York City.
"Dear Mr. Hickey:
"Your very kind letter of the 28th ultimo is to hand with enclosures, that I am very glad to receive, and for which I thank you very much for your kind thoughts of me at all times.
"I am just about to rejoin the Erin on her way for another long race and I am going to take the earliest opportunity to read all that spicy news that you were kind enough to send me from time to time, it is so encouraging and

AMERICA'S ANGEL OF MERCY

HON. FRANKLIN D. ROOSEVELT
President of these United States

Promoter and Founder of the Woodrow Wilson Foundation and Famous
Yachtsman. Get Behind Him, Brothers, without delay, and give Three Rousing
Cheers for the N. R. A.

METROPOLITAN
432 FOURTH AVENUE NEW YORK

Office of
Theodore Roosevelt

December 27th, 1917.

My dear Brother Hickey:

Three cheers for you and yours •
sons! I am so pressed for time I can only send you
this line of acknowledgment.

Faithfully yours,

Theodore Roosevelt

Mr. J. J. Hickey,
243 East 19th Street, City.

HERBERT H. LEHMAN
ALBANY-NEW YORK

November 18, 1932.

My dear Mr. Hickey:

I want to thank you sincerely
for your good wishes, and to tell you how deeply
I appreciate them.

Kindest personal regards.

Sincerely,

Herbert H Lehman

Mr. John J. Hickey,
Grand Union Hotel,
34-36 East 32nd Street,
New York City.

embracing, to hear the goods news of my friends and the grand old U. S. A. and I appreciate your every thought of me at all times.

"No words of mine can thank you for your many letters that helps make my life one of happiness and contentment, far better than the doctors, so that I have much to thank you for, and your friendship for me and your many fine letters to me makes you a good humanitarian always doing something for humanity and friends whom you never forget.

"I earnestly hope that this will find you well and fit, and in the very best of good health for, after all, what is a man's wealth when he has not the good health to attend to his duties? attending the wants of the poor and disabled, both at home and abroad, that I love so dearly to benefit.

"I earnestly hope and trust that this will find you well and in the full enjoyment of both good health and happiness, and with kindest remembrances, believe me to be, as ever,

"Yours sincerely,   "THOMAS J. LIPTON."

This is the last letter received by me from my good friend, and like the story of the Prince of Wales, in Alberta, "The last match" a poem and a midsummer nights dream, of good times and old friends.

After the passing away of Sir Thomas, I thought it timely to ask this gentleman, John Westwood, a few questions, among them was the question of what had become of the Liberty bonds that I sent, and gave to my dear old friend Sir Thomas in war time of June, 1918, and May 10th, his birthday of 1919.

Knowing full well that our own country needed money, and it would help a lot in the publishing of my books, knowing that the good old Chief did not need any souvenirs in his beautiful home on high, and that these gifts should be sent back to the giver of same.

I recall having written Mr. Westwood that the third Liberty loan bonds were to be called in, and that he should put the third Liberty loan bond through Sir Thomas's bank, so it would find its way to Washington.

But to this he made no reply, which makes me think that he had put the $50 bond through in his own name, and had forgotten the transaction.

But this he should not do, for the bonds were the property of Sir Thomas Lipton, and not that of John Westwood, his secretary, he should at least have made a memorandum of the transaction, and if not, than why not?

You will find his answers to my letters here inclosed, and my answer to same sent him forthwith, with a copy of the letter of thanks that I received from Sir Thomas, June 20th, 1918, that explains itself, but the mystery of which needs explaining.

"THE SIR THOMAS J. LIPTON TRUST

"70 CORNHILL, LONDON, E. C.
"10th February, 1932.

"Dear Mr. Hickey:

"Once more I have to acknowledge receipt of your very kind letter, enclosing some very important cuttings, which I am looking forward to read when I get a little time to myself.

"With regard to the Liberty bonds you wrote about, we have so far been unable to locate them. I have written Mr. Field, at Hoboken to inquire what he may know about them, and if they come to light, I shall be glad to communicate with you again.

"I hope you are keeping well and with kind remembrances,

"Yours sincerely,

"JOHN WESTWOOD."

"Mr. J. J. Hickey, Hotel Elton,
"4th Avenue, New York City."

This is the very last letter received from John Westwood, after twenty years of constant communication. Why?

To set the mind of Mr. Westwood at rest and to keep him from worrying I mailed to him forthwith a copy of the letter of thanks that I received from, and signed by, Sir Thomas Lipton, June 20th, 1918. To wit:

"CITY ROAD, LONDON, E. C.
"June 20th, 1918.

"Dear Mr. Hickey:

"Very many thanks for your kind letter of the 24th ultimo enclosing the souvenir $50 War Bond and this I am very glad indeed to have. It is more than kind of you to think of me in this way and I can assure you that I very highly appreciate your kindness.

"I shall treasure the bond as a memento, first of all for your own good self, and also of that most important event in the history of the world—the union of the 'Stars and Stripes' and the Union Jack, in the great cause for which we are now fighting.

"Again let me thank you for your kind thought, and looking forward to the pleasure of meeting you and thanking you personally. I am with kind regards, and best wishes,

"Yours faithfully,

"THOMAS J. LIPTON.

"Mr. John J. Hickey,
"23 Duane Street, New York."

I hope that I have fully explained to your entire satisfaction the story of those two War Bonds, and the mystery surrounding them needs more explanation, but from John Westwood, not the writer.

But, I have always felt that if Sir Thomas, were given these War Bonds his first order would be: Mr. Westwood, send Mr. Hickey two British bonds right away as souvenirs, please.

It is mighty hard when old age comes upon us and we are forced to give up the business that you started and turn it over to one of those easy money getters of secretaries, but infirmities will come, in spite of all we may do, and pains and aches do not harmonize with business.

I recall that when Sir Thomas and his party were leaving for home May 1927, and I not hearing of any farewell being prepared for him, I took it upon myself to write His Honor, Mayor James J. Walker, in the matter, and received the following reply-to-wit—

P.S.—For want of space I am forced to utilize every inch of room, editor. Little did we know at this time that Mayor Walker would lose his job, and be in exile, forced out of office in 1932, and that fighting Irishman John Curry, ousted out of his leadership by the executive committee of the Democratic party, votes for 14 1/3 to 10 1/6. His friends and foes, gave him every chance to resign, but no, he would not quit.

"CITY OF NEW YORK, OFFICE OF THE MAYOR
"May 11th, 1927.

"Mr. John J. Hickey,
"Hotel Elton, 4th Avenue, New York City.
"Dear Sir:
"Mayor Walker is in receipt of your letter of May 10th and has directed me to advise you that arrangements have already been made for Sir Thomas Lipton's reception at the City Hall.
"The Mayor has directed me to assure you, however, of his appreciation for your interest in this connection.
"Very truly yours,
"EDWARD L. STANTON, *Secretary to the Mayor.*"

While stopping with Sir Thomas Lipton, at Osidge June, 1928, one day at luncheon with Sir Thomas and a party of friends, Sir Thomas asked me if it was true that I wrote to Mayor Walker about his leaving for home.

I answered, "Why, yes, Sir Thomas," taking the Mayor's letter from my pocket and handed it to the grand old Chieftain, and having read same he passed it around among the party present, and having read same, they were all pleased, each of them having some complimentary remarks to make of the matter.

Sir Thomas smiled and said I thank you, Mr. Hickey, you are always looking after my interests, not only in this case, but many others in the past and I appreciate your kindness very much, and all present drank to the health of Mayor James J. Walker, and the good old city of New York.

I thought it my duty to a good friend, and as a matter of fact, I never yet let an opportunity of that nature pass, for in the matter of a grievance of this nature, I deemed it my duty to write to the fountain head of the particular department, notifying him of the same.

We are all human, and subject to forgetfulness, and I have never known it to fail that these leaders or heads of departments, were very glad to right a wrong, if needed, and to thank any citizen, having the temerity to write him in the matter, none more so than was Mayor Walker.

It is a well known fact that we have had distinguished visitors coming here year after year willing to take anything they could get for nothing back home with them, but here was the case of good old Tom Lipton, coming to our shores often twice a year, each time bringing both his wealth and good cheer with his grand old stories to his thousands of good American friends.

No, sir, to my mind I was simply doing my duty, personally for more than thirty long years, I have been the first to meet Sir Thomas on his landing and last to say "Goodbye, Sir Thomas, come back soon again," and I was in a position to know and understand many things that led me to write up this grand old sportsman's biography, for I studied the same very closely.

I recall a remark made by one of our great writers, to wit:

"Biography *per se* has never interested me. I like to know the results of men's lives rather than the details of how they lived. It has been said that you cannot understand a man's work unless you understand his life." This is well said, and to my mind words of wisdom. But I have given both sides of this subject my attention, and that enables me to write this story from every angle of his life and times, in fond and loving memory.

I was a devoted follower of Mayor Walker, and his dear old Dad, meeting them often in the past fifty odd years of my citizenship, and membership of the Democratic party, my heart bleeds for him today, or any other poor fool. I am quite sure that I am speaking the minds of all others who came to these shores to benefit by the helping hand held out to us all.

Under the banner of Thomas Jefferson, all men are equal, and your chances of prospering in America is up to yourselves, follow in the footsteps of men like Tom Lipton, always be honest in your dealings with mankind, and always remember that Christ died for us all, and must be honored and obeyed, and by our prayers obtain His assistance, for it is impossible to get along without it, never turn your back on God, and God will never turn His back on you, for to my mind, the un-Americans of today thought that they could get along without the assistance of God, and what is the result today, here we are suffering from depression, that is leading on to starvation.

I am proud to be called an American, and I offer up my prayers, not only for my dead, and my family living, but for the heathen, and the blind that would if they could destroy the country that gave them protection, and the bread that they eat, they are not worthy of. "Forgive them Father, they know not what they do."

And, in conclusion, let me advise my readers to honor and obey our leaders. God-given men like President Franklin D. Roosevelt, who is doing all in his power to bring prosperity back to this, our beloved country, and we must, all of us, jump upon the band-wagon and say "God bless America, we are ever ready to serve you, even to the giving up of our lives and our firesides."

I do not deny the fact that I liked Jimmy Walker, and I put up my money and gave up my time to help elect him Mayor, he being my party's choice, and this awful depression, stealing upon us like a burglar in the night, brought sadness and unemployment with it, and knowing how hard the Mayor and his Unemployment Committee were working to help these unfortunates, a mighty hard contract.

I have published the second edition of "OUR POLICE GUARD-IANS," and finding no encouragement for the poor book publisher, I wrote Mayor Walker and his Committee that I would employ ten men or more daily, they to go up through the office buildings with a card from the Committee, stating that all was well, and raise from one dollar to three for a copy of this book, I having sold the first edition for three dollars per copy they sure could sell them and make a good day's work out of their sales, for all that they would make was to be theirs, I wanted nothing out of the 500 books offered.

I received a letter of thanks from the Mayor and his Committee, who told me that they could not get a man to sell books, they wanted money only, and I made the same offer to the Prosser Committee with the same results, and thanks to my good friend, Michael J. Delehanty, of the Delehanty Institute of Civil Service learning, I myself personally went to the classes among the Rookie Policemen, many of them out of a job, and at their own price I sold the 1,000 books in three weeks, working late and early, and it is with their returns, that I am trying to place this book on the market, but alas, not a Chinaman's chance up to date. But God is good, and with President Roosevelt in the White House, killing off this horrid depression, God willing, I may yet succeed, for while there is life there is hope in the N.R.A.

God help the poor book writer, he is up against it, for it is no pleasure in compiling and writing a book, but it is a darn sight harder to get it before the public, and while I have undertaken this tremendous work of writing up the life of that great sportsman, and two other books, namely, "New York Day by Day" and the second edition of "Our Police Guardians," I will never give up the ship, in spite of oppression, or depression, and the dammed cowardly Communists. I am going to keep right on trying.

Those of us who have been personally acquainted with Sir Thomas for more than a quarter of a century, feel the sting very keenly, for we know that it will be mighty hard to replace this grand old man of sportsdom.

Sir Thomas Lipton's honesty and charming personality, and whole-souled sportsmanship and philanthropy will live through the ages, and his name goes down to posterity written in letters of gold.

He died as he lived at peace with the world, but Heavenly Father, it is mighty hard to believe that his, Sir Thomas's last request to send for Sir Harry Lauder, his boyhood chum, was denied him, and no one to come forward to explain why, but sooner or later they will have to explain themselves or have the thousands of friends of the grand old Duke know the reasons why.

When I recall the many pleasant evenings that I have spent chatting with our late lamented friend, both at his lovely home in "Osidge," London, and his suite at the Hotel Biltmore, New York City, owned by

another boyhood chum, the late John McEntee Bowman, who shortly after followed Sir Thomas to the grave, leaving behind him a charming
wife and two pretty children, among them young Jack McEntee Bowman.

And before moving to the Biltmore, he, Sir Thomas, stayed at the
Hotel Commodore and the grand old Waldorf-Astoria, that the 18th
Amendment to the Constitution, the prohibition law, put the skids
under, being forced to close her doors, leaving us alone to mourn
our loss.

You will notice later on in these chapters how John Westwood often
held me tied up either in the reception room, 618, or his own room, 614,
telling me that Sir Thomas was busy with friends, while as a matter of
fact, he would be sitting alone in his room, 222, praying that some
good old friend would stop in on him, and when he discovered that I
had been there several hours and had not gone into his room, he would
bawl me out, thinking that it was Mr. Westwood whom I was interested
in, for I could not tell my good old friend the real reason why I had
not called on him when first I arrived, and why? John Westwood
was always present, he seldom left us alone, that is why.

There was an invisible government organized by his employees, and
they were then functioning, and if John Westwood, the head mogul of
this invisible government, said you were not to see Sir Thomas, then
you would not be allowed to see or speak to him, unless by accident,
that he, when tiring of his room, would walk into the reception room,
618. No, sir, not even be allowed to pass the threshold of the reception
room, Room 618, and this same thing was also in force at the factory
in Hoboken, N. J., for often at the request of Sir Thomas, I would
journey across the Hudson, to visit that dear old gentleman, and find
myself up against a brick wall, and leave them to themselves, for any
old friend of Sir Thomas, like General George Washington when he
crossed the Delaware, was met by the English army in derision, and
no old New Yorker could so far disgrace himself to be held up by a
New Jersey fireman and his lookouts. Not at all, man, for I was a
peace- and not a fight-promoter, and respected my dear old friend,
Tom Lipton.

For the invisible government ordered that no person should be allowed to take the elevator before answering a thousand or more questions as to who you wished to see and why you wished to see him and
on what business and many other questions, for dear old Sir Thomas,
on reaching the eightieth milestone, lost many of his facilities; his
hearing and eyesight were getting worse every year, and the invisible
government knew this, and they had organized to profit by the same,
and did they? Well, God only knows at this time but just as sure as
there is a God in heaven, the story must and will be told and the guilty
made to suffer.

I often sit alone and picture to myself, Sir Thomas and myself riding over the moors of old Highgate hill, once the fighting ground of Dick Turpin, and his bonny Black Bess, who robbed the rich and gave it to the poor until the day that proved to be the last of Black Bess, and the arrest and conviction of the famous highwayman.

Arrested, tried and convicted of many crimes, including murder, he was sentenced to be hung on a Tyburn tree, at Hyde Park corner, a dreary old spot on which many devoted Catholics were hung, drawn and quartered, and otherwise butchered in the dark days of the Protestant Reformation, among them Sir Thomas More, and many other notables who had given up their young lives in the "Faith of Our Fathers," a spot that I often visited when stopping at "Osidge," the guest of Sir Thomas, after having visited Paris, France, a member of the American Legion, in 1927-1928, for I stayed one whole year visiting every country in Europe and the Near and Far East.

In Hyde Park corner, one visiting London will find a tablet commemorating those dreadful scenes of the 15th Century, the spot on which the Tyburn tree stood at the time of the Reformation, and if visiting Sir Thomas at Osidge, one would most likely take a bus, and they all pass through Hyde Park corner near the site of the old Duke of Wellington mansion, and the home of the Duke of York, second son of King George and Queen Mary, and his beautiful wife and children.

I speak of the Duke of York and his wife, for she is the most lovable woman that I met in all my long travels, always smiling and a kind word for all. I recall that after the funeral services over the remains of Sir Charles Russell in June, 1928, the well-known English barrister at law, at St. Patrick's Cathedral, on Ashley Place, Westminster, I attended a meeting at 10 Downing Street, the home of England's Prime Minister, and there I met the Duchess of York.

Sir Thomas and John Westwood were at this funeral, for Sir Thomas knew the father of this dead man, for Sir Charles Russell was one of England's greatest lawyers and, by the way, had charge of the affairs of Sir Thomas, and the Lipton, Limited. They were waiting for me to go to Osidge. I tried to beat that visit, but had to go.

We will return to the Highgate hill. But good-natured Tom Lipton was no highwayman, but a real Christian lover of the poor, and he gloried in being in a position to donate to the poor school children on their way home from Sunday school, gloves, stockings and other articles of wear to keep them warm all winter.

On his first trip out he would drive to certain street corners along the broad highway and there distribute wearing apparel, and on his second trip on other corners he would meet the children and give them boxes of candy to make them cheerful and happy.

I happened to be chosen for the first trip, and as Mr. Waghorn would open the many boxes of clothing, hand them to me, and I in turn hand them to Sir Thomas to distribute, a very cheerful episode happened that day that I will never forget, to wit:

In the midst of all the happiness and laughter there came a cry from the wilderness, as it were, and like a motor from a clear sky, up jumped one wee little noble English nipper, and he shouted from outside the crowd, "Hey, Tommy, give me a pair of gloves, size 10, will yer?" and everyone present laughed aloud, and Sir Thomas turned to me and said, "Did you hear that, Mr. Hickey?" I answered "yes, Sir Thomas," and to me it was very pleasing, for none but a brave little English lad would dare to make such a request.

All that afternoon he would repeat the story and even after dinner at billiards, with his old friend, Doctor Goodheart, and myself, Sir Thomas would again repeat the episode, and he would say, "Yes, it harkened my thoughts back to my boyhood days in Glasgow, when after school the boys would say, 'Come on, Tommy Lipton, and start the games.'

"How happy I was then, penniless, and how I often wish that I could once again be called plain Tom Lipton, for riches do not always bring happiness, but very often unhappiness, particularly when one is growing old and feeble and not able to attend to business."

On the afternoon of the episode, Sir Thomas had other guests, among them two beautiful young ladies from New York, a Miss Rankin and her friend and fellow traveler, a Miss Mayo. Miss Rankin, by the way, is the daughter of Mr. William A. Rankin, an advertiser with offices at 340 Madison Avenue and an old-time friend of Sir Thomas, and Sir Thomas took the two girls along on his second trip out to distribute the candy and they spoke of their experience for many days after.

And often in years later when we would be swapping stories in his room at the Biltmore, he, Sir Thomas, would invariably speak of that same old episode on that very cold Sunday afternoon along the moors of Highgate hill, for it always gave him much pleasure, and on up until the day of his death.

Sir Thomas did not forget his guests that day, for he gave the two young ladies two pairs of gloves, and myself also, and I have mine yet, and hope to keep them until death, for they were always keeping before me that picture of the long ago. I also recall that when in 1914, after the Shamrock IV sailed out of Portsmouth for America, and while the tender was taking us to the dock of the Royal Yacht Squadron, Sir Thomas gave to my friend, George Doherty, Justice of the Peace of Londonderry, Ireland, and myself two very fine ties, with Shamrock IV worked in, and I have mine to this day.

And now to think of it today, and Sir Thomas lying in the cold, cold clay, it is mighty hard to think of, among his old time friends.

THE BIRTH OF TOM LIPTON

Part I—Chapter II

Sir Thomas Johnstone Lipton first saw the light of day in a tumbled down old shack in the city of Glasgow, Scotland, May 10th, 1850.

The reason why Tom Lipton was born in Glasgow was that the hard times in the Emerald Isle drove Mr. and Mrs. Lipton, like thousands of their race, into exile.

"I got up with heart and hand, and sold my little plot of land
And bade farewell to Ireland, poor Pat must emigrate."

Yes, dear readers, those were the unhappy days in old Ireland, when one could not call his soul his own, and those of us living today, who still have recollections of those unhappy times, must and will say, "May the Lord have mercy on you, my Father, and Mother, dears, you certainly had your fill of trouble, forced to leave home and loved ones to read the signs before you of 'NO IRISH NEED APPLY.' " This was in England where my folks landed.

Mr. Lipton, the poor man, made no progress in Scotland, for things were very bad there and like England, her own people came first, and the father of our hero, young Tom Lipton, struggled along, picking up a few shillings here and there, praying to God to help them raise their lovely son.

But with all of their misfortune they were determined to give young Tom the best education they could, and Tom Lipton would go to school for, as a matter of fact, he liked school, and he was blessed with the opportunity of being regular, for even as a boy he was looking far ahead.

Fortunately for young Tom Lipton, he was born so polite and honest that he would be hired by the shopkeepers to run errands, and this aided him to hand over to his mother a few bob, or shillings weekly.

But young Tom Lipton was not at all pleased at this way of living. He wanted a steady job, one that was sure and dependable, so that he could help mama and dad, and do his little bit to bring happiness into his poor unhappy, unfurnished home, an eyesore to this brave lad, who was fast growing into manhood, and he determined to change his life by a steady job.

Tom Lipton was, to my mind, a born leader, for his schoolmates swore by him and every day after school they spent several hours at their games.

But it was no use, he had to go hunt up a job, forgetting his school and playmates for he must help Mother, and he would travel through the town often hungry and footsore, like many others of us poor exiles, going often to bed hungry, praying for better luck tomorrow.

My young days, like those of Tom Lipton, are so similar that I do not have to refer to my notes while writing his life's story, but mine was still more distressing for they come in later, and more brutal years, just when commerce was improving they passed laws to punish all stowaways, and in my case I was forced to hide under a sailor's bunk, with just enough room to get under and stay there until it was quiet, and then get out to change my position and while in that dreaded state, I was handed a panacin of chops and gravy with several sailor biscuits, but owing to my want of room I could not eat them, falling asleep exhausted, trying to nibble at a chop, dumping the whole lot over my clothes. Heavenly Father, when I think of those days I shudder.

And when safely riding down to Land's End, I was awakened by a so-called friendly sailor, I was rushed out of that position so that the mate in his rounds to see if all his men had reported before the pilot left, would not see me. I was put down an old hatch that was never opened unless in a case of emergency at sea, and falling down on the many coils of old ropes and sails, I fell asleep, and soon was awakened with a big fleet of water rats eating up the fat and gravy that spilled over my clothes. My God, I was frantic, and cared not what happened to me, but could not dare try to lift this hatch to get out.

But for some reason or other I heard the gingling of chains, and soon the hatch was raised and a gruff voice shouted out, hey you, get up out of there, the captain wants to see you forward, and more dead than alive, I dragged myself up the jacob, and out on deck, and then to be bawled out by a gruff old sea dog, Captain Welsh, and ordered ashore, I not knowing whether it was night or morning, for we were a half mile from shore, in mid-stream off Gravesend, land's end. I had to use diplomacy to sneak into the pilot's party, for I had not a red copper in my pockets. At last I reached shore, and discovered that it was after eight p. m. and the pawn shops closed, 21 miles from London, my home, and forty-eight hours after kissing my folks goodbye, heart broken, but happy to have me return safely, but I never told them of all the hardships that I was forced to undergo, for I did not want them to worry or lament at my terrible ordeal, so I kept it to myself and again looked for a job, and after weeks and weeks trudging around London, I took the "Queen's" shilling (A BOB), joining the 10th Huzzars, the "Prince of Wales' own," this was in 1879. When we were on the verge of the world's war that we were forced to fight and win, from August 1st, 1914, until November 11th, 1918. No, no, not November the 7th, 1918, of said and distressing memories. Please do not be angry at my telling this, my part, of my early life's story, but knowing that most people love to read of such romances, I have submitted it to you, so that you, too, will learn more about the life of a poor unfortunate stowaway, trying to improve his future standing in this world with the sad thoughts of how hard my dad had to work to keep nine of us on a pound a week, for I dearly loved my fond and loving family, and I wanted to help them all.

And praise and thanksgiving to God, I succeeded, for when leaving my loved ones like Tom Lipton, I promised them a whole lot, so to do that I lost no time in getting a job that paid the highest salary, that of longshore life, hard work, but the only job for one with little education and in one year and nine months I having sent them a five-pound note when able; then I succeeded in paying the passage of my father, my mother, three brothers and three sisters, finding a home for them, and looking up a job, they were soon on easy street and my promise fulfilled.

I then married and fathered ten children, and while Sir Thomas Lipton was building up his fortunes, I was building up a stable of two-year-olds—until the hand of death entered my home, taking with it my darling wife Mary and three children, in February, 1912, of sad and loving memory.

Returning to the ups and downs of young Tom Lipton, he landed a job as an errand boy, at a meagre salary of four bob a week, and he paid every attention to his job, and after a year there he plucked up the courage to ask his employer for a raise of a shilling a week, which was denied him. We find young Tom Lipton again out of a job, and looking for a ship to take him away to some unknown country, for he afterwards hated Glasgow, and the next we learn of Tommy Lipton, he is a stowaway on his way to the grand old U. S. A.

But it may suit you best to have Sir Thomas, himself, tell his story.

We next see Tom Lipton in the role of a stowaway, and after a rough, stormy trip he was put ashore on a pier not far from good old Castle Garden, in which I landed some ten years after Tom Lipton got a job.

This Lipton fellow was a cunning kid, and a good mixer, and after two days at sea, he having been told that the passengers' tickets had been collected, came out of his hiding place and mixed up with his fellow countrymen and countrywomen, and was not long in hearing their stories, and put this information to good use forthwith.

Having been told of a good-natured Irishman named Pat McQulligan, and his wife keeping a boarding house at 17½ Washington Street, near the old spot well known to you and me, as Castle Garden, he booked up with them as a boarding house runner, a pretty lively job in those days, for the toughest men of little old New York followed that line of work. But Tom Lipton and his brogue had them all beaten to a frizzle, as Theodore (Teddy) Roosevelt would say in the good old days of the past.

It was simply to pick up a little money that Tom Lipton grabbed this job, for he was determined to spend his time in Southland, and having made his little pile, or enough to dress him up and pay carfare, he arrives in that grand old city of the rip-roaring south, "New Orleans," and her "Madri Gras" yearly, pleasing the ladies and the babies and making the old men happy.

Young Lipton was not long in New Orleans when he ran into a very fine old Irish lady, a rooming house keeper. You will notice several stories of this lady and Sir Thomas in this book that I know will be pleasing to you.

But it was not comfort and happiness that Tom Lipton was hunting for, it was money, for having made good up to now, his only thought was Mother and the promises made, so he stopped at nothing to get this money, working both night and day, either on the plantations, or floorwalker in some fine, big store, for his honesty and charming personality carried him safely through these trying ordeals always.

And after all Dame Fortune is a good old soul, for she will hand out to the one to pay back to the other, and Tom Lipton, with his good old detective instinct, never forgetting the mean employer in Glasgow, got hunk.

At last he found his financial feet, however precariously, and he had not been many weeks in Glasgow before he had rigged up a small store in Stobcross Street, determined by hard work, fair dealing and honesty to make a success of it and he did all right, but how, and under what circumstances?

"Give good value." "Be civil to all." "Treat all alike, rich and poor" —were a few of the maxims that Tom Lipton lived up to always.

"But it was my first 'bold advertisement' I put out that made the venture go. I was not long in Glasgow when I bought two of the fattest hogs I could find, dressed them up with lettering on both sides, 'Lipton's Orphans,' and hired two Irishmen, in green costume, and without even getting a police permit, I sent them roving, and my, what an explosion followed.

"I told them to keep away from the tramway cars, but the pigs got warmed up and had a little fun for themselves. They circled around the men, twisting their ropes, knocking the men down flat on the tramway line, holding up traffic and I got hailed to court."

So you see what a paltry shilling, just 24 cents, will do, for in this case it no doubt changed the whole of Tom Lipton's future life, from that of a Glasgow storekeeper or worker to that of a multi-millionaire and the world's most famous sportsman and dean of the yachting world.

The refusal of this shilling raise did not cost Tommy Lipton any worry, for to use his own words, "If I cannot make a living in my own home town, then I will go where I can make a living among strangers that love and appreciate a good honest boy, looking towards the U. S. A."

And the next we see of Tommy Lipton, we find him looking for a steamer outward bound for New York, with a bundle of clothes under his arm, walking along the docks, as bright and as chipper as ever.

It did not take young Tom Lipton long to locate his boat, and jump aboard like an old-fashioned full-fledged able seaman, and picking out a good, quiet spot awaited future developments. So far, so good, but the life of a stowaway is not a happy or a healthy one; my own first attempt to leave home for far off Australia, on the blooming big English four-master, the "Dunbriton," after taking a pierhead jump, endangering my life in the darkness surrounding the great Royal Albert Docks at 3 a. m. taught me enough.

But young Tom Lipton fared much better than I, for he struck a good job after meeting a kindly old Irishman and his wife in the boarding house on Washington Street, whom, if so inclined, could make this his home forever. I had to go and hustle to get a start, and thanks to my dear cousin, Kate Donovan, Mrs. Edward Joyce, I, too, succeeded.

Imagine, folks, in after years both before and after I had first met my grand old friend, Tom Lipton, then Sir Thomas, I patrolled through this same grand old street, but Washington Street had lost its beauty and wonderful history, for a different race of people assembled there. Among the conglomeration were Sirians, Arabs, Moslems, in fact, every kind of a wanderer, from far off Palestine and Turkey, the Irish had grown wealthy and retired, many of them to heaven, I hope, among them Pat McQulligan, his wife, and Battery Dan Finn—gone but not forgotten.

Then poor little Tom Lipton began to count his dollars and cents, and hours looking forward to his return, and to make his parents happy he had mailed to them a "Five Pun" note, twenty-five good American bucks, for Christmas, and that made him happy. Now that you have heard my story of the early life of Tom Lipton, of the lion heart, let us go on with the case.

My word, if Sir Thomas were here today to hear the hip-hip-hurrah made by the sporting men of Europe, headed by Tom Sopwith, handing in their challenges for the coming yachting season of 1934, he would be happy.

Young Tom Lipton was so well liked by his boss, Pat McQulligan, that he at once offered him a part of his business, for his good wife, being sickly, had not borne any children, and poor old Pat wanted Tom Lipton to stay with him as a part of the business and on his becoming the adopted son of Paddy McQulligan, Tom Lipton would be entitled to all his wealth at the death of his foster father, but that did not suit Tom Lipton's plans, as he wanted to go South among the cotton and hemp plantations, knowing that that was the best place to earn and save his money, and with that thought in view he bid goodbye to his dear old friends, the McQulligans, who, with tears in their eyes, kissed him goodbye, and all Washington Street was in mourning all that week, for the stones in the street knew Tom Lipton.

And before leaving, the McQulligans had him promise them that in the event of his not making out good down South, their previous offer was always standing on his welcome return. Young Tom Lipton thanked them and off he went, arriving in New Orleans, he soon got fixed up in a rooming house and, having saved his every penny, he was getting real rich.

He plugged along until he had saved the sum of $400, and being very lonesome for home and Mother, he booked passage for Glasgow. On arriving there, he was greeted by the whole town, as a devoted son, a poor-born son, had at the moment return a rich man. The people just went crazy over young Tom Lipton, the wonderful traveler and future business man in their own grand old city of Glasgow, Scotland, "with haste to the wedding of Bonnie Dundee."

After all the excitement was over, he took a much needed rest. He having made good the promise he made his mother about a barrel of flour and a rocking chair and other things, he wanted to go to work and complete his promise of a carriage and pair to drive his mother all about town. He more than made good, and this is how he did it:

Tom Lipton hired a store and fitting it up with teas, coffees and most everything needed in a poor man's home, he had but little money left. To help him win back some more money, he gave up his furnished room and slept under the counter at night, waking in the morning he swept out the store, he dusted off the counters and prepared to greet his customers, who would say: "Good morning, Mr. Lipton, I hope that you are well this morning. God bless you, let me have a half pound of tea, and a pound of sugar and some coffee and oatmeal." "Yes, mam, I will," and in two shakes of a lamb's tail her order was filled and she on her way. So it went on for many months, until Tom Lipton, seeing that he was doing a pretty nice business, and being tired of doing the chores of shop, he thought he could afford to hire a wee lad to run the errands, and sweep out the store and dust everything well, every morning.

Tom Lipton by that time was the talk of the town, and one day he said to one of his customers, "Do you know of any willing, honest boy who would like to work for me? His salary will not be much for the first month or two, but it will be more than I ever got in my boyhood days in Glasgow."

"Why, yes, Mr. Lipton. My boy, James, is not working and would like to take your job." "Then send him around in the morning and I will put him to work forthwith at five shillings a week, salary or wages, same to increase from time to time, and without request, good morning."

The boy showed up and a fine kid he was, but dressed very poorly, and kind hearted Tom Lipton took pity on him and one evening said: "Boy, don't you leave this evening until I am ready to go with you."

The boy did as he was told, but he, thinking that he was to lose his job, commenced to cry, and his grand old employer hearing him, said, "Don't cry sonny boy, you are not going to lose your job, so put on your hat and coat and we will be off," and away they went to the village tailor.

Tom Lipton ordered this man to fit the boy out in a suit of clothes and send the bill to him. "Very well, Mr. Lipton. I will do as you say," and he very soon had the boy in a very fine, new suit, and it made such a change in his appearance, that even his mother did not know him for the moment.

Next morning saw the boy on the job bright and early. Happy and carefree he went about his business, every now and then looking through the big mirror admiring his new suit, that fitted him so well and snug.

But, lo and behold, the boy did not show up the following day, and this vexed Tom Lipton some, but he went right along doing his own chores, and he awaited the coming of the boy's mother. Soon she happened along with her bit of blarney, and this is the conversation that took place: "Good marning, Mr. Lipton, I hope you are well this marning." "Good morning, Mrs. McSwiggin, I am very well, I thank you, but I miss your boy. Is he sick?" "No, no, Mr. Lipton, you so kindly bought him a nice suit of clothes, and now that he looks so respectable I sent him out to look for a respectable job."

And that was how that grand old Samaritan was served. But he soon forgot all about that episode. His business kept on increasing, for he grew to be a great advertiser of his wares, and the name of Tom Lipton was known for miles around for the unique way he had of advertising.

But Tom Lipton deserved great credit, and he got it, and with the good peoples credit came their money, laying the foundation stone to Tom Lipton's millions of today and his wonderful sportsman's record the world over for to know him is to love him.

"I always did things," he would say, "in a humorous way, ever ready to help one then, as I am today." "I would have my store windows plastered with humorous signs and drawings of the famous artist of that time, both comic and sentimental," more cheap advertising, for Tom Lipton, and his world renowned "Two Orphans." The poor pigs that did not even know their own mother, that didn't want to, for Tom Lipton was very kind to them.

"When I opened my store in Aberdeen, I had two large mirrors, set up so that one could see themselves on entering, thin and emaciated, and the other showing you as you left the store, fat and plump, smiling and happy, and on the first sign was painted: I am going to Lipton's, while on the other sign was painted, Hurrah! I am just coming from Lipton's."

"On another occasion I hired an aeronaut to go up in a balloon and drop ten thousand telegrams addressed to one of my shops, and I offered a reward to the first twenty people that would arrive with a telegram."

"Naturally the shops were swamped with people bearing telegrams, and of course this brought me much more advertisement, and it got so that the editors of the papers would send a man down to copy my next story for the press, and this helped me along more than anything else, for all other newspapers would copy from the first and I was then on easy street."

"For all the local and out of town papers would carry the news, to London, and from there it would travel the world, setting the people talking on the subject, many of them no doubt wondering to themselves what kind of a fellow is this Lipton, anyhow!"

"Thus the Lipton shops spread 'like an amiable epidemic,' through Scotland and on, on, across the border line and into all of England leaving the news in the large towns and then into the suburbs."

And inside of the next ten years the ex-stowaway, and former ex-errand boy had an army of ten thousand employees working for him.

This is where young Tom Lipton showed his ability, in the advertising of his public exhibition, and without even asking for a police permit, to have, or to give such a public exhibition on the streets of the great city of Glasgow, for never before was such an exhibition even thought of.

This was the making of him.

And every now and then Tom Lipton would think out some other such scheme, and by so doing, kept the name of Lipton and his "two orphans" before the people of Glasgow, yes, and even before the whole world, for the papers of every country gave this novel story space, and the story of the Irish boy immigrant's return to home was very much talked about, even in the lobby of the House of Commons, for even the members of the House of Parliament enjoy a good joke at times, moreover the Irish Parliamentary party, when the joke is presented to the people by one of their own.

And the wee little store of Tom Lipton on Stobcross Street became one of Glasgow's most interesting sightseeing points, and the people would be seen marching along the street in both single and double file for months after, and the sightseeing lorries instead of saying as the sightseeing bus operators of today say, particularly in New York, "Come folks, take a ride down through Chinatown, see the Chinese Theatre, the Joss House, and have a plate of Chop Suey with Chuck Connors and Steve Brodie."

No, No, in Glasgow they would say, "Come folks, take a ride down to Lipton's Wee store and have a cup of tea, and a talk to 'Lipton's orphans.' "

Barnum's circus story was again repeated, "Yes there is one born every minute" and he was right, they fell right into line and followed the crowd along the long, long, trail, onward and upward to the Lipton store.

This brought prosperity to this poor stowaway boy, for he opened one new store after another, and every time that Tom Lipton opened a new store he would have handbills printed and circulated all over town, inviting the people to take part in the grand parade on Saturday night, and the crowd would be so great that it would be necessary to call out the Police Reserves, and not being satisfied to get into the hearts and pockets of the good people, he had to get in on the records of the Police Department, thereby setting the tongues of the whole Department wagging about the audacity of that Wee little Irish American youngster, Tom Lipton.

Tom Lipton, lived his life in the fear of God, and you know the result, he made good his prophecy the day he left his home and motherland to go seek his fortune, in the land of the God knows where, but the stout rugged constitution of Tom Lipton often carried him through, to what he is today, a credit to the world, and a charming sportsman to know, and to follow.

I often think, what a wonderful picture it would be for the screen today, that of little Tommy Lipton, the poor Irish boy, cheering his dear old Mother with kind words of comfort, praise and future happiness, in the following remarks, so dear to the hearts of a good son to a fond loving Mother, to wit:—

"Dry yer eyes 'Dinna greet Mither.' Some day I will return and buy you a fine silk dress, and a horse and carriage, with a fine big house and servants to make you happy all your life. Also that barrel of flower that I promised you with all the other fine things."

"Just you wait till I go to work, for when I grow up to be a man I am going to work with all my heart, even if I am forced to work my finger nails off to fulfill my promise to you 'Dinna Mither.' "

It is a waste of time to try and tell you folks more of Tom Lipton's hard struggle, for you are already aware of that, also of how young Lipton made good every promise, not only to his dear old Mother, but to the whole world at large, and right here in dear old New York, he got his first start, and this he never forgets, always willing and ready to tell his story, of how the good people of this grand old city, and their hospitality has helped many a poor boy or man out of a rut, and we, the adopted sons of this lovely little spot in the ocean, love to think back to those unhappy times and we pray to, and ask God, to guard, preserve and watch over our glorious country forever and forever, with peace and prosperity knocking at our doors, and the constant prayers of our unfortunate exiles, after receiving and witnessing the many shining examples of American hospitality, is that the good Lord, and his Blessed Mother will be always as good to America, as America has been to us poor, friendless kids of the long ago.

Blessing us with the honor and glory of living to raise our sons and our daughters to fight for, and if need be, die for, to preserve the liberty of our own good people, as well as for the good freedom loving people of all nations, and may the good Lord, preserve and take care of our great and glorious Democratic President, the Hon. Franklin D. Roosevelt, in his present hard fight for the peace and prosperity of all nations.

God bless our homes and firesides, the aid we are pleased to give those of our brothers in distress, and the blessings of God, follow the N.R.A.

And while still in the thirties he was a millionaire, and was still finding his best fun in hard labor, and even now in his seventy-eighth year he is a masterpiece, and keeps all the boys of his office tired trying to keep up with him. Sir Thomas Lipton, today loves to tell the story of his hardships and tribulations of the past, and he also enjoys a good laugh when telling the story of the two Irish pigs, and their Irish drivers, and the many other novel ways that he doped out for advertising purposes, the only free advertising that he ever received.

"It's a good thing to be born poor," Sir Thomas would often say, "for the rich boy never realizes the value of money."

Certainly, few boys have found money more difficult to earn, or have earned of a harder school to know its value.

It is also delightful to sit and listen to Sir Thomas, telling of his latter day career, and there is one story more than another, that he likes to speak of and that is the time that he bet Harry Lauder 9-pence that he would be in New York before him, it is very amusing, therefore I will write it up for your pleasure and information—but in a latter page.

Of all the honors that have fallen to him, for his philanthropy, his fine sportsmanship and the high esteem in which he, Sir Thomas Lipton, is held by the Royal Family of England, is remarkable, for there is no other man in the world's history that has such a charming record, and all for his love of his dear, good, kind, Mother, peace be to her today.

It was one of Tom Lipton's earliest desires to build a home for his mother, this he did when his business was increasing more and more, daily he went house hunting for his mother, and succeeded in buying a big house for her at "Cambuslang," so that in this, as like all other contracts, this poor little Irish boy made good, and was happy.

After the death of his mother, Sir Thomas presented the house to the Nurses' Association. "I wouldn't part with that house," he said, if I hadn't a shilling in the world. This house will forever be known as the Lipton Memorial Nurses' Association Home, in which there is a room set apart for Sir Thomas Lipton, for all time.

From the day that Tom Lipton was discharged by the Justice of Peace of Glasgow, Scotland, for permitting his two "Irish orphans," his hogs to run wild, obstructing traffic and otherwise becoming disorderly, his Mother's prayers began to take root and with a firmer grip on her beloved son.

Sir Thomas appearing in court to defend his piggies, or otherwise known as Irish hogs, he became so popular, that his business increased a hundred fold and he opened one store after another, always kind and charitable, his name became a household word, and business kept increasing.

He then thought it was a fair time to start his stores over in London and with that end in view, he opened stores all over London, and being so liberal with his money, subscribing to the charities of which the women of the Royal household were Patronesses, he was respected and admired by all, and Princess, afterwards Queen Alexander and himself became close friends, and that brought her husband Albert Edward on the scene, for he, having read so much about this little Irish Gossoon and his publicity pranks he asked to have Tom Lipton presented at court and this gave Sir Thomas a wonderful boost, and from that day on, the young Prince and Thomas Lipton were often seen together and this set the aristocrats of London, near crazy.

They could not understand how the young Prince of Wales would ignore them for that small little tradesman, Tom Lipton, the London Grocer, but our dear old friend, who would be a millionaire even if he had chosen to take part in a Barnum and Bailey circus, for he knew how to make money, and what was more, he know how to keep it, and make it double, thereby fooling the high hatted swells of London, and let me tell them something else that they did not know, and that is the Young Albert Edward, Prince of Wales, being himself a big wholesouled, broadminded man of the world, grew tired of this bickering, and he just dropped these selfish gentlemen from his list, just as he dropped another one of his society ladies, a Mrs. Brooks, naming her the "Babling" brook for the more that they tried to separate H.R.H. and Sir Thomas Lipton, the closer and warmer his heart went out to his friend Lipton, the savior of mankind and friend, and faithful son of the British Empire, and this while these men were gabbing their heads off, that was all, Sir Thomas not saying a word, worked on, as was his custom, eventually winning the love of all nations.

YOUNG TOM LIPTON'S FIRST SETBACK AND DIPLOMACY

If young Tom Lipton had received the shilling a week that he asked for more than sixty years ago, it is probable that today he might be found in his old job, living from hand to mouth, or perhaps a retired merchant, or shopkeeper in Glasgow, never to be known as Sir Thomas J. Lipton, "Knight Commander of the Victorian Order" or Sir Thomas J. Lipton, the "Irish Baronet" or would he be a welcome guest, and near friend of the King of England and have the power to save a man's life sentenced to be shot for having led his brigade to fight against the British Army in the Boer War of 1899, who after the war was arrested and charged with High Treason, or would he be in a position to win the hearts of all America. This story will be told in full later on.

This is the story of Tom Lipton's early life, as he told me himself to wit :—

"I had been engaged as an errand boy at four shillings a week, and I thought that I was worth more, so I plucked up courage to ask my master for a shilling raise, and to my utter surprise and disgust, my request was emphatically denied. I left him to better myself and got another job, that being my first setback, I was a little bit disheartened, but not for long, for when I thought of that mean man I was glad I left him."

"Many years after I received a letter from the head of that same firm, asking me to look after a young lady, a member of the Red Cross, who was about to sail on the *Erin* for Serbia, as a hospital ship.

"I found that she was a friend of the wife of the managing director, who said that he would be greatly obliged to me if I would do whatever I could for this young woman. I knew that he was not aware that I had ever worked for his firm."

"So I had him rung up and I told him that it would be quite all right about the young lady he spoke about, I then asked him if he ever worked in Glasgow?" He answered, "Why yes, I did, many years ago." "Did you wear a frock coat in those days?" I asked. "Oh, yes, I did," he replied. "And then I up and told him that the only previous communication I had received from his firm was a letter written in pencil, refusing me the raise of a shilling a week, in wages, while working for your firm."

"This man was so amazed that he shut me off, forgetting to hang up the receiver."

TOM LIPTON'S STAR OF HOPE WAS FAST BECOMING A
REALIZATION—HE WAS SUMMONED TO COURT THERE
TO MEET THE PRINCE OF WALES, AND AFTER THAT
MEETING, THE POOR LONDON GROCER, ENTERED THE
LONG TRAIL OF INTERNATIONAL SPORT.

PART I—CHAPTER III.

And from that day, he came to the conclusion that there was
no place in International sport for two such rough riders as, Dunraven
and Lipton, and he took off his coat to work, by taking up where Lord
Dunraven had left off, and this decision was so well received that it
changed the whole life of the former London grocer.

He was always welcomed to the Queen's Palace and received in
state by the young Prince, who had been a long time looking for one
of his subjects, who had the brains, the money, and the courage to
right the wrongs, or the mistakes of Lord Dunraven.

This was very pleasing to both Queen Victoria and the whole Royal
family who had heard of Tom Lipton, and his charity, honesty and
charming personality, and this brought about the summoning to Court
of this young Irish Scotchman, who dared to institute his wonderful
methods of advertising that appealed to the Prince, and this is what
happened that day.

Here my friends is the inside story of how Sir Thomas Lipton took
to yachting, and why.

In the year of our Lord 1895, Lord Dunraven, who had challenged
for the America's Cup, and who passed away at about the time that
we were waiting to hear of the successful launching of *Shamrock V*
and *Enterprise* April 14th, 1930, but whatever his complaints were,
may he rest in peace.

One evening while the late King Edward VII of England, then
Prince of Wales, who was himself a first class yachtsman, felt very bad
about the talk that was then going on, regarding Dunraven and his
complaints, both at home and abroad, and he told Tom Lipton, just
how bad the Queen and himself felt about the matter. It was then
that Tom Lipton arose to the occasion, for he never let an opportunity
pass him through life.   .

The young Prince, always noted as a lover of peace, never looked
for trouble but he often prevented trouble when he saw it coming
his way, he said, "something must be done and done quickly, for I
value the love and respect of the American people too much to have
a petty little thing like a cup be the cause of us being at all unfriendly,

and someone must challenge again." It may have been a chance thought of the carefree young Prince in 1898, but to Tom Lipton, it was just what he wanted, and he bade the Prince goodbye, and left for home to plan out his future course, and he lost no time, and here we are today, we see this grand old man still trying to make good.

Thomas J. Lipton, the unknown and uncared for simple tea merchant of that day, did not have to cater to the snobs, for the Heavenly Father had given him the brains and the manhood to seek better company, and he went them all one better by entering the ranks of sport and good fellowship.

And he startled the world by building yachts—building a freak yacht, and he named her after his fatherland the *Shamrock,* 1st and knowing full well that the *Shamrock* 1st needed a protector, he built one of the greatest steam yachts of that, or any other time, and he named her the *Erin,* and having provided himself with a sailing yacht and a floating palace of a steam yacht, he requested the Royal Ulster Yacht Club of Ireland, to issue a challenge for the America's Cup, and from that day to the present, his name has become a household word, and will forever so remain.

The Prince of Wales had heard about this Lipton fellow, and he asked to meet him, often they met, and forever after the future King, and the so-called poor broken down tea merchant became the closest of friends, for the young Prince grew to love Sir Thomas Lipton, for he was a man after his own heart.

And they constantly met either at Buckingham Palace, or on board the beautiful steam yacht *Erin,* and when the miserable aristocrats, who before had at all times looked upon Tom Lipton as a usurper, were breaking their necks to be given an introduction to this great Dick Whittington, of sportdom.

But Tom Lipton, while he will always forgive, will never forget, and when these craving aristocrat wouldbe's, were introduced to him, he met them just as they should be met, with an air, both civil and strange.

But those blokies thought that there was a gold mine in the knowing of this great tea merchant, for Tom Lipton was growing greater and greater every day, so they implored of him to organize a Lipton Limited and they handed over their wealth, and Sir Thomas organized the greatest corporation the world ever knew and it was known the world over as the Lipton Limited.

But there were some who could not see this Irish tea merchant so close to Royalty, for the young Prince of Wales was a sport lover, and he, too, loved yachting, and he had built a beautiful sailing yacht and named her the *Britannia,* and the challenge issued to the New York Yacht Club by the Royal Ulster Yacht Club of Ireland, having been accepted, and the greatest pleasure that Prince Albert Edward ever enjoyed was the sailing of his beautiful yacht against Tom

Lipton's *Shamrock* in her tryouts along the English, Irish and Scotch coasts, before leaving for New York, in the year of our Lord, 1899, and in spite of the many handicaps, Sir Thomas Lipton, and his *Shamrock I* gave a pretty good account of himself, but lost to a much better yacht no doubt, or at any rate a home product, that was not forced to cross the wild Atlantic ocean on her own bottom.

This endeared Thomas Lipton, closer to the heart of the young Prince, for to think of it, there were so many multi-millionaires in England, and not one of them would dare undertake this great risk, and yet an unknown poor Irish tea merchant was willing to spend his time and money to try and win this great trophy—the America's Cup.

And on the return of Thomas Lipton, and *Shamrock I,* the young Prince was more oftener than ever to be seen in the company of Tom Lipton, and they became very close friends, all of which gored these snobs to desperation, and what did they do?

Why, they thought that if they could build a yacht to beat Sir Thomas and his *Shamrock* so that they could then be welcomed into the inner circle of the Prince of Wale's party, but were they? why no.

Several of them built yachts and fast sailors they were too, but did they win the favor of the Prince from Thomas Lipton? why no, not at all, for their friendships grew so ripe that no power on earth could shake them, and Tom Lipton, knew all that, and he kept right on building yachts and issuing challenges to sail for the America's Cup, and here he is today in his 80th year better fitted and respected, than ever before, in the year of our Lord 1900. Sir Mortimer Singer, built the yacht *Lulworth,* about this time, and after sailing her for a few years and finding himself in the same identical position as he was before building her, he sold her to a Mr. Alexander.

Paton, a Mersey yachtsman who, it is believed, will continue to race her, the *Lulworth* in the same class as *Shamrock V* this season off the English coast, with the *Astra,* another one of those birds that was built to beat Tom Lipton and his *Shamrocks,* but did they, or can they? I know that they did not the day that I sailed with them off Harwich for of all the seven starters, *Shamrock,* sprang over the finishing line a mile ahead, and that is just how Tom Lipton has been keeping those highbrow friends of his for many years just about a mile behind him.

For when King Edward VII ascended the Throne on the death of his grand old Mother, Queen Victoria in 1901, Tom Lipton, became a favorite at Court.

This class of sailing champions now consists of the King's yacht, the *Britannia,* Sir Thomas Lipton's *Shamrock,* Lord Waring's *White Heather,* Mr. T. B. F. Davis', *Schooner Westward, Ho,* and the two new twenty-one and a half meter yachts *Astra* and *Cambria,* built for Sir Mortimer Singer and Sir William Barry, June 1928.

That, dear reader is the story of how this poor little Irish lad, whom none of the highbrows of England cared to meet or know, firstly, but were mighty glad to be introduced to him in later years, received his first baptism, and reception into Royalty and officialdom of the then, Great Britain, by a warm reception through the main doors of Buckingham Palace and usually led into the Throne room and there received in State by His Imperial Majesty, King Edward, VII. A he man, loyal to his friends and to his people, yes a real old-fashioned Democrat, and a broadminded man of the world.

Albert Edward, the Prince of Wales, before his mother died was ever welcomed by the nations of the world, but that up-start of Germany, the Kaiser Wilhelm II, had to behave himself or get a wallop from Prince Eddy, and let me tell you that Prince Edward the Prince of Wales was no slouch with the gloves.

And he kept the peace of the world, as requested by his grand old mother, who when Kaiser Bill went on a rampage, would say, "Eddie, you go over to Berlin, and tell your crazy cousin to stop his nonsense, at least while I am living" and Prince Edward would call Sir Thomas and away they would go and Emperor Willie would go back into his hole, and I often think how happy the world would be if the hole was closed up and he inside.

Tom Lipton's "STAR OF HOPE" had set, and playing a lone hand, and playing it so well, he was recognized and glorified by the whole Royal family of Great Britain, and what was the result? read on, good friends, read on and the whole Royal family of England, remembers that Sir Thomas Lipton with his honesty and charming personality and a free and open pocketbook, has done more than any other man in history to cement the friendship that now exists between these two great English speaking nations.

And what could be better than to see us as one united body, both England and America, like father, and daughter, always united and happy, what other pleasures can take the place of peace and happiness, constantly existing between these two great world nations, who are in a position to both rule and govern the world today, by forcing peace on all other nations, unless it be some bulldog nation that is blind to their own best interests as was Germany and her Emperor in 1913, and 1914, bringing about the destruction of the whole civilized world today, that alas we will be many years recovering from. He kidded himself along in 1933, thinking that the coming of Hitler, would restore him to the throne, but nothing doing, no, no.

Then is it not but fair and just to a man like this grand old Dean of that noble sport of yachting, that they should at last rally around his, the standard of Sir Thomas Lipton, the standard of honesty and fairness, would to Heaven that we were blessed with more men like Sir Thomas Lipton, then this hard cold old world would be far better to live in, and that grand old policy of the past would again be supreme, that of "All for one, and one for all." All praise be to you Sir Thomas, for your one long request will shortly be granted, and if this promise is not redeemed at this time, what is the difference if it is all sport, and looking to this kind of sport causes a very heavy outlay of both time and money that the poorer classes are in turn blessed with.

That point alone is a mighty one, for any man that will bring about the opening up of the rich man's purse, must surely some day be recognized both by God, and country, for it is simply following the miracles of our own good Lord, when he sat in the party of hundreds and all they had to eat was seven small baskets of fish, and just as God gave them plenty to eat in the days gone by, so too is Sir Thomas Lipton, giving our workmen a chance to live happily with their wives and families today, for every time that he arrives he brings with him both comfort and cheer.

Tom Lipton summoned to the Palace of Kings, by H.R.H. the Prince of Wales, every now and then, there to meet the Royal family, ever after having proved himself he became a Royal favorite and always welcomed to Buckingham Palace.

And from that day onward, while becoming despised by many of the sore headed aristocrats, he was welcome by Queen Victoria, and the poor London grocer became popular, his sun had risen, and his early dreams were realized.

He having won the hearts of Princess Alexandria, and her court by his nobleness and charitable heart, meeting them often, beautiful Princess Alexandria of Wales, after conversing with her husband Prince Albert Edward, was instrumental in having young Tom Lipton, summoned to the Royal Palace.

Having won the hearts of the Royal family, young Tom Lipton, then went out to win the hearts of the world, and it made no difference what color or creed, he was always ready to give them a helping hand, that is why this Irish Scotch, stowaway kid won out, for he was the most talked of boy in the British Isles, and that helped him greatly.

And after several conversations with the young Prince of Wales, and he, Tom Lipton, knowing from same, the feelings of the whole Royal family after the unfortunate Dunraven episode, that was his cue to go marching onward and upward, and from that day on he became a great lover of sports, and pastimes, taking up yachting as his favorite pastime, he built *Shamrock I,* and that pleased the young Prince and his mother very much, and did eventually bring about his summons to the Court of Victoria, and raised to the proud position of that of an Irish Baronet, with which title he, Tom Lipton, was greatly pleased, and his stocks went up 100 points.

He became a member of the Royal Ulster Yacht Club, and having hunted up the greatest yacht builder in the whole British Isles he gave him an order to build the fastest and best yacht, and in so doing, spare no money, but be sure and give a good, fast sea-going yacht, and he then requested the Royal Irish Yacht Club to issue his first challenge, for "America's Cup" 1899.

He raced, and having given a good account of himself, and by his well known good natured honest charitable heart, from that day on he won the hearts of all America, for his smiling face in defeat and his cheerful goodbye, but I will be here again next year, not having much money and few friends he inwardly felt dismayed, until that grand old financier, the late J. Pierpont Morgan clapped Tom Lipton, on the back and said, "Young man I like you, you have proved yourself, and before you leave I am going to see and have you elected an Honorary Member of the New York Yacht Club," oh, boy, how that changed him.

Tom Lipton was a happy man, and on his return was welcomed with open arms, for his actions in America, made of him the foremost diplomat in all Europe, and that is saying a whole lot, but young Tom Lipton, a diplomat without portfolio, did more to bring back peace and happiness to both countries, and the Dunraven matter soon was given the gate, and young Tom Lipton knew his onions and he kept right on, with this good work, and he proved himself to be one of the world's greatest peace promoters thereby killing off the fight promoters of that time and there were many, in both countries.

For there were troublesome times existing, for with the Dunraven scandal we had President Grover Cleveland, twisting the Lion's tail and he just issued his defi, in what was known as the "Cleveland" message, but thank Heaven by the efforts of the then Sir Thomas Lipton, and the wiser heads of both countries, that warlike feeling has passed forever.

It would be mighty hard for me to try and tell you my good friends of all the honors that were showered on the head of the poor London Grocer for he still had his enemies both in Court and out of Court, ever ready to knock that poor despised London tea merchant, who had broken into Court and there to become a prime favorite over night, to them, sad to relate, something that the poor simps could never get over, Warrau Warrau.

Having been Knighted by Queen Victoria, on the recommendation of the Prince of Wales, and the young Prince so happy at the state of peace wanted to have his mother grant more honors, but Tom Lipton, was not looking for honors, not at all man, not at all, he was looking for a bright and a happy future, and he went right along building this his house of happiness only to be undermined and thrown to the ground, by the very men he fed, and many of whom he kept out of the poorhouse, it is sad to relate.

But Tom Lipton carried on, and having built Challenger No. two, and three, and again meeting defeat his same old genial Irish smile winning for him day after day thousands of American friends, and on his return, he was requested to exercise his power at Court by the late Charles Stewart Parnell, Ireland's un-crowned King, and his party, who would not dare ask the King or Queen of England any favors.

But young Tom Lipton did, and this the greatest favor of all, that of reprieving a subject from execution, who with his army dared to take up arms against his own country in the "Boer" war of 1899, and thanks to Tom Lipton the life of Colonel Arthur Lynch, and his followers of the Irish Brigade were saved, something no other human on earth could do, but Tom Lipton, did.

There will never be any occasion for a controversy or an unfriendly feeling existing between those two great English speaking nations, that must stand shoulder to shoulder more so now than ever before, with the wild ranting of the Russian Communists throughout the world, ready to destroy all governments, we must keep our eye on the gun, watch and wait, and always be ready.

We have done all that can be done to civilize them and bring to the whole world peace and prosperity, yes we gave them our money and man power and now today, they are banding together to prevent the payment of this just debt, so what can they expect of us, in the future, and what war or world destruction may again follow, can we of America or England rally to their assistance, why no, they will have to fight their own battles, and like the miserable rats of American gunmen, kill each other off the map.

But don't forget that Tom Lipton did have reasons to find fault often for the fact alone of our building four or more yachts to prevent *Shamrock* carrying away the American Cup, but no, good old Sir Thomas Lipton, sang low and kept out of all foreign arguments or entanglements, and left American yachtsmen to settle their own quarrels and misunderstandings.

Always praising the American people he was quite contented to leave himself in their hands, the grand old soul, hated arguments, and never asked for any favors, but it may have been better if he had, years ago, for he may have been favored with some amendments to that age old Deed of gift.

I don't have to tell you of all the good that Tom Lipton, has done not only at home and in this country, but every country in the world, for there never was a time when he was more happier than the time that he was dispensing charity, and became one of our greatest Philanthropists.

Would to Heaven that he had been blessed with the winning of America's Cup, if only for a year, and place it beside his dear mother's picture at home, now a handsome nursing institution built by Sir

Thomas in memory of his guiding star, his fond loving dear old mother.

I am free to say, that if Tom Lipton had won the cup he would be living and with us today, but alas, that cannot be, how happy we would be if he was given the opportunity to say Mother Dear, my ambition in life has been fulfilled.   I have fought my battles through life, always on good sound principles of honesty and square dealings.

For the information and guidance of my readers, permit me to lay before you the hardships and abuse that a poor boy has to put up with when leaving his home and loved ones, whom he may never see again, to go wandering through the world alone and uncared for, our Heavenly Father our only friend, thanks to him that does all things well, for those that love and follows him through this hard road, of misery and discontent.

Of course some of us have had it much harder than others as Stowaways for a poor Kid, with maybe fifty cents in his pockets cannot be tipping the unmerciful dogs, who although earning a salary, is willing to grab your last cent, you meet those wolves in every day life, but on shore it is much different than on shipboard, for I paid dearly for my experience.

If I must say it, a boy leaving home under such circumstances, must be of a noble heart, or he would quit, stay home and be a burden on his poor but fond loving parents, raising a family of twelve on a very poor salary, and this no blue blooded son of Erin, would have the audacity to do.

And often after the cruelty one has to undergo, on his voyage over, balks and sits down on a bench in Battery Park, with his eyes piercing the dark clouds towards Erin or any other land, that he may have sailed from, quits and gets nowhere at all, unless in jail for begging, or maybe a more serious offence of robbery, and then his life is blighted for all time, and sad to relate, we have met many of these foolish boys who quit, more's the pity.

But our hero young Tommy Lipton did not quit, not at all man, not at all, for with his droll talk and his Irish blarney, he bucked the waves and sea kidding the hungry employees along on his way over, and telling them of what he will do for them when he becomes an American millionaire.

Landing in New York with about enough to buy a bed, and little supper he ran into a grand old Irish boarding house keeper, and soon is seen bringing newly landed Immigrants to his Irish Boss, thereby showing his willingness to work and make good, the rest of this story you will read elsewhere in these chapters, that I am sure you are going to enjoy its reading.

Tommy Lipton, made good, in his every undertaking for he had his Mother's prayers and these God heard, and directed his Guardian

Angel to aid and assist, that poor little Irish boy, and protect him from all harm, and help him, and as he travelled along through life, he never forgot his own early ups and downs, and I will submit a story to you that will show the humanity of Tom Lipton or Sir Thomas Lipton in after years. To wit—

To show to the world that his riches did not make him high-hatted I will quote this little story, and you may judge for yourself the kind of a man Tom Lipton was without or with, these riches.

A few years ago a meeting of the Lipton Limited of which Sir Thomas was the Chairman, and going over the respective reports, both financial and otherwise they came upon an item in the financial report of a shortage of about 280,000 pounds owing to the laxity of some of his employees.

Well, what did Sir Thomas do, did he run out to get a Cop, why no, he was too humane for that, but he asked to be heard and he made the following proposition to the Board to wit, and this is what he said:

"Gentlemen, of course you understand that because I am chairman of this company, do not say that in case of a shortage, that I must make good all losses, but in this case I feel that it would be unwise at this time to take the guilty ones to Court, for in the first place it would be giving us publication and advertisement that we do not want."

"Secondly, it would be the means of ruining some poor woman and her family, by exposing the case, and that we must not do under any circumstances, for it would not give the unfortunate men a chance to pay us back this shortage, by discharging them from our employ.

"This is my proposition Gentlemen, I will hand to your honorable body a check for the above losses, and will call the men before me and tell them just what I have done, and what I expect them to do in return, that is to remain in their respective positions, and pay back all they stole from us, and my propositions being well received by the men, who went to their homes with light hearts and a beautiful smile, and they paid much more attention to their work, and paid back every shilling of this shortage, and I still kept them in my employ for years afterward," always enjoying the friendship of their good hearted human employer, that to my mind used fine judgment, in this as in all other cases, too numerous to mention here.

Sir Thomas was a happy man, for his having paid the bill and thereby keeping Scotland Yard away from the offices of the Lipton Limited, and he prides in his actions and is ever ready to tell the story, to his friends for King Solomon could not do any better, or even as good, as did Tom Lipton.

The fact of Sir Thomas, becoming so successful, in his many under-takings I would have bet my life that he would some day be successful in winning the America's Cup, for when a man is backed by Royalty, his fortune is made.

You my friends will read in this work, how I the writer thought to take a leaf out of Sir Thomas's book, by mailing to His Majesty King George V, a copy of my previous book, namely, "OUR POLICE GUARDIANS" it carrying among its pages the beautiful story of King George, and his Son the Prince, of facing death on the bloody fields of Flanders to cheer the boys in the mud holes and trenches, that I am sure would be pleasing to his subjects.

And be it known that the sector, visited by the King, and his Son, had been won from the enemy by dint of hard fighting, under the leadership of a British General and his command, ably assisted, by the present Police Commissioner of New York, Major General John O'Ryan, and his noble heroes of the U. S. A. Twenty-Seventh Division. It was a noted fact that these two great Generals did mighty fine work, and a friendship sprang up between them and their commands that will live forever, and in another chapter of this work you will read of General O'Ryan, and his fighting division, sailed for London in 1930, for the express purpose of a re-union of their brothers in arms, and a wonderful time was enjoyed by all.

But I was not so lucky as was Sir Thomas, I don't know why, I often feel that the Tom Lipton two orphans must have looked cross-eyed at me, to think of my breaking in where Sir Thomas had left off, be that as it may, my book laid in Buckingham Palace quite a little while in April 1928, for on April 10th, I received a letter from a grand old gentleman, Private Secretary to the King, a Lord Sandringham, who passed away, April 1930, at the time that all the world was happy at the successful launching of both *Enterprise* and *Shamrock V,* April 14th, 1930. I will submit to you a copy of the letter in question, to wit—

"BUCKINGHAM PALACE.

"The Private Secretary presents his compliments to Mr. John J. Hickey, and begs to return herewith the book which he has been kind enough to forward for the King's acceptance, as it is contrary to rule for His Majesty to accept books from those who are not his own subjects, unless the works are submitted through the London Embassy or (Legations) of the Countries to which the senders belong.

Unfortunately Sir Thomas was away at this time, so I could not consult him as to the mode of procedure, in such a case, yes I did ask Mr. Westwood's opinion, his answer you will see in copy, in this book.

Unfortunately I was sick, just about able to crawl, and not in a frame of mind to go Hob Nobbing with Royalty, for if at all well, I certainly would have delivered this copy of my book through U. S. A. official channels. His Majesty the King, so long as that I had undertaken the task, I would have successfully put it over in right Royal style, but alas, human nature.

I have no regrets for that little transaction, not at all, only that I was not in a fit condition to clean up as I should, but I ask forgiveness of His Imperial Majesty, King George V, and all whom this matter may concern.

I had the pleasure of visiting Lord Sandringham, at Buckingham Palace and had quite a delightful chat with that grand old gentleman. I saw King George and Queen Mary, and all the little Kings and a jolly old bunch they were, always smiling, and friendly, so why not I be happy, for the late King Edward VII, blundered in not leading Dick Crocker's Derby Winner "ORBY" by the head and into the stud in 1909, and I too blundered in this matter, yes we all blunder more or less, I don't blame that grand old ruler, not at all.

But such men as was the aristocrats of that day that blundered and blundered over and over again, for even after Sir Thomas had granted their requests and organized the Lipton Limited they still blundered, because it was bred in them to hate a poor good natured whole-souled commoner, but they lost out.

King Edward VII, of jolly old England thought a lot of Sir Thomas Lipton, and often visited him on board the *Erin,* when at anchor in Portsmouth, Isle of Wight, where he delighted to spend hours in the company of this great yachtsman.

It may surprise many when I state that King Edward, of England thought much of Ireland, and when Prince of Wales, would often run over and spend a few days travelling and hunting the game that old Ireland was noted for in the happy days of the past, gone alas forever. Yes it is a noted fact Queen Victoria, herself loved to visit old Ireland, a son was born there, Prince Patrick, Duke of Connaught. Also of its leaders he thought much, for King Edward was noted for his love of fair play, and he knew that these good men, were simply doing their duty, and he has proven that in many of his acts, when the opportunity presented itself.

Sir Thomas Lipton became quite a favorite with the King, because of his many acts of a charitable nature, and in building his *Shamrocks* to go over the ocean, to sail against America's best sailing yachts to at least try and bring back the former "Queen's cup that England had held so long and was proud of, until taken from her in the great sailing races of 1851, and forever after is known as the America's cup. King Edward VII, was very broad minded, he loved his people, and his people loved him, very much, and above all was never slow in recognizing and appreciating acts of this nature, and it is for that one reason more than any other that he lives in the minds of many, not only of his own people but also of the peoples of the world, for the good name of King Edward VII, will never die.

And for the present King, George V, the son of King Edward, who is at this time fighting a wonderful fight against death, we think very much of, and the prayers and well wishes of all the world are manifesting itself, for we are desiring very much to hear of King George, recovering fully from this terrible sickness, that he has battled with for the past month of 1928.

And there is no man living that will welcome that good news than will the subject of this story, Sir Thomas Lipton, and his many friends and his associates the world over, for none more than Sir Thomas, is aware how King George resembles his father, in both sport and good-fellowship, and whose good name will, like his father be ever remembered, and respected by all.

I recall that to release Col. Lynch, Michael Davitt, wrote the King, he giving Sir Thomas the letter to deliver, and after the release he kept Davitt's letter as a souvenir, would to Heaven I could print this whole story in this work.

Sir Thomas Lipton did many services that pleased the Royal family and it was a suggestion of the Prince of Wales, in their conferences that made Sir Thomas, decide to take up where Lord Dunraven, left off.

Going out and looking for the best designer to be found, he ordered his *Shamrock 1st,* and raced to bring back the America's Cup if possible, but more than the America's Cup, he sailed to win back the love and the respect of the American people, and although he lost the cup, he did win the people of not only America, but of the entire world, for his charitable heart. And the young Prince and his Mother the Queen and Royal family were delighted. In later years the King told Sir Thomas, "how he had been watching his benevolent work for several years, aiding and assisting the poor all over the country, and such work appeals to me at all times."

"But said King Edward, when I heard of your challenging America to race for the 'Queen's' or 'America's' Cup, I was thunderstruck to think that a poor boy, but a few years ago, who had accumulated a fortune, undertook to bring the cup back to England, I thought that was wonderful, and I asked to have you presented to me at Court.

"To think that we have so many millionaires in London, Englishmen, that do not bother their heads about England's welfare either at home or abroad, while you, a poor Irish Scotch boy, is spending both your time and money in the advancement of England, and her sporting public, it is amazing to say the least, Lipton, I am for all time your friend."

It was Sir Thomas that brought the great American fighting champion John L. Sullivan, over to England, and introduced him to the King, who was carried away with the Big Boy, from Boston, Mass., and his laurels, and many knockouts, for be it remembered, King Edward was no slouch with the gloves.

HON. ALFRED E. SMITH, *Former Governor—The Happy Warrior*

THE LATE SIR THOMAS LIPTON

THE CHEERFUL LOSER AND HIS WELL-KNOWN
IRISH SMILE

COMMODORE HAROLD S. VANDERBILT

AMERICA'S SUCCESSFUL DEFENDER OF THE
YACHTING RACES OF 1930 AND 1934

And it was whispered to me confidently that John and Albert Edward put on the mits and fought a pretty hard four rounds, after which they both dressed for dinner, and spent the evening together. It was good old Charley Mitchell, England's fighting champion, that made this meeting possible.

They say that history repeats, well before leaving with the American Legion advance guard for Paris, August of 1927—I asked Jack Dempsey, if he was going to visit London this year, and he said why yes, providing things are right, and I said that Sir Thomas would like to have him, Jack Dempsey, call on him at Osidge there to spend a few days, Jack said alright Mr. Hickey, I will meet you at the Hotel Savoy, July 10th next, but things were not quite right with Dempsey, so that he did not visit London, or Sir Thomas, at all. We all know the cold dirty deal they dealt out to our champion Jack, at that time.

SIR THOMAS, today owns more prizes in the shape of medals, cups and others, his winnings for the past thirty-five years, and titles, he carries more of them, than does any other man living today. Sir Thomas, had these cups, plaques and others, photographed and autographed and sent me a copy.

But as a matter of fact, Tom Lipton is not a title hunter nor never was. These titles all came to him for services rendered, in the way of charity to the people in general, and the world in particular.

But Sir Thomas is too fond of sport to lay off the game, and he will be heard from again pretty soon, for he would give up his every title or cups to win our "America's" cup, not that he is at all covetous not at all, man dear, it simply is a case of a man setting his mind on something and he never quits until either God calls him or he wins the cup, that is all, for any man that has known Sir Thomas Lipton for a quarter of a century as the writer of this story, will agree with me that Tom Lipton, is one of the cleanest and most respected sportsmen that the world ever produced.

Yes, I admit that Sir Thomas had a bee in his bonnet, for the cup, and who can blame him, he has the money, and he has the ambition, and he is blessed with a charming Irish personality, that will carry him anywhere, and perhaps eventually win him the much merited America's cup, who knows?

And that is why this noble Irish character, is braving the wild storms of the Atlantic ocean to issue his fifth challenge, for the cup, but I am reminded of the handicap that confronts Sir Thomas and his *Shamrock V* and the remarks of Colonel Duncan F. O'Neill, a hero of the great war.

Colonel Neill is a very unassuming gentleman, but a braver man, or a better sailor it would be hard to find, he is known as the Commodore of the Lipton fleet, and I will quote to you a statement made by Colonel Neill, several years ago when being interviewed by a newspaper man, to wit—

"It would be unwise to design the challenger until some changes had been made in the rules governing the cup contests."

"According to Colonel Neill, friends of Sir Thomas feel that the rules of American waters and those under which European races are held, diverge so widely that the differences form a big obstacle in competing for the America's cup, since the yacht built particularly for this race is virtually useless for competition in European races."

It is possible according to Colonel Neill, that representatives of American yachting, including those of the New York Yacht Club, holders of the cup, may be invited to conference where rule changes, by both parties may be discussed, with a view to similar conditions, for all races.

The Colonel hastened to add that British yachtsmen do not feel that the American yacht race rules are in the least unfair, but they feel that it would be better if both American and British yachtsmen built their yachts under the same conditions.

Now folks, you have the real reason why we have not had a yacht race since 1920—the handicap is too great, to try again, although this conference may be called together any day to consider as per request, before Sir Thomas orders the Royal Irish Yacht Club, of Ireland, to issue the challenge.

It is not at all fair, something should be done to help bring about a race, for in every case where there is a yacht race it means the spending of millions of pounds and dollars, on both sides of the ocean.

Be it remembered that Sir Thomas Lipton have been battering away, spending his money and his time to try to win the cup, since his first challenge in the year of our Lord, 1899—and while fast closing on to eighty years of age, this grand old Veteran is still going strong.

And be it known to all here present, that owing to the wonderful fight put up by Sir Thomas and his *Shamrock I* in 1899—Queen Victoria, called Sir Thomas to Buckingham and Knighted him, and for all time he should be known hereafter as Sir Thomas Lipton, Knight Commander of the Victorian Order, and a title that is coveted by all, but is seldom bestowed. Some great recognition for a poor Irish lad, my word.

"Sir Thomas said I have spent more than $5,000,000, to try to win the cup and I have no regrets, or do I regard this as money lost, for I value much the friendships made, of such men as the late President Theodore Roosevelt, and many other great Americans, among them Ralph and Joseph Pulitzer, the Hon. John J. Fitzgerald, ex-Mayor of Boston, and many others too numerous to mention."

The following letter dear people completely changed my plans from a newspaper man to that of a wandering Irish Jew, all dressed up, but nowhere to go, and with your indulgence, I will tell you why.

MEMORIES OF THE HAPPY PAST

PART I—CHAPTER IV

I had been in communication with Sir Thomas, and to my surprise I received the following answer, to my letter, forwarded to Sir Thomas at this moment, for my mind was made up to travel, but under different circumstances.

"S. Y. ERIN, At Southampton,
"Isle of Wight, England, June, 1914.

"John J. Hickey, Esq., 306 Washington Avenue,
"Parkville, Brooklyn, N. Y.

"A thousand thanks for your very kind wishes and I earnestly hope that same may be realized. I appreciate your kindness in taking it upon yourself weekly the trouble of mailing to me all the good news from my many friends over in your lovely country, they are always a pleasure for me to read, and I am more than grateful to you for them, always.

"Hoping that I may have the pleasure shortly of being able to thank you personally for your kindness, when next I cross over to America, and with my kindest regards and best wishes,

"Yours respectfully,

"THOMAS J. LIPTON."

Well, Well, by all that is good and "Pius"

I was elated, and I answered this letter from Sir Thomas, forthwith, and this is just what I penned my dear old friend, no, no I lost no time beating the bush about it, I simply told him that I was coming to see him, and to look *Shamrock IV* over, and then make for blooming old London town.

Yes Sir, all of my plans were made to meet my dear old friends of the past forty years there, to renew our old time friendships, never thinking of the plans that my dear old friend had also made to give me the time of my life, a part of my troublesome history never to be forgotten, for the next thing that came to me was a letter saying Mr. Hickey, I am delighted.

And this was the happy message, "Greetings, come on the next steamer, and I will have my Steward, Mr. Chambers, take the best of care of you on board the *Erin,* and a steam launch will be awaiting you at the Royal landing stage at Cowes, Isle of Wight."

Well, imagine my feelings, then in the employ of the New York "Herald," at Herald Square, under the direct supervision of my dear good friend Mr. Frank Flaherty, one of the finest Democratic New York citizens that it was ever my good fortune to meet, a "Prince", known and respected by all.

Meeting Mr. Flaherty, that morning, I told him that I was very much desirous of taking a rest, for I had so much to do after my wife's death just one year before, in the way of taking care of her offspring, and seeing to it that all of my children should be properly taken care of I then asked him to lay the matter of a vacation before the Board of Control, and he laughed at my audacity, but said Yes John, I will do that.

Next morning he met me with that same old kindly spirit, and a smile saying, old pal, your request has been granted, and I hope that you will have the rest you need so much, and report back to me in two weeks, back in your old form and ready to resume business, but did I, well read on.

I soon got in touch with the White Star Line and learned that the *S.S. Oceanic* was leaving New York in a week for Southampton, and I booked up on her, not knowing at the time that this was to be her last but one trip from this or any other port, for she was blown up on her next trip, bidding my dear old friends of the Editorial Staff among them a grand old gentleman, a Mr. Edward Drew, who asked me to keep in touch with him always, I did.

I soon packed up, saw as many of Sir Thomas's friends as time would permit, got their messages and bid goodbye to my adopted home, New York, my family and friends whom I thought I would never see again, for one on such occasion never knows what's next, and when off Sandy Hook, I wrote my goodbye to Frank Flaherty, asking for an extended vacation, and after seeing the beautiful lights of good old New York pass from view, I retired to try and get a sleep, but that was not to be, for although happy, my mind was not at rest, nor did I get a good sleep for several days, thinking of all that I was leaving behind me maybe forever.

My word, when I look back to that glorious July 4th, 1914, with happiness and prosperity in every land, and the Stars and Stripes flowing from every house and building with my fellow citizens walking along Fifth Avenue, and one band after another striking up some beautiful tune in honor of the day we were celebrating, my heart sank, and my tears flowed, in spite of the fact of my being an old retired New York Bobby, but it was to be, for I at no time ever forgot my duty and love for my adopted country, and all that I owed her, and my fond and loving family.

My Mother and Father, three brothers and three sisters whom I had paid the passages of to bring them to America, and my ten children, at the same time were Motherless, and the fact that my dear old Mother was fast losing her reason with old age, and the sad thoughts that my Father was killed by a fall from a New York street car, in 1893, my oldest brother Lawrence had fallen from a building on which he was working, in the City of London, 1880 and my oldest sister married, also died from a fall in New York, 1898, and at the moment I am re-writing this history on the 22nd year's anniversary of my darling wife Mary's passing away, may the Heavens be their beds.

No doubt some of my readers will term this writing babyish, that may be so, but let them place themselves in this same position, and it's a hundred grand that they too will resort to the same babyism, that is if they are human, and picks up where I left off, roaming in far off Foreign lands across the deep and dark blue sea, remembering the lock of hair, that your darling Mother gave to thee.

When I sailed away July 4th, 1914 all the world was happy and peaceful, no thoughts of war, and it was my intention to go to London to see the fights between Gunboat Smith, and Georges Carpentier, that Smith lost on an unintentional foul, that Mr. Corri, the referee, should have overlooked.

And on the next night, the Willie Richie and Freddy Welsh fight, but I had not made any mention of this in my letter to Sir Thomas, so that when I arrived in Southampton July 11th, 1914, I booked up at "Hoopers" Hotel and wired Sir Thomas that I was here, and soon received a telegram from London reading as follows: Dear Mr. Hickey, I am staying over in London to see the fights, go and make yourself happy in the *Erin,* I will join you after the fights, my word, but Jack Hickey, the old Bowery Copper was travelling in auspicious company, oh yes, I say he was, this has a moral, always be polite and sociable, ever ready to do a good turn, and never let an opportunity pass you by, and you too may get in the aristocratic swim, who knows?

Now to sum up, this little history, Sir Thomas is dead, and the *Erin* is in Davy Jones' locker, Frank Flaherty is still going strong, and may be nominated for Senator this fall, and my dear good friend Ed Drew is living in retirement in an apartment in the Bronx, forced to give up his writings on account of his age, and by the way, it may be well to know that Mr. Drew, in his younger days was an able writer. I was astonished to learn that Mr. Drew had written a long story, in the N. Y. "Herald" of my visit to Mr. Croker. I recall while stopping in Dublin, Ireland, August 6th, 1914, I wrote Mr. Drew, that I had spent the day before with the late Mr. Richard Croker, former leader of Tammany Hall, and a mighty fine leader at that, and after lunch he took me through his Irish stud, and introduced me to his wonderful Derby winner "ORBY" who had won the blue ribbon in 1909, and through some dam fiddling among King Edward's staff, the usual custom of the King, taking the derby winner by the head, was overlooked in this case, and Mr. Croker took that to heart, one sad mistake of King Edward VII.

My but what a wicked old rogue is Dame Fortune when she wants to be! for it makes no difference how hard one tries to avoid trouble, he finds it impossible, and God knows that Sir Thomas Lipton, had his full share of his worldly troubles. The fact of his being chiseled out of the Cup in 1914, and the sinking of the *Erin* in 1915, but later on, the beautiful steam yacht the *Victoria,* that Sir Thomas had hired to accommodate his friends for the America's Cup yacht races of 1920, ran aground and was near sinking. Not a moment was lost, and she was saved and drydocked forthwith, and it was with happiness and glee, that she escaped serious injury and at the races she would be, and we the guests of Sir Thomas had a wonderful time on her after.

And on each of these occasions, Sir Thomas came within an ace of losing his life, but. thanks to Divine Providence and the prayers of a fond loving mother, Sir Thomas was saved, only to die in the hands of thieves, ingrates, a few years after, more's the pity.   At least so it appears to date.

So that there will be no misunderstanding, it may be as well to know that when my Dear Wife Mary, died, I commenced to lay my plans for a visit to my old home in Ireland, and to do this I had to first see that my children were taken care of, so I consulted a very fine old friend, a Catholic Priest, who was devoting his life to the upbringing of Catholic boys whose parents had died.   I had been one of his promoters in this worthy cause for many years, sending my check yearly to pray for my dead, and the future happiness of my children.

This good Padre, promising to take care of my three minor sons, I placed them under his care, and had all provisions made before laying out my plan of travel to the Dear Little Emerald set in the sea, old Ireland.

And having taken care of these details, and working right along saving my dollars and cents, and when fully well satisfied that I was doing my duty to my children, I commenced to take the matter of a vacation up with my Boss, Mr. Frank Flaherty, General Manager, for Gordon Bennett, and the Bennett Estate, Mr. Bennett then living in France, why, I don't know, this was none of my business.

And after Mr. Flaherty had made the way clear for my vacation, he told me that on my return I would couple with my own work that of a couple of old fakirs in his employ for twenty years or more, that never had the nerve to ask for a vacation, and that was the reason why I quit my job, and went my way, knowing that I could never starve while my pension was going on, a small one, but nevertheless a God-send monthly.

Now folks you have heard my confession, all of which may be verified if you think it necessary.   We will go along with the story.

I can never forget the very kind reception that this old New York Cop received that day, after the fights in London, and the days following, from both Sir Thomas and his party, among them was Commodore Marks, of the far off Australian yacht club, Lord Hardwicke, who was to sail on *Shamrock IV,* then about to leave for New York for the yacht races, of 1914, but war having broke out, these races for the America's Cup, had to be postponed until after the cursed war would be over.   I never could fathom why, we were at peace with the world, and the races could well have been run off.

When the war was a reality, Commodore Marks joined his Regiment and with Colonel Duncan F. Neill, fought hard and, often, within an inch of their lives, both of these good men winning the D.S.O. and lived to return to be honored by the British government, for their wonderful records on the firing line, and are both living today, and doing well.

Sitting around the festive board in the saloon of *Erin,* Sir Thomas sitting at the head of the table, would ignore all others present to ask his old friend Hickey, about his friends back home in little old New York, and roaring Bill Thompson, former Mayor of Chicago.

Sir Thomas would say, "Tell me Mr. Hickey, how are my old friends the Hon. Morgan J. O'Brien, Commodore Taylor, Commissioner R. A. C. Smith, and many others, of course we had no Mayor Walker, or Police Commissioner Enright, Whalen, or Mulrooney, and a host of other friends of Sir Thomas, made since that time, but how that grand old warrior did chuckle after hearing about his old friends, and Mr. Hickey, was drinking the good Lipton Tea, Bushmill whiskey all through the long line of questioning, and then we would go up on deck and play quoits and other games, until something new would get on the mind of Sir Thomas about his friends in America, and he would say: Come Mr. Hickey, I was thinking of Mr. or Mrs. so and so, and I having moved around the city a lot before leaving home, was well able to explain his many questions, for you never knew an old New York Bobby, to get absent-minded under such circumstances, not at all man, not at all, for they stay up nights to get their information.

And Sir Thomas never once forgot to ask about his grand old friend Former President, and Colonel Theodore (Teddy) Roosevelt the man, and a one hundred per cent American, of whom Sir Thomas thought very much.

This was again repeated in Osidge in 1928, but the friends of Sir Thomas had increased, for Enright, Walker, Whalen and others were on the job.

For further reference, and so that we will be able to keep our records in proper shape, and it being a part of the autobiography of Sir Thomas, I take pleasure in submitting same to you folks, to wit—

All arrangements were being made for the yacht races in 1920, postponed from 1914, and we the invited guests awaiting the call to steam out to the S. Y. Victoria, hired by Sir Thomas to take the place of the *Erin.*

Sir Thomas was a happy man that day, moving around the deck introducing his guests to each other before the race started, among them were many old friends, namely, the Hon. Morgan J. O'Brien, his wife and family; Commodore Willard U. Taylor and his beautiful bride, now his wife and mother of two fine young sons; Police Commissioner Enright and Mrs. Enright; Deputy Fire Commissioner John Hannon, and a committee of the firemen that saved *Shamrock IV* from being destroyed by fire on City Island, at the drydock of Mr. Jacobs in February, 1919, and many other notables.

Oh, yes, there was one grand old famous Indian fighter in no less a real representative of the American army fighters of old. I speak of that grand old general, Nelson A. Miles, sitting happy and comfortable among the ladies whom he delighted with his presence and whom he highly entertained with his famous battle stories. Of course, the younger generation did not know, nor can they speak of, the wonderful fighting ability of that grand old warrior of fifty years ago; but we, the old-timers, always have honored and respected him and all America was proud of our native son. But there was one other man present in the person of "Roaring" Bill Thompson, Mayor of Chicago, who has been quoted often as ringing the nose of King George V, of England, a decent and honest ruler who was never known to do anything dishonest to either his people in particular, or the world in general.

Sir Thomas knew nothing of Mayor Thompson's private life. All that he knew was that he was the Mayor of the great and glorious city of Chicago.

But I had reasons to be sorry for the Mayor's presence, if for no other reason than that he gave the aristocrats of London food for gossip.

Constantly looking for news of that character, so that they could weaken the standing of Sir Thomas with the King and the whole Royal family by notifying the King that Sir Thomas was entertaining this terrible man that would utter such remarks about the pulling of the nose of His Majesty, and whatever else they cared to add to the same. Yes, this was their chance.

I, having been requested to call upon Sir Thomas several days after the races, the question came up of the races and his fine body of guests present day after day. It was then that I thought it high time to tell my little history of Bill Thompson, not so much because when I mailed him a copy of my book, "OUR POLICE GUARDIANS," with bill for the same to the Mayor, he did not respond, or even return my book, with return postage guaranteed, and he was not the only one, for I also mailed a copy to his successor, and many other notables of New York society, and received neither money nor my book, among them several learned judges, and that wind-jammer, "Babe" Ruth, for it is an old and a true saying that opportunity makes grafters of many, and I have had my fill of this sorrowful experience.

My only thought was of my dear old friend of long standing, Tom Lipton, and what his excuse would be should the King ask him about the matter.

And after making these remarks to Sir Thomas, he answered, "Heavenly Father, why Mr. Hickey, I knew nothing about that at all.

7th May 1926

To my good friend
John... ...
With best wishes
Yrs faithfully
Thomas Lipton

THE LIPTON TROPHIES

KILLARNEY
1914

THE AUTHOR TRAVELING THROUGH IRELAND

SIR THOMAS LIPTON
The World's Famous Irish Yachtsman, and Honorary Deputy
Chief Inspector of New York Police.

Mr. Westwood has all and full charge of mailing these invitations, not me, unless I may suggest the names of old friends like yourself.

"My time is constantly taken up in business. I have no time to learn the private character of these men; I have no other means of learning of them unless from an old friend like yourself. Please keep me informed of such matters, won't you, Mr. Hickey. Write me a personal letter when you think it advisable to have me know the truth of such cases please!

"I am very much pleased and I thank you for having called my attention to this matter. In case the King may question me about the story, don't forget to write me and I will return an answer myself personally. I thank you, who in all of our long friendship have never let such matters pass you."

I don't know how you, my readers, may think about this as in all other cases I deemed it my duty to a grand old friend, that was all.

I promised Sir Thomas that I would and did right up until the races of September, 1930, but received very few answers. Why? Well, all that I could make out of it was that John Westwood, who had sent out the invitations, did not like to hear my remarks to the Chief. There was one letter in particular and a very important one at that; I wrote Sir Thomas and mailed a copy of same to John Westwood, that if acted on might have placed a much better aspect on the races of 1930. These letters Westwood claims he never received, but I don't know why. For that I am very sorry.

You know, my friends, how easy it is to give a man a black eye, by one that to do you an injury by making false reports, particularly when that man is more than three thousand miles from the scene, and not aware of what is going on behind the scenes.

But human nature won't permit a friend to be lied about, not at all, and many of my letters from Sir Thomas, in this book, will substantiate my remarks.

But from that evening on how cool John Westwood got towards me, and it often cropped up at later meetings, no doubt, he thought that I was butting into his business, and that of the invisible government then functioning. But that did not disturb me a little, I would lay down my life to protect my friend, and at that was simply doing my duty—to your entire satisfaction, I hope.

And I, knowing that I was not to receive my invitation to view the races from the deck of the *Erin*, I wrote John Westwood that business would not permit of my being a guest of Sir Thomas this season, for Newport was too darn far from the Bowery, and too expensive to travel to daily, so that I contented myself by staying home to add to the many pages of my book, my autobiography. I recall writing my congratulations on his successful voyage over, to my old friend, Duncan Neill, at

New London, but received no answer. Westwood received all mail, and it was up to him, not Uncle Sam.

But it is a loss of time for me to be writing in this strain. I simply want you folks to know the truth, and how miserably I was served by John Westwood for standing by his boss, my good friend. You are not dumb heads and surely know right from wrong; use your own judgment, and if you arrive at the conclusion that Hickey was wrong then I will abide by your decision. That's all my good and noble readers—that's all.

I, having been denied the seeing of Sir Thomas by John Westwood so many times when I would call from the hotel office, I determined to wait and meet him returning from some function, and get him taking the elevator, only to get rats from Sir Thomas, rather than to tell him the truth.

But you don't want to be listening to my complaints. I am simply making them so that my readers employing secretaries will beware, or, like Lord John Dewar, you will want one committee watching over the rights and interests of the other committee in jail. It is not proper to trust any man too far, particularly the one that you entrust with your private affairs, business and money, and to avoid that, get married, but pick a real woman, not a gold-digger, or you will jump out of one hell into another.

Here is how my dear old friend used to write. Oh, how I long for them today:

> "CITY ROAD, LONDON.
> "May 10th, 1923.

"Dear Mr. Hickey:

"Your very charming and artistic birthday card to hand, and I am deeply grateful to you, for you never have forgotten me in all these so many years, and that is very thoughtful of you.

"I assure you that I deeply appreciate your kindness very highly, for the fact of being remembered by my old friends like your own good self, hoping this will find you fit and well, and looking forward to meeting you in dear old New York soon again, I am,

> "Yours faithfully,
>
> "THOMAS J. LIPTON."

Little did I think, dear people, that I would so shortly after be changing my book from the autobiography to the biography of Sir Thomas, and after that first race of September 13th, I would not go to Newport on a bet, but we, the guests of Sir Thomas, spent several happy days off Sandy Hook, for it was one continuous round of pleasure. This is one of the features, to wit:

Every morning Mr. Borden, from Rumson, N. J., would bring his hydroplane along side of the steam yacht *Victoria* and take a party up and give them a view of the sloops while racing. You would always find the present Mrs. Commodore Taylor, whom, I am proud to say, is the mother of several beautiful children, always in the lead, the first to step on board the air machine and the last to leave it, and it would do one's heart good to be near that gay young sport, "Grace Darling." Number two: Commodore Embury McLean, another one of my old friends, with Mr. William H. Ranken (Mr. Ranken was closely connected with Sir Thomas in the advertising end of the firm), and Miss Ranken, his pretty daughter, and I met at "Osidge," the London home of Sir Thomas in 1928, and another typical American girl, fond of all kinds of outdoor sports. Miss Ranken and her friend, Miss Mayo, played plenty of golf and tennis while stopping at this beautiful castle, "Osidge," eleven miles outside of London.

Another grand old friend of Sir Thomas' of many years was present, that was Commodore A. Jarvis and wife, of Toronto, Canada. Thomas A. Edison and son, Richard E. Enright, Police Commissioner, and Mrs. Enright, Grover A. Whalen, then Secretary to Mayor Hylan, his wife and family, Commissioner R. A. C. Smith and daughter, the Hon. Justice Morgan O'Brien and family, John J. Hickey and family, and last, but not least, the Hon. George Doherty, Justice of the Peace of Londonderry, and a very fine gentleman he turned out to be, for when Mr. Doherty and I joined the party, knowing full well that birds of a feather flock together, Sir Thomas introduced us and we were friends ever after, and when Justice Doherty heard the band of the line of battleship the *Shannon,* playing the "Wearing of the Green," he was amazed, grabbing my arm, he said, "Glory be to God, Mr. Hickey, it's little did I think that I would live to hear a British warship playing our old Irish battle hymn or march."

And while all work and no play makes Jack a dull boy, and maybe that is the reason that I am so dumb! Well, to get back to my good friend and fellow sufferer, "Rory O'Moore" George Doherty, who said, "In the name of God, let us go down stairs and drink to the *H.R.M. W. S. Shannon,*" and we did. From that time on he kept me in fits of laughter. I enjoyed it, so, too, may you. However, look upon it as a cocktail between working hours, for I never before tasted a cocktail so pleasant and amusing.

Perhaps a little comedy, followed by a sorrowful death, may not be out of place, to wit: I, having been asked by Sir Thomas on leaving that I take care of Mr. Doherty, and wanting to have him see all the principal points of interest, we arrived in London at 2:30 a. m. and up at 9, to attend Mass in St. George's Cathedral, Lambeth, where I spent my boyhood days; so, too, did Charley Chaplin, the great comedian, who was born there; and I, being a fad on walking, for even today I must walk at least two miles a day to keep me fit and well, but my genial Irish friend was no walker, but my plans had to be carried out, and they were keeping us walking until 11 p. m., for every time a bus drew near he was for the bus, but not seeing me running he quit and would sit down on the curb, until he saw me near out of sight, and then poor George, and his little bandy legs would be seen running to beat the band, for if I left him, he, too, would be lost and unable to find our hotel, the "Caledonian," Harpur Street, West London, and on passing Westminster Abbey, he wanted to rest up, but this could not be, under the circumstances, for I was on my way to St. Patrick's Cathedral, Ashley Place, to hear one of the greatest, and last but one, sermons preached by Father Hugh Benson, a wonderful talker often heard here in America, but the poor man worked so hard in his preaching that he became ill and died in 1914.

Father Benson, may God have mercy on him, came of a noted family, his father being the Protestant Archbishop of Westminster with his palace quite near St. Patrick's, but Hugh Benson embraced the Catholic faith, and sure there was no crime in that, was there? However, both Father Benson and Father Vaughan, both now dead, and the present Bishop or Cardinal Bourne of Westminster, have brought about the conversion of thousands of the aristocracy of England, doubling that of any other three men of the church, and I was in duty bound to be sure to get two seats that evening for the great big Cathedral was packed to over-flowing by the most prominent men and their families of all London, and elsewhere. I saw the notice by accident after Mass on the bulletin board of St. George's Cathedral, or I would have missed this. I would not let that memorable episode pass me, if I never eat or rode, and right on the site on which I handed His Eminence, Cardinal Manning, out of his cab, away back in 1879—or 80, to bless and consecrate the ground, one great and glorious happening in all of my long life, could you blame me to present myself there that evening, of Sunday, July 20th, 1914?

With all due respect to my eminent friend, Justice George Doherty, who was a devil among the pretty English lassies, and never tiring of their company, I knew that it was not right to use him so, but that is why I never in all of my travels, asked for or did I want a companion, for I love to walk and take in the sights, something that I may never live to enjoy again.

I had promised Sir Thomas to be sure that George D. would be at the pig market Wednesday. Next morning being Monday, I let him sleep to mid-day, and after dinner I took him on another walk down through High Holborn, into Lincoln's, into the Strand Temple Bar, Trafalgar Square and the Thames Embankment to keep him from abusing his good friend, Hickey, that wanted to learn the eminent and fitting Justice something he never knew before. That was, the sayings and doings of London town.

But, as a matter of fact, I thoroughly enjoyed his company, for he kept me constantly laughing, for often I expected to be placed under arrest near Scotland Yard, for kidnapping, for the moment he would sit down on the curb he would have a committee of ladies around him pitying the poor man, so far from home, and then they would appeal to me, and again I would have to call upon my diplomacy to shut them up, and call it a day.

Next day the same old grind, walking my dear old friend to Hyde Park, St. James and the Green Parks, to Buckingham Palace, advising him to send his card into King George, whom he thought very much of, he having to take the oath of obedience to the King or Queen of England, to become a Magistrate.

Then back to the hotel to take supper and pack up, put him on his train at Euston Station, to get over to Ireland to buy more pigs, maybe the Tom Lipton's two "orphans," but I was tired, and glad he left for home, goodbye.

Against the wishes of the American Consul in London, I paid a hurried visit to Paris the eve of the declaration of war, August 1st, 1914, for the dark clouds were fast gathering, and war dogs barking loud and strong. I was forced to pack up and fly back to London next day. Yes, I saw Paris.

But I left home to see the world, and to return without seeing any part of it was too much for my blood, and I booked passage to Ireland, and after seeing all Ireland sailed home with the Hon. Justice Daniel F. Cohalan and his pretty family, like my own large and commodious, September 27, 1914, I did not go to Ireland to fight. I have had all I wanted of that in my early days.

And now I want to live and die in peace. But I did join up with the City of Cork volunteers before leaving, to give aid and comfort. My first visit after nearly forty years, in 1914, was a most happy one, but my visit in 1927, while visiting Paris, France, with the American Legion, was not so happy, and I don't want a repetition of it. God forbid; but I love Ireland from the bottom of my heart, for there is but one Ireland.

But, how strange; just at the very time that the Cosgrave government has been defeated and is giving up its power, along comes an important document that must be considered and signed, namely, the "Dominion's" report, and when Mr. Patrick MacGilligan, the Free State Minister for Foreign Affairs, read and presented the document, describing the findings as constituting "the most important constitutional document submitted to the legislature since the Anglo-Irish treaty," it was received with great applause by the good men of Ireland there represented in the Dail, but the few that are called the followers of De Valera, laughed and scoffed.

And after all arguments, pro and con, the bill was called for a vote and to the surprise of the government, received a majority of but thirteen votes, and yet they want us to believe that they are the real friends of Ireland. The back of my hand to them patriots.

Ireland is depending on the good people to buy her bonds. Are they at this time going to be disappointed? Why, no. The good wealthy Irishmen and Irishwomen—the bright stars of America today, will never forsake their motherland. God bless them all, for God gave it to them, and their families, all of them devoted followers of the Catholic Church, and William T. Cosgrove for Ireland's next President, and again old Ireland will be happy. April 3rd, 1930.

A member of the Cosgrave administration came to our shores today, and it was given out that he was to be taken for a ride by De Valera's brutal followers, but P. C. Edward Mulrooney, soon stifled that report, having a body of picked men to meet and greet the gentleman, and protect him. Yes, this good man was well protected, and the bonds went over the top.

Having bid goodbye to my dear old friend, Mr. Doherty, I wandered to the House of Commons and, having sent in my card to our honored leader of that time, the able successor of the late Charles Stewart Parnell, Mr. John Redmond, I was escorted to the strangers' gallery, to hear the members arguing on the Home Rule for Ireland Bill, just passed and the amendments that were introduced by our sore-headed members of the enemy party, the Tories.

And after this session, which terminated late in the following morning, I was introduced by Mr. Redmond to many of his followers, including his noble brother, William K. (Willie), who gave up his life in the cause of Ireland's freedom leading his men in battle on the bloody fields of Flanders, so that Willie Redmond, M. P., is no more.

And our able leader, Mr. John E. Redmond, who had undermined his health in his long fights to bring about the happiness of his people, missed his brother's company very much, for from the first day that I met them as boys, taken by the hand of good old John Redmond, M. P., at the "Reformer's" tree, in grand old Hyde Park, fifty years before our present meeting, and ever after John E. and William K. Redmond were never separated, until the fire of the German enemy separated them once and for all.

And, I am sorry to relate, the strain was too much for our leader, and he, too, was forced to take to his bed and passed away. The victory of his many years of fighting for Ireland being won, he died peacefully in the arms of his fond, loving wife, another victim of the late great world-destroying war. Peace be to the Redmonds, they had done their bit, and are today resting in their heavenly home, absent, but not forgotten.

And while writing this story, I am sorry to relate that another Redmond has been called upon to cross the greate divide. I speak of the noble son of our late leader, Captain William Redmond, M. P., and a devoted follower of our present leader, Mr. William T. Cosgrave of the Irish Free State.

I spent several days in London looking up my old haunts and the few of my old friends still in the flesh, but I felt rather lonesome without my dear old friend, George Doherty, Esq., J.P., and pork butcher of Londonderry.

I had heartily enjoyed the company of my old friend for the past week, for we were not over anxious to mix up with the society folks, other than to play a few deck games while loafing about on the *Erin*.

It seemed to me as if I had met Mr. Doherty before, and we stuck to each other like lost brothers. His charming Irish brogue and personality had me enchanted, but when he had gone, my spirits dropped considerably, so that my doctor prescribed a wee drink of Irish, three times a day.

And with this allowance, I greatly enjoyed a pint of stout and mild, and a blooming big cheese sandwich, or a pint of half-and-half, but at that I was lonesome and London failed to hold me any longer in her embrace, so, having made my last visit to the House of Commons, leaving at 2:30 a. m., I found that the last car and bus had gone. I walked back to my hotel tired and footsore and weary of my staying any longer, for I was Ireland-bound.

I packed up my belongings, paid my hotel bill and arriving at the Euston Station, I booked for Hollyhead, and thence to Kingston, Dublin. My word, when I found myself once more on that grand old Irish coast, with land not yet in view, I having taken with me from London a little of "Kinnahan's double L" I bid ould Ireland "the top of the morning."

And after that I felt like a new man. I was so happy thinking that I was nearing dear old County Cork, and in a few more days would be at the grand old bog fireside, in the "Boreen" beyant in the corner. I then sang a few old come-all-you's, the songs of my childhood, and while singing that grand old song of "Come Back to Erin," I fell asleep, for the steamer had many more miles to go before reaching land.

Much correspondence passed between us in the many years of friendship, and for your information and guidance, I will publish in this work some copies of these many letters, that I hold dear, and tightly tucked away among my most endearing possessions.

"OSIDGE, LONDON.
"26th January, 1911.

"Dear Mr. Hickey:

"Sir Thomas Lipton, who has just sailed for Ceylon, wishes me to write you and thank you very much for your kind thoughts of him, and the coming year of 1911, which he highly appreciates and reciprocates in the fullest measure. The Chief trusts that you and yours are well and enjoying good health and prosperity.

"With all good wishes, from Sir Thomas and myself,
"Yours respectfully,
"JOHN WESTWOOD.
"Mr. John J. Hickey,
1841 Coney Island Avenue, Brooklyn, N. Y."

"CITY ROAD, LONDON.
"28th May, 1914.
"Dear Mr. Hickey:
"Your letter of the 19th instant, with the enclosures addressed to Sir Thomas
Lipton is to hand, and I shall take the earliest opportunity of placing same
before Sir Thomas, who I know, will greatly appreciate your courtesy.
"Yours faithfully,
"Mr. John J. Hickey,   "JOHN WESTWOOD.
306 Washington Avenue, Brooklyn, N. Y."

There were no thoughts of horrid war at this time. This letter I
answered by stating that I hoped to leave for Ireland on or about July
4th, and would advise Sir Thomas on my landing in Southampton on
my arrival there about July 10th or July 11th, 1914.

And on my landing in Southampton, I wired Sir Thomas, then in London, and received a telegram forthwith. The rest of this story you
will find in another chapter of this book.

"CITY ROAD, LONDON,
"8th August, 1914.
"Dear Mr. Hickey:
"Your letter duly to hand. I am afraid, however, that there is no chance
of the races taking place on the dates fixed and will have to be postponed
either to a later date this year or until next year.
"I think the chances are that it will have to be next year.
"I trust that this will find you well.
"Yours faithfully,
"Mr. John J. Hickey,   "JOHN WESTWOOD.
"Caledonia Hotel, Harpur Street, London, W. C."

"CITY ROAD, LONDON,
"4th September, 1914.
"John J. Hickey, Esq.,
"Turner's Hotel,
"Georges Street, City of Cork, Ireland.
"Dear Mr. Hickey:
"Many thanks for your letter of the 1st inst., also the very fine postcards
inclosed in same.
"In reply to your inquiry, I am pleased to state the *Erin* is now on her way
back to England, being due at Falmouth tomorrow (Saturday) but it is at
present uncertain where she will be laid up, as Southampton is at present a
closed port.
"With kindest regards and best wishes,
"Yours faithfully,
"JOHN WESTWOOD."

It will be mighty hard for me to forget that grand and glorious
day of July 19th, 1914, for both happiness and sunshine reigned supreme. John Redmond, the Irish leader, had just won one of the
greatest victories in Ireland's history, the Home Rule for Ireland Bill,
and the whole world and its people were rejoicing, with bonfires burning on the hillsides of Ireland, and a picture of happiness and sunshine
in every home.

But, alas, inside of the next week or two, the dark clouds of misery
and bloodshed and world destruction; the people unhappy with death
and starvation staring them in the face; with the wild man of Europe
and his hungry hordes; the Kaiser Wilhelm and his blood-thirsty followers being held up by that famous hero, King Albert of Belgium, and

his army, his action saving the world's destruction, for while King Albert was fighting, all the other nations affected were sleeping.

Then came the blasing of trumpets and the rattling of sabers. France woke up and declared war, August 1st; England, turning heaven and earth to try and avoid this, the world's greatest conflict, but it was no use, she was forced to enter, declaring war on Germany August 4th, 1914, and poor me in both countries at the time of their respective declarations; Paris August 1st and London August 4th, of the sad and deplorable year of Our Lord, 1914—followed by old Ireland, that is always fighting, and after the British warships, playing their heart's delight and grand old battle hymn "The Wearing of the Green," nothing on earth could keep them out of the fray.

I, staying up nights in the cities of Dublin and Cork, to see the poor fellows off to go unprepared into Ostend and there to be shot and maimed in the terrible battle of the "Mons," one of the fiercest of all battles, only to return to Ireland, that they had just left happy, singing, "It's a long way to Tipperary, it's a long way to go, it's a long way to Tipperary, to the sweetest girl I know," armless and legless. My God! What a sight.

Kaiser Wilhelm the 2nd had not yet arrived on the scene, but prepared to the minute; for, remembering well the speech of Prince Bismarck, in 1862, "Germany was growing, and they must have more territory and that could not be obtained by the pen," the remarks of Prince Bismarck to the German Parliament in 1862 stuck in his gizzard. But Bismarck was no longer connected with the present German dynasty, and Wild Bill was shouting out, "Bismarck, my Bismarck, my kingdom for a Bismarck." It was then too late, for when the Kaiser ordered Prince Bismarck out of his palace, he was "kicking his best schoolmaster out of doors," for if King Edward VII of England, or Prince Bismarck were living there would be no unmerciful World's War, for it was madness to start one at the time, with all nations looking to get a slap at Germany, and they did.

Sir Thomas was indeed a very happy man that week, and all that he seemed to be interested in was in his old friend, Hickey, telling him about his grand old American friends, and the seventeen guests around that festive board, of course, were happy, for they learned more about America, and her hospitality from that old-time New York Bobby that week than they ever heard before.

And after Sir Thomas would order a cocktail for each, we would adjourn to the upper deck and play the regular ocean voyage games, "Quoits," and maybe a quiet game of cards, and when it came to the goodbye forever, every member of the party were so sorry, and expressed themselves so, many times, and I, too, had many reasons for being sorry at this farewell.

I had never been blessed with meeting such a fine group before.

THE DEPARTURE OF *SHAMROCK IV* FOR AMERICA
JULY 19TH, 1914

PART I—CHAPTER V

This was one of the grandest days in the history of this grand old seaport, for King George V and Queen Mary were there backed up with 350 warships, and happiness reigned supreme the world over. It seemed to me that all England and a goodly part of Ireland and Scotland were present and, of course, the little old U. S. A. was also represented, on that glorious occasion, for without America the world would be lost.

Yes, sir, Southampton and the towns for 100 miles around were on sea on that memorable occasion, but the two policemen that guarded that port, for I never saw but two cops in the twenty-four hours, and that speaks well for that pretty little seaport. And when I say twenty-four hours, I say that advisedly, for when eight bells had struck we would find the tender ready to take us back to Southampton, two miles away, there to meet these same old two bobbies again.

I will never forget my feelings that beautiful day, standing with the many guests of Sir Thomas, bidding goodbye to the brave boys that were to sail the *Shamrock IV* to New York, 3,000 miles way, to win new laurels.

Under the command of Commodore Duncan F. Neill and Lord Hardwicke, who was to take the tiller on her trip, it seemed to me that our parting was a farewell, and not a so long one, for I could not fathom how a small, frail, little wee piece of wood and sail could survive the terrible storms and the high winds of the roaring Atlantic, when the biggest and prettiest ship afloat, the *S.S. Leviathan,* was getting knocked around on her different, and oftentimes troublesome, passages, and in my heart I said goodbye.

But that grand old scout, Sir Thomas, would say, "Don't you worry, Mr. Hickey, Duncan Neill will take her over safely, so look forward for an early telegram, for Neill will send me a word or two just as soon as he is prepared."

And when Sir Thomas called me to him the following day and read the long looked for telegram, reading as follows, "All is well, Sir Thomas, and will make the trip in 21 days," the grand old sportsman smiled and I became a much happier man, and enjoyed my stay aboard the *Erin* in a more pleasanter mood after listening to that very fine reading from my old friend, the Commodore of the Lipton fleet, far out to sea.

Sir Thomas also remarked that he, too, would have been with them but he had been summoned to London. Something had gone wrong at the factory and he must return to adjust it.

You all know what had happened at that time, a something that was to bring about the destruction of the world, the people of the Balkan states were up in arms, because on July 28th, 1914, a poor innocent boy of 17 shot and killed an enterloper to his country, an enemy, as he thought, in the person of Prince Ferdinand of Austria.

And that was the spark that Kaiser Wilhem of Germany, Austria's ally, was waiting for many years to plunge the happy world into misery, pitting father against son, and brother against brother. Heavenly Father, how my dear old heart bleeds when I think of it. I, an exile from Erin, and a devoted and loyal adopted son of these United States, caught in the midst of this terrible ordeal, and at the moment three thousand miles away from home and loved ones, who had gone to visit his old home and friends after forty years.

I recall as a boy in London, when in 1862, Prince Bismarck, one of the world's greatest diplomats, and adviser to German royalty, in a speech in the German Parliament, said among other things, the following:

"Our population is fast growing, we must have more territory, and that cannot be obtained by the pen." And in the year of our Lord, 1879, we were on the verge of the World's War, that was fought in after years, 1914, and I know it to my heart's content for I booked up to fight for Ireland and England against the robbers who would strip us of all, if they could.

No other country wanted war, not at all; they were not prepared for war, but Germany must have it, she wanted more territory, and she got it in hell. And here we are today, in 1934, we find Dictator Herr Hitler paying back to her ally, Austria, something that was owed her, but not in gold. No, no.

This brought about the postponement of the coming yacht races, and Sir Thomas turning his beautiful yacht the *Erin,* over to the Government to aid and assist the dying of all nations, as a hospital ship only to be in a few short months or weeks blown up by the enemy, Commodore Neill joined his regiment and won victory after victory, while Sir Thomas was being at different times within an ace of his life, trying to protect his doctors and nurses of the British and American Red Cross, but America, had not at this time entered the fight, but when she did, April 6th, 1917, she cleaned up fighting side by side with our Irish and English brothers helping that grand old English General, Haig, who was fighting with his back to the wall.

The mind of the author is often carried back to the beautiful days of 1913-1914, with happiness on all sides, no thoughts of war for nothing could be further from one's mind, but when it was forced upon the world with such able soldiers and statesmen of our Allied countries, it was met with a spirit of determination and final victory, thanks to the nobleness of the art of the following heroes, and their fighting armies, to wit:—

King Albert of Belgium, Lord Kitchener, Earl Grey, backed up by Ireland and her fighting heroes under the able command of Ireland's Parliamentary leader, Mr. John E. Redmond, and his hero of a brother, William (Willie) Redmond in thanksgiving to England for the Home Rule Bill just passed by the Members of the House of Commons, to make Ireland and her leaders happy, but at what price glory. Major Redmond, M.P., shot down leading his men into battle on the bloody fields of glory, this bringing about the death of his brother, John, the very able leader and successor of the late Charles Stewart Parnell, followed shortly after by Captain William Redmond, M.P., son of John E. Redmond, the Irish leader, but I am not writing the world's war history, although the one was born of the other, and should have been stifled at her birth, and the wishes and requests of our noble President, Franklin D. Roosevelt, ignored by our House of Representatives, both the Democrats and Republicans of both houses acting shamefully towards the liberator sent to us from the Heavens to save his people, and all mankind.

You will recall that a like dirty action was repeated under the grand and glorious administration of President, the Hon. Woodrow Wilson, when he asked of the House of Representatives and the Senate something badly needed than at law, to help us, they too ignored that great man's requests, among them seven able bodied Congressmen, elected by the Democratic party of this great city, something never known before in history,—shame on you all.

But when it came to Prohibition, even they having their stomachs and cellars full, while our poor soldier boys were dying for a drink in the dark trenches of the bloody battlefields of Europe, this cowardly mob of men passed the 18th Amendment, and when our President vetoed the bill, these same misrepresentatives met and passed the bill over Mr. Wilsons' veto, but they all went the way of the unjust, one of these same men I saw at the funeral of that eminent Jurist, the Hon. Victor J. Dowling, March 26th, 1934, and from a fine, big, healthy man, he is today a miserable looking specimen of that great legislature, that we, the voters of New York, sent to Washington, D. C. year after year, until that sorrowful day, when he and his pals were bigger than our President, and refused to do their duty to us, their people.

Yes Sir, you can take it from me that these same gentlemen that dared spit in the face of our President, March 25th, 1934, will meet their ends and will die by the roadside, while President Roosevelt, will resign supreme.

A funny stunt of Sir Thomas, and his friend, Mayor John Fitzgerald of Boston, and well known Irish wit, and all of Sir Thomas's diplomacy was shown to the Prince of Wales that afternoon, all of which young Albert Edward thoroughly enjoyed and he laughed to beat the band, and told Sir Thomas that he would like to meet this good natured Irish gentleman, the Mayor of Boston, Mass., of the U.S.A.

The Prince of Wales had heard all about Boston, many years ago, for at the time of our late great heavyweight champion of these United States, yes the whole world, John Lawrence Sullivan, visited England at the request of England's great boxer, yes, fighting champion, the late Charley Mitchell, and when the Prince's attention was called to this visit, he asked to have Mr. Sullivan visit him, and they spent a very pleasant couple of hours together, for the Prince was a lover of the Noble Art of Self Defense, and like the late President of these United States, good old Theodore (TEDDY) Roosevelt would don the gloves with his old friend, the late professor Mike Donovan, every afternoon, the Prince donned the gloves with John L. Sullivan, and they sparred several rounds, for like all good men of his type, that is broadminded, as in the case of young Tom Lipton, Albert Edward, Prince of Wales, all men were equal to them, rich or poor, he took delight in meeting them.

And on John L. Sullivan's return to America, it was his pleasure to let his friends, in particular and the public in general, know the kind of a man the young Prince of Wales was, and how hard he could hit, and this was very pleasing news to all, for now that they have all passed on, we must not forget them, but always remember them in our prayers, for they made good.

But to get back to my story of the landing stage of the Royal Yacht *Squadron,* Sir Thomas laughed heartily when I asked him if that was the same landing that was taken over by his big hearted friend, Mayor John Fitzgerald of Boston, Mass., and later on at the luncheon table aboard the *Erin,* I asked Sir Thomas to tell the story to his guests, and he was mighty pleased to do so, for it gave the society ladies and gentlemen something to talk about.

I spent a very happy week on board the *Erin,* or visiting *Shamrock IV,* on the drydock in Gosport, she at the time receiving her finishing touches and preparing to take her long ocean sail, to dear old America, the land of the free, with no beer, but plenty of Lipton's tea.

I shall never forget the morning of *Shamrock IV,* sailing out of Gosport. I thought that day was not unchristianed like to ask Col. Neill, or any other man or handful of men to endanger their lives to sail a wee small yacht over the raging billows of the Atlantic ocean.

Destroy that stone wall that you folks have built around the America's Cup, and by so doing show to all mankind that we Americans are human.

And at the same time you will be giving your opponent a clean break and by so doing, show the world that you are not afraid of losing this dirty old lump of silver, shaped in the form of a cup, or to be more plain about describing the cup, we will call it a tailor's thimble.

If you men of the New York Yacht Club, had the fear of God in your hearts, you would have done this twenty years ago, and Sir Thomas would be then living in happiness, in the position of a retired London grocer, who through his hard work and honesty and his charming personality became a millionaire, and made good in his every undertaking.

And that includes the winning of the America's Cup. Maybe?

My word, what a happy old gentleman Sir Thomas would be, sitting on top of the world, and having no business with grafters and fakers, constantly on the lookout to see when and how they could rob the old gent, for his books will show how often he has been robbed, and by the "System."

I, the author of this work, may be Irish born, but take it from me that I love America, and all that she stands for, other than the 18th Amendment or Prohibition law and its thieving ministers full of hypocrisy, whose God is the almighty dollar, and we are cursed with many of them, unfortunately. I must not overlook that damnable un-American, birth control gang.

I arrived at Castle Garden, as did Tom Lipton, with but fifty cents in my pocket, but always ready and willing to make a dollar, but honestly, and losing no time in declaring my intentions to become an American citizen, and knowing that I had several years to wait, and having to fulfill my promise to my parents on leaving home, I became a longshoreman, for I saw that they were the only people that were making any kind of money. This being the only job for a man with little education, trade or calling.

In the years that I was forced to wait before I was entitled to my full citizenship papers, I went to night school, studied up, and made good to my loved ones, then married an Irish lass from the County of Tyrone, "Tyrone, among the bushes," a Mary Ward, may the Heaven's be her bed to night, for she was a wonderful girl.

We married, and she mothered ten children for me, 5 boys and 5 girls and having done her bit, going so far as to destroy her health as a good God fearing Catholic, she did God's work, and mothered what he sent us, and when but 48, she became ill, and having suffered the torments of hell, she died.

I had joined the New York Police force, served my time and was retired when Mary died, leaving me with five minor children, whom I sent to school and watched over them carefully, raising my sons to volunteer their services to fight for their country, and they but minors at the time, and now they are all members of the 'finest' police force the world over, New York's Blue Birds.

I did much myself during the war to show my own patriotism, selling and exchanging Liberty bonds and War saving stamps, to the amount of $175,000, that and other things done by me, ought to be enough to prove my love of this country and my right to back a friend. I was then appointed a Captain of the United States War Stamp Committee, from Washington, D. C. And of this appointment I assure you I was very proud, to know that I was able to help my country and her allies, when badly needed, I thank God.

In the series of races for the America's Cup, off Sandy Hook in 1914, the list of guests comprised of many members of both the army and navy of all good friends of Sir Thomas, and they thoroughly enjoyed the pleasure of the notable races out on the briny ocean.

There was one man in particular there that day in the person of Lord John Dewar, the great London whiskey king, and boyhood chum of Sir Thomas, he was happy of course, when the Racing Committee notified Sir Thomas that his *Shamrock IV* had won the second race that day, that of July 15th, 1920, and Lord John gave vent to his feelings that day, whooping it up with a wee cup of Lipton tea, or I should say whiskey.

And I am free to say, that we Americans might be happier, had we the pleasure of drinking whiskey instead of tea, although I enjoyed several drinks of Lord John's Scotch that night, but many of my compatriots did not have that pleasure, thanks to the riff raff of Methodist ministers, who voted away our rights and liberties with the prohibition curse of that time.

Out of this series *Shamrock IV,* had won two races and by adding one more would have won the Cup, but the next day being very stormy and there is no denying the fact that if the Skipper of the *Shamrock IV* had nerve and sailed his yacht, the cup would then be the property of Tom Lipton, and my word, how happy he would be, and the thousands of dollars he would save.

We, the guests, both men and women travelled down to Sandy Hook, and there were no reasons why, when being asked by the racing committee: "Captain Burton, do you wish to race today?" Burton, passed the buck to Sir Thomas, and why? Well I understand it was because he had his wife on board the *Shamrock IV* and that should never have been allowed, no, no, not at all.

Of course, you know the result of Skipper Burton failing to do his duty not only to his employer but to the men that were promised a bonus if the *Shamrock IV* had won the cup, and they were willing to sail the race, for the sake of their wives and families, but alas, that was not to be.

The answer that Sir Thomas made to the question of the racing committee, was, "No, Gentlemen, I would not endanger the lives of my men for all the prizes ever produced," and to the Skipper he shouted, "Take in sail and get back to your moorings forthwith," but my the poor old Chief was angry.

And he gave Burton a good dressing down, for among other things he told him that he was the Skipper of *Shamrock IV,* and not him, and he gave him to understand that when a man employed as the Skipper of one of the yachts, then he is the boss, and he, Sir Thomas, never interferes with him and his workings, or for that matter, anyone else in his employ.

The "moral" of the *Shamrock's* crew was very troublesome, and *Resolute* won the next three races and America keeps the cup. And *Shamrock IV* was sure enough in the bag, and this, to my mind, commenced the dirty work to place our grand old friend and his yachts on the tobogganing slide.

But in spite of all that, Sir Thomas, the never say die sport came back again with his *Shamrock V,* got a damn sight worse dose, for *Shamrock V,* did not have a Chinaman's chance and why? You tell me, all that I know is that it was a cowardly shame, and the responsible ones, sooner or later must answer, but will they? Yes, if I can bring it about.

My God, my heart bleeds for this grand old yachtsman, that was never known to do an unkind act, to either man, woman or child, always playing the game fair and above board, then why be so infernal mean with him.

Sir Thomas never wanted to leave Sandy Hook, for he always respected the rights of his good yachting friends along the coast, who always had a chance to see the yachts working, often in a hard fought contest, and ever since yachting began in America to win back the Queen's or America's Cup the races were held at Sandy Hook. Then why were they transferred, only the racing committee of the N.Y.Y.C. can answer that.

Many new yachtsmen of the army and navy of both America, England, and other countries, and each day during the races, Sir Thomas would introduce the writer to them all stating that Mr. Hickey is a retired member of the Police Department of New York, and is today the historian of the Department that he so ably served in the past. Each day there would be a different list of guests and it being the wish of Sir Thomas, that Mr. Hickey should be present each day so that when Sir Thomas and Mr. Westwood were engaged elsewhere the writer would be entertaining the guests, and it goes without saying that I thoroughly enjoyed every minute of my stay, one happy excursion, at that.

Every now and then Sir Thomas standing aft, and I standing forward, he, to have a little joke on Hickey the Cop, would send the

THE WHITE HOUSE
WASHINGTON

March 8, 1916·

ear Sir:

The President deeply appreciates the
ndly words of your letter of March 7th,
he asks me to thank you cordially for
ng written him, as well as for the good
which you manifest.

Sincerely yours,

Secretary to the Presiden

John J. Hickey,
New York City.

, THE WHITE HOUSE
WASHINGTON

ato Generale d'Italia

NEW YORK Feb. 25th,1927.

Mr. John J. Hickey,
Hotel Alton,
353-4th Ave.,
New York, N.Y.

Dear Sir:

I have been requested by his Excellency
Premier Mussolini to forward to you, herewith enclosed,
check for $ 2.00, covering the fee for the book "Our
Police Guardian", which you sent him, and which he has
greatly appreciated.

Yours very truly,

Royal Consul General of Italy

BUCKINGHAM PALACE.

The Private Secretary is
commanded by The King to
thank *Mr. John J. Hickey*
for *his* letter.

7th March. 1919.

GENERAL HEADQUARTERS,

BRITISH ARMIES IN FRANCE

*With heartfelt good
wishes to the New York
Veteran Police Assocn.*

D. Haig. F.M.

16 March 1919

S.Y. ERIN.
Southampton.
24th April 1914.

John J. Hickey Esq.,
    306. Washington Avenue.
        Parkville.
            Brooklyn, New York.

Dear Mr. Hickey,

A thousand thanks for your very kind wishes and I hope they will be realised.

I much appreciate the trouble you have taken in sending me the clippings, which were most interesting and I am very grateful for them.

Hoping that I may have the pleasure of being able to thank you personally for them when I come across to America, and with all good wishes,

Yours faithfully,
Thomas J Hinton

rubbernecks of women forward to have Captain Hickey give the information they desired.

Poor me, with my yachting cap, blue coat and flannel pants, would have to use all the diplomacy at my command to tell them something, for I knew as much about yachting and yachts as did Nan, the newsboy.

My, how Sir Thomas would laugh, for each time I looked his way I could hear his laugh, and hear him say, to some of the guests, in his joking old way, "Captain Hickey is in trouble, and wished he was just about five miles away," but he kept on kidding me the live long day, but I took that in good part, for as the woman said long ago, "It pleases you and it don't hurt me."

My, how I would like that Sir Thomas was here today, to enjoy his kidding in the same old way, off Sandy Hook, aboard the Steam Yacht, the *Erin* tickling the ribs of his friends all grinning, in that same old yachting style, with the same old friends, such as Lord Dewar, and his famous Scotch, and my grand old friend, George Doherty, J. P. and his real good old Irish brogue.

But it's no use, that can never be, he bade farewell to yachting, Neptune and his boiling sea, to enjoy the beautiful rest in Heaven, that is handed out to none, but the good and the blest.

Well, let us imagine that we are back to July, 1914, happy and free, with all our old friends, and Sir Thomas in high glee, enjoying the different deck sports, and waiting for Squire Borden, and his hydroplane the racers and racing to see, a picture no artist could paint.

Ever mindful of the debt that he owed to the Fire Department of New York for their having saved *Shamrock IV,* in 1919 from destruction, he invited the Commissioner, Chief, and all the officers and men that could be spared to be his guests the first race day, and Commissioner Hannon, and twenty men had a very fine day's sport off Sandy Hook that day, and they never forgot the pleasure, for they were entertained in royal style with the best of eats and of course, drinks galore, for they were on a foreign ship, and 12 miles off shore, and with the many stories told to them all by Sir Thomas, and after the winning of that, the first race by *Shamrock IV,* they departed in high spirit.

The *Victoria's* launch running us over to the Atlantic Yacht Club House, the headquarters of Sir Thomas, the telephones were kept working calling for their cars and off with them to spend the evening seeing the pleasures of Coney Island, then home, to sleep, the sleep of happiness, the end of a beautiful day. Mrs. Enright, in the absence of her husband, the Commissioner, who was very busy, and when I called up Police Headquarters, Dick Enright was soon on the job and after a good meal we too saw Coney Island, Oh Boy. Sad to relate but John Hannon died, and the Atlantic Club burned down in 1933.

Imagine to yourselves, my dear good people, trying to write up the history of a lifelong friend, his happy and unhappy days constantly appearing before your mind, such as the meeting of H.R.H. the Prince of Wales in 1898, the meeting of that whole souled New York Banker, J. P. Morgan in 1899, giving him confidence and good cheer, brightening up for all future contests, with inspiration and good cheer. And that happy day in 1923, the Enright reception followed by Sir Thomas, receiving the freedom of Glasgow, his natal city, followed by his meeting with Count George MacDonald in 1929, and his winning of the hearts and good wishes of all America, followed soon after by the grand reception accorded him in his visit here in 1930, by the Police Commissioner of the time, the Hon. Grover A. Whalen, followed by that wonderful reception accorded to this grand old warrior, by the Hon. Mortimer Sullivan, Mayor of Newport, Rhode Island and the good people of that grand old yachting colony, the home of American aristocracy and sport lovers.

And then to look back at the deplorable and heart-breaking days of July 20th, 1920, his first greatest setback, and this after hearing of the injury to the *S. Y. Victoria* that he had leased to take the place of *Erin* for the Cup races of 1920, his grand old floating palace of a floating home filled with happiness and cheer, sank by the enemy, February 15th, 1915, and all of the insults and grunts that he has been forced to swallow ever since that memorable day of the Burton blunder.

But all of these sad events were but a piker to his treatment here with *Shamrock V,* in 1930, and by none other than his own employees, is there any wonder that he died of a broken heart?

But nevertheless I will try to the best of my ability as a memorial to a grand old friend, to present this history in proper form, for as I stated in my opening, I am not a graduate from any school or college, but a lover of facts and you may take my word, when I say to you that this history is founded on facts, figures, and the many letters enclosed.

Speaking of the serious and nigh fatal accident to the *Victoria,* this worried Sir Thomas quite a bit, and when he came to himself, his first act was to send a letter to her owner who, as a matter of fact, Mr. Arthur Meeker, Vice-President of the Armour & Company of Chicago was with his family on board at the time, and whose lives were saved by the crew of the tender sent out to their assistance.

Sir Thomas in his letter of sympathy and condolence to Mr. Meeker, was deeply impressed and mighty glad at the saving of these lives, for it would have been the sorrowful ending of a glorious day, and while Sir Thomas, had surrendered his charter of the *Victoria,* just the day before, nevertheless he felt mighty bad, *Victoria* giving both joy and comfort to Sir Thomas and his guests at the Cup races of

1920, and it was a noted fact that the *Victoria,* next to *Resolute* and *Shamrock IV,* was the center of attention.

But the sad loss of the *Erin* and the poor hard working nurses and crew trying to steal a few hours of rest and sleep, only to be blown up was the most severe blow of all, for many reasons, principally because she was the floating palace of Sir Thomas for many years, something that no other yacht could ever boast of after, for Sir Thomas had a hunch, not to spend any more time afloat than he could possibly help, so he made *Osidge* his home, permanently, but could never forget the *Erin,* for the *Erin* was his home.

It would take long to tell you of all the happiness and joy that we, the guests, enjoyed that week of the series off Sandy Hook, and even to this day when we meet the happy days spent on the *Victoria,* July, 1920, will be spoken of among the former guests of Sir Thomas, and among them were many men of prominence, all titled persons, but a bunch of good royal sports.

SIR THOMAS ON HIS MISSION TO FAR OFF SERBIA, IN THE INTEREST OF HUMANITY

PART II—CHAPTER I

Sir Thomas, having appealed to the British Government to sanction his wish to fit out the *S. Y. Erin,* as a hospital ship, for the purpose of doing something for humanity, and his request being granted, he nobly braved the dangerous waters, the submarine and aeroplanes and other like implements of torture to attend to the poor unfortunate people dropping by the way side, eaten up with terrible fever, and this is what he did, and how he did it.

Having fitted his yacht out with everything that he thought was needed, he sailed to the danger zone, carrying with him a number of British and American Red Cross nurses, under the supervision of doctors Donnelly and Ryan of New York. And they having worked for several months, both day and night in face of the eminent danger of the German guns and aeroplanes that was constantly being played on them, and even though they had seen to it that the word hospital and the Red Cross flag be painted on both sides of the *Erin,* the villians kept up that horrid fire.

But Sir Thomas and his assistants worked right on, he having to spend much time ashore, so too, did his assistants, taking a desperate chance on their lives at every turn, forgetting themselves to try and save the life of one or more human beings afflicted with the dreaded fever, and at what a sad and sorrowful cost, but they were making good most every day.

But the ruthless enemy never let up their murderous designs until one night when the Skipper of *Erin* heard an S.O.S. coming from another one of their outfit, a hospital ship torpedoed, and having done all that could be done and returning to their base, the Germans sank the *Erin.*

Yes, and this in the wee small hours of the morning, when the tired out angels of mercy was trying to get a much needed rest, the *Erin* taking with her six of those poor creatures of nurses and crew, a crime against humanity, and in spite of their cowardly work they kept up their fire on the miserable little hut that was ran up to shelter them ashore.

Was that warfare, or was it murder in the first degree, I leave you my readers to judge, and what was the consequence, the poor nurses commenced to drop dead, one by one, and the injured Sir Thomas sent to their respective homes and loved ones. Both doctors

64

Donnelly and Ryan, also were stricken down, and taken away from the frightfulness, for their Heavenly Father had called them to him, and soon Sir Thomas was stricken and near followed.

But again his Devine protector was at his side, and with the prayers of his fond and loving Mother, and in spite of his own illness he could not stay in bed, knowing that his assistants were in dire distress, he visited them and consoled them to the last.   It is a sad and a long story to try to picture to you, and to one that saw much of these happenings while I was visiting over there, my heart will not allow me to dwell on the tragedy, but will do the best that I am able to, but its a pitiable tale to tell, and to think of it, that the same ungodly powers that forced this cursed war upon the world, are again looking for more, and how or why God in Heaven permits them to go on I don't know.   These same scoundrels catering and begging for our friendship after their late bloody encounter, how under Heaven can any man, woman or child condone the murders and cowardly murderers of the past, I know that I cannot, or ever will, or any other father or mother.

But the men and women of today are too prone to forget, until death enters their own household, and they then come to realize their stupidness and love for their fellow man or woman.   My God, when you read in these pages of all that took place in Serbia, and the sufferings of our devoted angels of peace and longevity, your blood will run cold like mine and you too will feel as I do, towards the pirates that slaughtered them, and when you again regain your composure, you too will speak your mind.

I have among my many friends good Germans, and while they are getting the luxuries of the world from this great and glorious country, they are first, last and all the time, faithful to their Fatherland, in spite of what has been done in the past, yes, and they are ever ready to give up the good money that they made here to foster another dreadful war.

That, to my mind, is inhuman, and should not be, and if it was not for the darned crooked politicians and shoemakers of this country, this would never be, a hungry lot of scoundrels looking to pick up every conceivable dirty rotten dollar, thereby biting the hand that fed them, and bucking against that wonderful God-given document, the Constitution of these United States of America, violating all obligations, that they have sworn to protect, and that should not be, for under these circumstances you must be an American, pure and simple, or a damned rascal of an enemy,—come show your hand, damn you.

Our grand old Chief labored day in and day out for many months, but Sir Thomas would not quit even in spite of the fact that he too was taken ill with the fever, he was there for a purpose and the humanity of his heart would not let him leave that sickening sight, until he had won the day, by driving the dreaded disease and madening fever away from their shores.

While talking with Sir Thomas in his suite at the Biltmore, October 6th, 1929, he told me that all the time that we were in Saloniki, we were in eminent danger, for the enemy knew the moment that we landed and our mission over in Serbia, and they tried day and night to get us, for they were constantly firing on the Red Cross Army depot, until Dr. Donnelly, could not stand it any longer so he visited Sir Thomas and asked him to procure an American flag, to hoist outside our little quarters.

Sir Thomas Lipton, true to his word obtained a very fine large flag, and he gave it to Dr. Donnelly, who thanked Sir Thomas, and the Doctor said, "Sir Thomas, I hope that this American flag will save the lives of those dear girls, that left their happy homes and firesides to come out here to do God's work, and entirely in my charge, and for whom I am responsible."

"But should the enemy get us, kindly see to it, that we are all sent to our homes in America, and I would deem it a big favor, if I am killed, or die, of this horrid fever, you will have my body wrapped up in this American flag that you so kindly bought for us, and may God bless you."

Sir Thomas made answer, "Yes, Mr. Donnelly, I will see to it that your wishes will be carried out," and they were to the letter, for the terrible fever was raging madly, poor human beings lying in the gutters unknown and uncared for, and soon Sir Thomas was afflicted, so also was Dr. Donnelly, and five of the Red Cross nurses, all lying at the point of death for many days, and the thoughts of his promise to the doctor caused Sir Thomas to leave his bed, and make inquiries about Dr. Donnelly, and the girls, and again the prayers of his dear old mother, followed Sir Thomas, for he lived to fulfill his promise to Dr. Donnelly, but the doctor and five nurses passed away, far from home and loved ones, peace be to them all. The *Erin* and nurses were blown up like rats, after answering an S.O.S. of another hospital ship sinking.

Sir Thomas paid great attention to the wants of the nurses of the Red Cross, that had unfortunately contracted that dreadful fever, many of whom are at rest, having died from the effects of that fearful disease. Sir Thomas, the good samaritan, he is never fearing for himself, rolled their bodies up in the Amerigan flag and laid them down to sleep the sleep of peace on the shores and the mountain side of what is today the bloodiest battlefield in all Europe, Salonica.

This good man, Sir Thomas, after having successfully dodged the shells and the bombs of the enemy, contracted that infernal man-killing disease, and he is today just a mere shadow of his former self.

When the time comes, that the supreme Being on high, the ruler of the Universe that does all things well, calls upon this good man, then the curtain will go down on the life of one of this world's noblest sons, and the prayers of this, our America, will forever be, peace to this good man's Soul. To know him, was to love him.

I recall a letter received a short time ago from Sir Thomas, in which he said:

"My dear Hickey:

"I am still weak, but my heart goes out to your beautiful country, and I am longing to be there, but alas, it would be a crime for a native son to leave his own loving Mother Country, while she is suffering and bleeding, in the interests of Humanity.

"But, my heart bleeds and forever goes out to your noble American Men and Women of the Red Cross. Some of the nurses, both gallant and brave, belonging to the Amreican Red Cross Society, and the Sanitary Commission in Serbia, that I brought back, are now in the Grace Hospital, Detroit, Michigan. I hope to pay them a visit when I get over to your dear country America, they did noble work out here. Good bless them all. I am so anxious to see them again, hoping to meet you soon, I remain,

"Faithfully yours,

"THOMAS J. LIPTON."

The grand old angel of mercy having been called home, and thanked by the two governments, he lost no time in booking up a sea trip, that could not be given for publication, or the damned enemy might get him on the high seas, but Sir Thomas was happy, for I was informed that he was about to take a long trip to others, no destination, but to J. J. H. New York bound.

Sir Thomas loved America for many reasons, one of which was that he at all times enjoyed a better rest here than in any other country, and of course, *Shamrock IV* on this side of the water gave him much trouble and lots of worry, and he had to give her his attention, this may have well been avoided, had the races been run off in 1914, but such is fate.

You can readily see by the reading of this letter the love and good-fellowship of this grand old sportsman for America, and her angels of Red Cross nurses, in fact for everything American.

If this space and time would permit of my telling you of the many private conversations that passed between Sir Thomas and the writer and in all of said conversations, the one topic was always America, and her people. But it must not be supposed that he had turned his back on the land of his birth, not at all man, not at all, for he was ever willing to make any sacrifice to aid and assist her, and her allies to win that late infernal world's war.

Yes, dear friends, Sir Thomas worked hard, both late and early, to have the enemy understand, that peace will reign on earth to men of good-will and that the warm heart of British friendship goes out to all mankind.

Oh, no, I don't have to tell you folks of these traits in the makeup of Sir Thomas, you know them and have known them always, for any man or woman broadminded enough to use the brains that the Lord endowed them with, has passed judgment of that kindly old gentleman, long ago, but do not blame the writer, for he loved the very ground that Sir Thomas walked upon. And be it known to all here present, that it was after being on an errand of mercy, in the matter of rushing to the assistance and rendering aid and comfort to the crew, the doctors, and nurses of another hospital ship, that the *Erin* was torpedoed, after her sinking, and returning to her the *Erin's* base, the hard worked nurses figuring on having a rest.

Sir Thomas, personally attended to the burial of Doctor Donnelly and his five Red Cross nurses, and after the burial he saw to it that all of personal effects of the dead were packed up and forwarded to their families.

True to his promise he ordered that each body should be wrapped up and buried in the flag of their country, and mailed a telegram to the next of kin explaining the whole sad case, working himself into a darn good fever, but he would not quit, until his full duty had been performed.

And all this time the enemy shells were falling all around them, horrid warfare among so-called Christians, how God permitted them to get away with it I don't know at all, their poisonous gas and every other contrivance that their dirty brains could produce, hell is the only place for them.

There was an awful death feeling hanging over the poor Serbians when Sir Thomas arrived there, and he bade them be of good cheer, and the doctor and nurses would attend to their wants, forthwith, and this cheered the poor souls, of men, women and children, many of them too weak to stand the strain any longer, keeled over and died, more or less with fear of the guns.

But Sir Thomas stuck to his task, and day after day, in every way, they were cleaning up both night and day, and the blessings of God descended on our grand old Chief, and the fever was driven out of that part of the waters, and then Sir Thomas took to bed and for a while his life was despaired of, but slowly and surely his brave old Irish constitution, stood by him and he recovered, but very weak, he busied himself to learn of those of the Serbian Government in charge if all was well.

And Sir Thomas was called to the palace, thanked and decorated by both the King and Queen, and blessed and thanked by the good people, of that former death stricken land, the poor old fellow was happy.

But all of the sorrows that he had passed through, with his doctors and nurses in driving this horrid fever out of the land, and the German

City Road.
London, E.C. 17th April 1917

Mr. H. H. Hickey,
    243, East 19th Street,
        New York City.-

Dear Mr. Hickey,

                Very many thanks for your kind letter of the 17th
March - St. Patrick's Day - and for all the sentiments which you
express, as also for the interesting papers which you so kindly
sent.   I am always interested in any American news and the
American papers for the last week or two must, I am sure, have
been worth reading.   Anyhow, I am sure you are feeling better
now that America is "all in" with the Allies.

                I do not know yet when I can get over to your
side; I have been hoping for this for a very long time now, but
circumstances have always been too strong for me.   I shall,
however, no doubt surprise you by appearing in New York one of
these days and shall hope to find you in the best of health and
spirits.

                With renewed thanks for your kind thoughtfulness
and wishing you the best of luck,

                    Yours faithfully,

The Champions of the Police Athletic Association of Greater New York in Newport, 1905, J. J. Hickey, Manager

JOHN J. HICKEY
Champion Long Distance Runner of the Police Department, 1895-1905

guns pointed at them were not half as bad as was the blowing up of the *S. Y. Erin,* for that was the worst sacrifice of all.

The *Erin* was blown up in the wee small hours, while the poor, tired out nurses and doctors were trying to snatch a few hours sleep.

I recall Sir Thomas writing me, stating that he was having great trouble with the Germans, and it got so hot that Dr. Donnelly pleaded with him to buy an American flag, to see if that would stop the German fire, but no, they still carried on. I also recall Sir Thomas telling the writer of the remarks of Dr. Donnelly when the long beautiful American flag arrived, he said, "Sir Thomas, if I should be killed here, won't you please have my body rolled up in that beautiful flag of my country and bury me in same," and the grand old noble-hearted Irish Baronet, saw to it that Dr. Donnelly's wishes were obeyed to the letter.

Sir Thomas, saw to it that Dr. Donnelly, and his dead companions were given fine funerals and their personal property forwarded to their homes and loved ones in far off America, and all at his own expense, for he idolized the very ground these God-loving creatures walked upon.

Often, Sir Thomas and I would be alone chatting, he would repeat these terrible scenes in Serbia, the good work done by Doctor Donnelly and his staff of nurses, that brought about the sorrowful death of these God-given angels of mercy, in their fight to save humanity.

And to take his mind off that sorrowful question I would tell him one of my old Police stories, and he in turn would tell of others, thereby for the moment he would forget the bitter past.

Mrs. Donnelly, the wife of the doctor, grieved much over the death of her husband, became ill and she too died to be with him in Heaven, and Mrs. Donnelly, the mother of the doctor, took upon herself the raising of young James until he was ready to accept the offer of Sir Thomas, and today that grand old lady at 82, her son John and grandson, James are living happy.

The following letter is one of many that I received at the time:

"CITY ROAD, LONDON, E. C.
"January 14, 1915.

"Mr. J. J. Hickey,
"Washington Avenue, Parkville,
"Brooklyn, N. Y.
"Dear Mr. Hickey,
    "Your letter of the 15th is at hand with enclosures, I thank you very much for same. And I shall mail them to Sir Thomas at the earliest opportunity, at the moment somewhere in Serbia, assisting in the noble work of saving the lives of the suffering people, in the hospital that he outfitted on board the *Erin.* Hoping this will find you fit and well, I am as ever,

"**Faithfully yours,**

"JOHN WESTWOOD."

Often, while sitting with the grand old Chief, he would delight over the fact that he made all promises good, for they weighed heavily on his mind, particularly the promise he made to Doctor Donnelly, on his dying bed.

The series of races postponed from 1914, were sailed in 1920. *Shamrock IV*, won the first and second, the *Resolute* won the fourth, thus necessitating the sailing of the fifth race.

The first, third and fifth were sailed over a course of fifteen miles to Windward off Ambrose Channel lightship, and return.

The second and fourth were sailed over an equilateral triangle of thirty miles in the vicinity of the Ambrose lightship.

The deed of gift also includes another clause which allows the defending club the privilege of not selecting its representative until the time agreed on for the start of a race, but it specifies that the yacht thus selected must thereupon compete in all the races.

Thus, if several cup defenders are built by members of syndicates of members of the New York Yacht Club, the identity of the yacht selected to defend the cup need not be divulged until the last minute.

Such a procedure, however, would hardly be likely, and, if two or more contenders are built, undoubtedly there will be a series of elimination races earlier in the season to select the defender.

Another clause in the deed of gift is that each course, must be completed within seven hours or else "no race" is declared.

In the last cup series the second start came under this heading. After *Shamrock IV*, and *Resolute* had sailed for five and one-half hours in light zephyrs over the triangular course it was plainly apparent that they could not complete the course within the required time, so that the race was called off. When the race was given up *Resolute* was 34 minutes and 12 seconds ahead.

The wording of the Royal Ulster Yacht Club's challenge virtually leaves in the hands of the New York Yacht Club the working out of the details of the series, with the implied suggestion that since working arrangements of the last cup series were satisfactory, similar arrangements for the proposed series would be acceptable.

Sir Thomas Lipton, was one of the easiest men in the world to get along with, for he left everything to the racing committee of the New York Yacht Club, and this they appreciated very much.

LIEUTENANT COMMANDER CHARLES OSCAR MAAS OF THE RED CROSS

As an illustration of the old saying that the world is small, and no matter how far away from home one may be, you will meet at some time, somewhere, someone whom you know, I will recount an incident.

It was at the height of the excitement in London, England, August 5th, 1914, and while walking along the Haymarket, I was saluted, "Hey, Hickey, old man, how are you?" Turning about to see who it was, I could have dropped in my track, for it was no less a personage than Mr. Charles Oscar Maas, an old time acquaintance, whose office was on Nassau Street, New York.

Our greetings were hot, I was going to be conventional, and say warm, but the word lacks that difference which is to be found between the two, hot and warm.

We talked of this, and discussed that, and he, being a lawyer, we reviewed several of the cases in which I, as Policeman, and Mr. Maas as lawyer, had participated. His position in London, was that of Chief Counsel, of the American Red Cross, in the World War. His surprise at seeing me in London was no greater than mine, at seeing him there.

We had lunch together and when I told him of my intentions of going over to Ireland, he tried hard to persuade me to go back home by the first boat leaving, but he had overlooked the fact that he was talking to John J. Hickey, one of New York's finest, and when he at last realized to whom he was talking, he broke out into a laugh and said, "Hickey, if I had your Sticktoitiveness I'd be on the bench today."

It did me a whole lot of good to meet Mr. Maas, at that time, for it is a pleasure for one to meet a man from his own old town, particularly at such a time.

Of course we had to speak of the war, but under the circumstances, the bellicose had to for the time being retire to the rear, and let friendship come to the front.

Before we parted he requested that I write him, and keep him posted as to my whereabouts and admonished me to make it my first duty to call upon him if through some mischance, I should happen, into trouble.

I promised to do so and although I wrote him several times, I never heard from him and, since then I learn that my dear good friend has gone to "blighty" R.I.P.

1914 to 1918

A COPY OF A FEW OF THE LETTERS THAT PASSED
THE CENSORS AT NIGHT

Part II—Chapter II

Here are a few of the many letters mailed to me by my good friend, Tom Lipton, and at a time when the poor people over there could not call their souls their own—Zeppelins flying all around them overhead. Yes, sir, and a letter as a word from a friend was very comforting, I am sure. God help them, they needed all the cheer they were able to get, but I kept our old friend Sir Thomas, quite busy, when time would permit, but my good friend came first always.

"CITY ROAD, LONDON, E. C.
"December 17th, 1914.

"Mr. John J. Hickey,
"306 Washington Avenue,
"Parkville, Brooklyn, N. Y.
"Dear Mr. Hickey,
"Many thanks for your kind letter of the 20th ultimo, and your kind inquiries.
"I am glad to say that I am keeping well, although, as you can understand, we are all very much troubled about this terrible war and the awful loss of life which it is causing.
"I only wish that I was free to adopt your suggestion and come over to your country for a spell, but this unfortunately is at present impossible.
"I am very interested to hear that you are writing a book of your travels and shall look forward to receiving a copy when completed, as I feel sure your book is going to be an entertaining work.
"The *Erin* is shortly going abroad on a special mission in connection with Red Cross work.
"This appeals to me very strongly and I am very happy to think that I am able to do some little bit to help win the war in the present crisis.
"While I am unable to go to America at the moment, I shall keep on looking forward to the pleasure of seeing you on my arrival at New York at a some not too far distant date.
"I trust that this will find you in the best of health, and with kind remembrances and many thanks for your courtesy in writing me.
"Respectfully yours,
"THOMAS J. LIPTON."

This is a sample of the many such letters received from thi. noble sportsman and dear friend, of which I am so very proud, to hold in endearment and fondest memory.

I am very sorry that I cannot find room for all of these letters but will try to do my best to insert them, for I know full well how you would like to read these many historical letters, that have passed between that grand old Warrior, your friend and mine, Author.

72

"Mr. J. J. Hickey,   "CITY ROAD, LONDON. E. C.
"The Elk's Hotel, Sacramento Street,   "May 17th, 1915.
"San Francisco, County California.
"Dear Mr. Hickey,

"Your letter of the 30th ultimo addressed to Sir Thomas Lipton is just to hand and I shall be glad to forward it to Sir Thomas by the first available mail.

"Sir Thomas is now at the moment in Malta, aboard the *S. Y. Erin* on his way to Salonica, conveying another hospital outfit of doctors, nurses, orderlies, clothing, stores and many other things to clean up the horrid fevers killing the people of Serbia by the thousands.

"So that it will necessarily be some little time before your letter reaches him.

"I am sure, however, that he will be very pleased to hear from you, and to learn your beautiful report from the Expositions of both San Francisco and San Diego, relating to the Lipton exhibits.

"It goes without saying that Sir Thomas himself would have loved to have been able to visit both exhibitions, for a stay at this time in beautiful Southern California, would be very much enjoyed by him.

"But, unfortunately he has other and sterner work in hand and at this writing it is impossible to form any reliable estimate when he will be free to once again join his friends in America.

"Many thanks on Sir Thomas's behalf for your very kind letter and hoping that you are keeping fit and well, with best regards,
"Yours faithfully,
"JOHN WESTWOOD."

"Mr. J. J. Hickey,   "CITY ROAD, LONDON, E. C.
"306 Washington Avenue, Brooklyn, N. Y.   "June 15th, 1915.
"Dear Mr. Hickey,

"Your very kind letter written on the grounds of the Exhibition of San Francisco, addressed to Sir Thomas Lipton, who at the moment is preparing to leave for home after that awful siege in Serbia, his doctors and Red Cross nurses having cleaned up in good style, are free.

"I note too that you are preparing to leave for your home in little old New York, that wonderful city, after many months of travel through the many States of the Union. Trusting that this will find you well, I will see that Sir Thomas will get your letter on his arrival.
"Yours faithfully,
"JOHN WESTWOOD."

I, having to utilize every inch of room in this, my first edition, I will like you to know the very latest news, of both countries' racers and coming contestants for the America's Cup to date. From a telegram just received.

Gosport, England, April 16th, 1934.

All of England are having a bully old time at the successful launching of the challenger, *Miss Endeavour,* she took the water in fine shape and a beautiful model she makes, and when Mrs. T.O.M. Sopwith, the wife of the owner smashed a bottle of champagne over her bow, at the same time saying, "I christian you *Endeavour,* and from the bottom of my heart, I wish you a cupful of luck," then the music started and *Britannia* ruled the waves and every Tom, Dick and Harry, and Harriett, started in to celebrate, and a blooming good time was had by all.

I learn that *Endeavour* will be longer than will be the *Rainbow,* our next defender, but to offset that, Miss *Rainbow* will carry 7,550 more sail than will *Endeavour,* and that is quite an item, and in the course of the remarks Charley Nicholson, again gave out his salve, remarking, "I still have something up my sleeve, that no one will know, but let him tell that to our big fine looking defender *Rainbow,* if fortunate to win this honor as defender. We Americans heartily congratulate Mr. Sopwith and may the best yacht win."

"CITY ROAD, LONDON, E. C.
"July 10th, 1915.

"Mr. John J. Hickey,
"Hotel St. Blaise, East 23rd Street,
"New York City.
"Dear Mr. Hickey,

"I am in receipt of your very kind letter of June 15th and the very fine information it contained and the vast amount of news the enclosures contained, concerning my American friends whom I have long been praying to see. Your information cheered me much and I appreciate your kindness very much for you never forget me, it makes no difference where you may be, you never once forget to write to me, all of which makes me feel very happy, and more anxious to visit dear old New York and my vast number of goods friends living there.

"I notice that you have been doing a tremendous lot of long distance traveling, and high mountain climbing, both below and above sea level exploring the many different countries visited by you, and the book of travel that you are now working on, should be very interesting and beneficial to all, particularly to those that are fond of travel and have, like yourself, enjoyed much travel but whose time was limited.

"You must have enjoyed your stay in the many countries, because your time was not limited, you certainly had a wonderful experience, the kind that I myself would enjoy with pleasure, don't forget that I want the first copy of your valuable book when published.

"You are at liberty to use my name anywhere or everywhere that will be of assistance to you, it makes no difference how far you go in this particular matter for I always have the utmost confidence in my old friend John J. Hickey. You may be called upon to go to extremes to get your work before the public, so don't be the least bit backward in keeping me informed from time to time, for in all such cases, we all need the assistance of our fellow man, in particular, and our friends in general.

"Unfortunately I have been on the sick list, something unusual to me, for while working hard in Serbia in the cause of humanity, I was troubled with dysentery and since then I have not been able to take food, and that alone is a mighty hard blow to me, always a good eater.

"But Heavenly Father, all that I went through in Serbia, I thank the Lord that I am as well as I am, for the torture endured and the attending of the sick and dyeing, and in death taking charge of their bodies, having them prepared to send to their homes, was enough to sicken any white man.

"Besides my not being able to take food, I have not been out of my house since arriving in England, and that is a mighty hard blow to me.

"But, once I take a turn for the best I will soon recuperate.

"I will be much pleased to hear that everything is going along with you to your entire satisfaction, because you are a hustler, and a persistent worker, and it makes no difference what the cause, old man Hickey will be found busy on the job so cheer up and some day when this world's war is over we will meet again, hoping never to part.

"With all kind wishes for your future and again thanking you for your kindness in sending to me all of this beautiful news as contained in your letters to me, and what your cuttings contain, and hoping to find you well and wishing to you every success, I am,

"Sincerely yours,

"THOMAS J. LIPTON."

I had visited Sir Thomas in 1914, and the war driving me back, I again packed up, and traveled the U. S. to the exhibitions of *San Diego* and *Frisco*.

"Mr. John J. Hickey,   "OSIDGE SOUTHGATE,
"Hotel St. Blaise,   "MIDDLESEX, LONDON, E. C.
"East 23rd Street, N. Y. City.   March 16th, 1916.
"Dear Mr. Hickey,
    "Very many thanks for your kind letter, I am glad to know that you are keeping fit and well.
    "It is certainly very kind of you to write me of so many interesting particulars.
    "I note that you met an old friend of yours, a William McCracken, at the Police Department Holy Name breakfast held in the Hotel Astor.
    "I have never had the pleasure of meeting this gentleman, but his people I believe were old friends of my parents.
    "They too came from "Clones" County, Monaghan, Ireland. I am sure that William McCracken will do well, as he comes from a very honorable family.
    "Kindly remember me to him when next you meet.
    "At the moment I am trying very hard to make another visit to your big city and it won't be long before you will find me looking for my old friend Hickey on the pier, and then we again will have one of those old time friendly chats about my many friends in America, and how successful they are.
    "Hoping to find you well and with all best wishes,
                        "Yours sincerely,   "THOMAS J. LIPTON."

For the information and guidance of my readers, I will state that the William McCracken, of whom Sir Thomas spoke, is, or was, a police officer in New York for many years, and he played an instrument in the police band, and we would meet at all the activities of the Police Department throughout the year, and after business have a social drink or two, and Bill, knowing that Sir Thomas and I were close friends, he would ask me many questions as to the state of Sir Thomas' health.

But, unfortunately, the hand of death was laid on the shoulders of this good man, and he, too, sailed up the long road to that beautiful land on high, in which Jesus hath said that "no tears shall be shed, in that beautiful land on high."

There was never a time that Sir Thomas neglected a friend, and the above letter is just a sample, and it satisfied the minds of many, for this good fellow, Bill McCracken, a member of the New York police band, Officer McCracken, to be right, would be found looking for his friend Hickey at the police festivities of the past. His mission was to inquire how his cousin, Sir Thomas Lipton, was, knowing our friendship, so I popped the question to Sir Thomas, and the letter above was his answer.

There are quite a number of cases of this same kind that I could tell you folks about, but I guess you have enough to satisfy your minds.

To the best of my knowledge and belief, Mr. McCracken buried his first wife and remarried, but I do not remember ever meeting them, nor do I know where they lived, or a gosh blam thing about them, but I sure was glad to hear Sir Thomas speak so highly of him, a pretty decent fellow,

Private and confidential.

"Mr. John J. Hickey,
"Hotel St. Blaise,
"158 East 23rd Street,
"New York City.

"OSIDGE SOUTHGATE,
"MIDDLESEX, LONDON, E. C.
"March 28th, 1916.

"Dear Mr. Hickey,
    "Many thanks for your kind letter of the 10th, Inst.
    "I note what you say about the publication of your new Police book and again I wish you every success, and assistance at my command.
    "As far as this country is concerned I do not think that the best written book that was ever published would be a success just now.
    "In the first place money is so exceedingly scarce, and every penny is required to help win the war, but cheer up, there is no doubt what the finish of the war will be, for it will be nothing short of a Victory for the Allies.
    "I am not yet certain when I can get over to your side, but it may be very shortly, if I can bring it about.
    "With all good wishes and wishing to you the best of good luck.
                                        "Yours sincerely,
                                                    "THOMAS J. LIPTON."

                "OSIDGE, SOUTHGATE, MIDDLESEX, LONDON, E. C.
                "27th May, 1916.
"Mr. John J. Hickey,
"Hotel St. Blaise,
"23rd Street, New York City.
"Dear Mr. Hickey,
    "Very many thanks for your kind letter of the 10th, and your very fine birthday card and enclosures all of which I appreciate very much.
    "Many thanks also for the information that your letter contained, for it was something that I wanted very much, and the press clippings they were highly interesting and I enjoyed them very much.
    "I am very sorry to learn of the death of your dear Mother, and please accept from me my heartfelt sympathy; no man can meet with a greater loss for there is nothing on earth that can take the place of Mother and her love, a man's guiding star through life.
    "With renewed thanks and trusting that this will find you fit and well and with all best wishes, I am,
                    "Very sincerely yours,
                                                    "THOMAS J. LIPTON."

My dear old Mother died May 9th, 1916, age about 84. Peace be with our dead.—AUTHOR.

"Mr. John J. Hickey,
"Hotel St. Blaise, New York City.

"PARLIAMENT HOUSE,
"WESTMINSTER, LONDON.
"17th of May, 1916.

"Dear Mr. Hickey:
    "Very many thanks for your kind and consoling letter of the 14th inst., with cuttings enclosed, which I have read with great interest and for which I am very grateful.
    "Messages such as yours are always most welcome and encouraging, at all times, particularly the present time.
                "Believe me, very faithfully yours,
                                                    "JOHN E. REDMOND."

I answered this to our great Irish leader, the able successor of the former chief, the late Charles Stewart Parnell, who with his successor, is sleeping in the great beyond. Peace be to them all.

And I gave to our great leader all the joyful information that came my way, to cheer him along through his hard-fought battles in Parliament, for I always liked the Redmond boys.

We would meet at the Reformers' tree in Hyde Park on Sundays. They were then boys, with their uncle, old John Redmond, Member of Parliament for many years, representing the County Wexford.

If the government of England had not listened to Carson, and had at that crucial time, given Home Rule to Ireland, without any frills, such as the amendments to the bill, Ireland would be happy today. There would not have been the drowning of Lord Kitchener, nor the Irish uprisings of 1916 and the terrible state that Ireland is in today, April, 1932.

The Irish leader, John E., and his loving brother, William (Willie K.), I am sorry to say, are botl dead. John died of a broken heart, and Major William Redmond killed leading his men in action in Flanders in June, 1918, his death bringing about the undoing of the Irish leader, for they were not at any time separated, always palled, eat and drank together. May the Lord have mercy on them both!

"Mr. J. J. Hickey,   "CITY ROAD, LONDON,
"Hotel St. Blaise, New York Ctiy.   "Nov., 1916.
"Dear Mr. Hickey:

"Sir Thomas has requested me to acknowledge receipt of your ever welcome letter of the 10th inst., as well as the bunch of cuttings enclosed, that you have been so kind enough to send him, all of which he is enjoying very much.

"Sir Thomas greatly appreciates all of your kind attention in this matter and desires that I inform you of that, also that he is at the moment in much better shape, improving in health daily, but only sorry that circumstances are such that he is unable to leave the country at present to get over to your side of the water. Nevertheless, he is living in hopes of his meeting his many good friends in America at some not distant date, not the least among them, is your own good self. Sir Thomas also thanks you for the American Liberty button you were so kind as to send him.

"Yours respectfully, hoping this will find you well and fit,
                                        "JOHN WESTWOOD."

                                        "CITY ROAD, LONDON, E. C.,
"Mr. J. J. Hickey,   "November, 1916.
"Hotel St. Blaise, New York Ctiy.
"Dear Mr. Hickey:

"Your kind letter of the 28th inst., with enclosures received, that he, Sir Thomas, has enjoyed the reading of so much, and for which he requests me to write and thank you for your kind attention to him always. Unfortunately, he is not yet in a position to say when he will be at leisure to get over to New York, but is constantly looking forward, to meet his old American friends again soon, would to Heaven it was tomorrow, that he was about to see his old friend Hickey waving a welcome from the dock in good old New York. Sir Thomas desires me to send you his warmest thanks and best wishes to which I need say I add mine. But it won't be long now.

"Faithfully yours,
                                        "JOHN J. WESTWOOD."

This was the time when the vile enemy were bombing all England, killing off the poor inoffensive men, women and children.

It made no difference what part of the world Sir Thomas may be, he never forgot writing to your humble servant. Those letters are many, so that I will just write of the letter sent me by Sir Thomas in 1915, when the war was raging on all sides, but at this time America had not entered the war.

The letter in question ran as follows:

"BELGRADE, SERBIA,
"July 17th, 1915.

"Dear Mr. Hickey:

"Many thanks for your letter just received, and your kind consideration of me. Would to God that I could embrace your kind request to once again visit my many friends in your dear old city, New York.

'But, unfortunately, under the existing circumstances, I cannot at this time. We are at war, and here I must stay to do everything in my power to help my country and her allies to win, and I am trying to do my duty in so far as able to aid and assist the distressed and wounded soldiers, and the fever-stricken people of Serbia, God help them, dropping in their tracks, eaten up with this unearthly fever, and in a starving condition.

"May God grant that his horrid war will soon be at end, and I will then join my many friends in grand old America, particularly New York, but alas, that cannot be now, and perhaps never, for our lives are in danger from early morning until the dark at night, in fact every twenty-four hours, they, the enemy guns, are firing shells to blow us all out of the world.

"But this cannot keep up forever, we must fight on, and some fine day we may have your great country with us, for without you Americans our cause will be lost.

"I have given the *Erin* over to the government and it was converted into a hospital ship, for the purpose of nursing back to health those of our boys and their allies who are doing great fighting at this time, but the enemy is so strongly enforced from day to day, it is mighty hard on us to try drive them off.

"It appeals to me at this time to think that I am of use in doing something for humanity at this particular time, when war is hell, at any time, but alas, we must fight on, for our brave countrymen will never quit, until peace is declared, whatever side wins, but it would be dreadful if England and her allies lost.

"Would to God, that I could do more than I am able to do for humanity. This work appeals to me, although never used to such work and the hardships following, and I thank God, I am keeping fit, and still able to do my bit.

"But with God's help I hope to meet you in New York at not a far distant date. Trusting that both yourself and family are well and wishing to you all good health and prosperity, as ever,

"Respectfully yours,   "THOMAS J. LIPTON."

I certainly was a happy man to receive such a very fine letter from my dear, good friend, one that only Sir Thomas could write under such circumstances, for this great sportsman was never known to forget a friend, in war, or peace time, and the more one knows of him, the more one loves him, for his charity and noble generosity, well known the world over.

Sir Thomas Lipton not only subscribed to the feeding and clothing of the poor of London, and they were many, but he also subscribed his money to help the poor of all America, and his name can be seen among the subscribers to the Christmas dinner fund of the New York "American," for one will always read the name of Sir Thomas Lipton for $500, and this has been noticed for many years, with many other contributions that are never published.

Then, why should we not love and respect Sir Thomas Lipton?

"Mr. John J. Hickey, "LONDON, E. C.,
"Hotel Elton, New York City. "21st August, 1918.
"Dear Mr. Hickey:
"I duly received your kind letter of the 14th and was very glad indeed to hear from you again, and to know that you are well.

"The Liberty Bond is also safely to hand, as I advised you in my letter of June 20th, and I need hardly to say that I very much appreciate your kindness in sending it to me, such an interesting souvenir and one which I shall always value very highly indeed.

"I am also very pleased to know that your sons are fighting with the Allies and so far are doing well. I earnestly hope that they both will be spared to you, returning safely after this terrible business of war is over. I am still living in the land of hope as far as my projected visit to the U. S. A. is concerned; at the moment I cannot say when I am likely to get away, but don't be surprised if I ring you up some fine morning and tell you that I am in Little Old New York. I hope this will find you in the best of health and condition with kindest regards and renewed thanks for your goodness,

"Faithfully yours,

"THOMAS J. LIPTON."

"Mr. J. J. Hickey, "CITY ROAD, LONDON,
"Hotel Elton, New York City. "6th November, 1918.
"Dear Mr. Hickey:
"Your note of the 17th of October addressed to Sir Thomas Lipton is duly to hand but I am unable at the moment to place it before Sir Thomas as he is now out of town and may be away for a week or two.

"I shall be glad, however, to keep the matter in mind, and ascertain of my Chief what he thinks about the various points in relation to your book, "OUR POLICE GUARDIANS." I am sure that Sir Thomas will be delighted to assist you, and to send to you what you ask, that is a photograph of *Shamrock IV,* and a photograph of himself, and one of the *Erin.* I will mail them to you at an early date.

"Yours faithfully,

"JOHN WESTWOOD."

"OSIDGE, SOUTHGATE,
"MIDDLESEX, LONDON, E. C.,
"25th of September, 1916.

"Mr. John J. Hickey,
"Hotel St. Blaise, E. 23rd St., New York City.
"Dear Mr. Hickey:
"I much appreciate your letter of the 7th inst. with the enclosures that you so kindly sent to me, all of which I read with much interest and pleasure, and for which I am deeply thankful.

"It pleases me very much to learn from you that the good people along the Jersey coast with whom you are spending your holidays speaks so highly of me. I trust from the bottom of my heart that I may always retain their good opinions and friendships, as I value this more than anything in this old world, and kindly say to them, please, that I very much appreciate their goodfellowship and kind thoughts of me, I thank you.

"I am sending to you a photograph of the Red Cross Hospital ship, the *Erin,* taken just before she was blown up by the Germans and sank with a sad loss of life in the Harbor of Salonica, Serbia, in 1915.

"I fully intended to be in America before now but, as you understand, the best laid plans get upset during these critical times.

"Hoping this will find you well, and your family all enjoying good health, for there is nothing in this world more precious.

"And again thanking you very much for your wonderful art of corresponding week after week, never for a moment tiring, but as the years roll on it seems that your strength and speed grows faster, I thank you.

"Yours sincerely,

"THOMAS J. LIPTON."

Dear readers, the photograph spoken of I hold among my most endearing possessions, not only because Sir Thomas kindly sent it to me, but the very fact that several old friends of mine, members of the crew, went up with her as well as several of the poor American girls of the Red Cross, who were trying to snatch a few hours sleep in the wee small hours, when lo and behold! a torpedo was aimed at the good ship, showing plainly, the Red Cross, painted on both sides for protection.

No doubt, Sir Thomas would also have lost his life at that time, but for the prayers of a good old mother, but God willed that he sleep ashore that night above all others.

And my good friend, Doctor James Donnelly, with a grand old mother, 80 years old, living right here in New York, also a native of Monaghan, went ashore that night after the Red Cross nurses had tucked themselves in for sleep, that turned out to be their last sleep on earth.

This was feared, for Dr. Donnelly asked Sir Thomas to purchase an American flag, thinking to stop the constant firing of the enemy, but nothing doing, and Dr. Donnelly asked Sir Thomas, in the event of his, the doctor's, death, to roll him up in the flag and send his body to New York, and that grand old Chieftain did this, and sent the nurses back home, with all of the belongings of each.

Much more could be told of this outrage, one that I shall never forget. While I am willing to condone many acts of rascality, this blowing up of a hospital ship I shall never forget or condone.

"Mr. John J. Hickey,   "CITY ROAD, LONDON, E. C.,
"243 East 19th St., New York City.   "17 April, 1917.
"Dear Mr. Hickey:
"Very many thanks for your kind letter of the 17th of March, 'St. Patrick's Day,' that the men and women of Erin love to celebrate.
"It is very nice of you to constantly keep me informed of these great celebrations, and particularly that of Ireland's Patron Saint, so dear to the hearts of the Irish people the world over.
"I admire your sentiments very much, for all the good things that you say about Olde Ireland, I heartily appreciate, for my Mother and my Father and all of the 'Liptons' through history first saw the light in lovely Ireland, and your kind words cheer me very much.
"Some day I hope to be free to witness that great celebration there to see the Lads and Lassies dancing and singing, 'Haste to the Wedding,' 'The Top of Cork Row' and other famous Irish ballads and songs that all of us enjoyed in our boyhood.
"I am always so interested in your American news for it pleases me very much and for the moment carries my thoughts back to the happy days of the past. 'Kind words can never die.'
"I am sure that you, like myself, are feeling better now that America, and here heroes have taken the field in helping to preserve the life and the Liberty of all freemen, and we are soon to find better results in our newspaper reports from the front. May the Good Lord, in his divine wisdom, aid and assist our brave fighting heroes in the allied army, soon to bring about victory with an everlasting peace and goodwill.
"I have been striving and working very hard so that I may be free to be among my American friends again, for I never tire of their company, or that

great America, that gave me my first start in life, Heaven help her, and her people, who are every ready to help the world.

"Hoping to meet you in New York soon again, and wishing you every kind wish for your future success and happiness.

"Yours faithfully,   "THOMAS J. LIPTON."

"Mr. John J. Hickey,   "LONDON, E. C.,
"23 Duane Street, New York City.   "13th March, 1918.
"Dear Mr. Hickey:

"I have duly received your many kind letters of the past, particularly that of the 15th ultimo, with the vast amount of good news that they always contain, and for which I thank you very much.

"I have been hoping for a long time to get over to New York, but it is utterly impossible under the present circumstances, but I am living in hopes some day of sailing over to see you and my many other kind American friends, for whom I hold the very highest regards.

"I trust that this will find you fit and well, and with my kindest regards and best wishes to all, I am,

"Yours faithfully,

"THOMAS J. LIPTON."

"J. J. Hickey,   "CITY ROAD, LONDON, E. C.,
"203 East 19th Street, New York City.   "3rd October, 1918.
"Dear Mr. Hickey:

"Very many thanks for your kind letter of the 1st ultimo, which has duly reached me, as also did the very interesting enclosures it contained.

"I am happy to know that you are well and jogging along in that same old happy go lucky spirit.

"Since you last wrote me, many things have happened and it is to my mind nearing the end of this fearful war, and its finish will be as we all desire for the Boches' game is up.

"There is no question that the help of the U. S. A. has come just at the right time.

"Thanks for the copy of your excellent poem. I was not aware that you were so gifted in this way, and I congratulate you most heartily on your warlike spirit and many fine verses, it contained.

"I am still hoping to get across the big pond to your lovely country to again meet my many friends in America, and this I think is now coming within measurable distance.

"Again looking forward to the pleasure of meeting you, and with my kindest regards and best wishes, I am,

"Yours faithfully,

"THOMAS J. LIPTON."

At this writing the grand old sportsman was feeling miserable, and in hiding from the enemy guns overhead, in the enemy despicable air raids over London, when one's life was constantly in jeopardy, both night and day.

Not at all a happy position to be in, moreover, that of a multimillionaire, and this reminds me somewhat of the policeman who resigned to go to war. He and I were side-partners on patrol, and confided in each other quite a lot, as comrades usually do. We would make a lap over our posts and resume our war talk hourly. He was a bachelor, but a darn good pal.

One bright morning when the war was raging on San Juan Hill, after we had answered return roll call, having patrolled the old 4th Ward from midnight to 6 a. m., we decided to inlist, and we visited the inlisting sergeant.

After a rigid examination, Pat Murphy and Harry Haywood were accepted and Jack Hickey was rejected, for big family and physical disability. Harry Haywood rose to sergeantcy and was killed in battle on San Juan Hill.

Pat Murphy, one night on sentry duty, stood erect and said: "What a damn fool I was to leave the police of New York, where I could sleep all the time! Here, if I lay down to sleep they will shoot me, and by golly, they will shoot me if I stay awake, so what in hell is a poor devil to do, at all, at all, for be jabbers, I'll be shot anyhow." Could it be that Paddy was half shot and didn't give a damn what happened, but the Boches never got him.

But, dear old Sir Thomas had his kidding cap on, even in danger, when he started out to kid old man Hickey about the poem that he had written, dedicated to the "Honor Legion" of the Police Department of New York, and a big hit at the time, feeling the sting, with two sons overseas, both in their teens; Mother dead seven years, I was in that frame of mind to write a war-time poem, with apology to Kipling, whose son was killed in battle just this same time, and that played heavy on the old poet's mind.

But Sir Thomas was highly pleased with my venture, so why worry, and my old comrade-in-arms, Pat Murphy, returned safely, so I still have another chance to get half shot, thanks to President Frank Roosevelt.   December 7th, 1933.

"THE HOTEL COMMODORE, CITY,
"May 10th, 1919.
"My Dear Mr. Hickey:
"Very many thanks for your birthday greetings which I very highly appreciate. It pleases me very much to be remembered by old friends and I am grateful to you for your kind thought.
"I trust that this will find you in the best of good health.
"With my kindest regards and best wishes, and looking forward to the pleasure of seeing you soon.
"Yours faithfully,   "THOMAS J. LIPTON.
"Mr. John J. Hickey, Writer,
"23 Duane Street, City."

"THE HOTEL COMMODORE, CITY,
"November 11th, 1919.
"Dear Mr. Hickey:
"I was sorry to be out and did not have the pleasure of my seeing you when you so kindly called here today.
"When I arrived, I was so buy and excited at meeting so many well wishers that I did not get the opportunity of talking to you as I should have liked.
"I would like very much if you would ring me up and make an appointment to come and have a cup of tea some afternoon in my own room, as I am looking forward to a long chat with you about our mutual friends, and the good old times gone forever, don't fail to come.
"As you can readily understand I will be very busy this week, working both night and day, and would like if you would get in touch with me early next week.
"I hope that you are keeping as well as I would wish you, and I am looking forward with great pleasure to my having a good long chat with you, and this without interruption, of any kind, and very soon I hope.
"With my very best wishes,
"Yours sincerely,   "THOMAS J. LIPTON.
"Mr. John J. Hickey, Writer,
"23 Duane Street, City."

I saw that Sir Thomas was having a wonderful time after landing, and not wanting to mar his pleasure, and being tired, I retired to my hotel to rest up. What with Police Commissioner Enright, and his staff of deputies, the police band and Glee Club, it was some welcome!

Next morning I received a letter from Sir Thomas, and I wired him forthwith, that I hope to have tea with him, after the Prince of Wales was leaving for home on the *H.M.S. Renown,* November 9th, 1919.

We met and had a very fine time, afternoon and evening, and on leaving, the last words that Sir Thomas addressed to me were the following: "Mr. Hickey, don't publish your book until after the yacht races next year," that of 1920, postponed from 1914.

This was the book of my world's travels through Europe and America of 1914 and 1915, on which I had worked until the time of our meeting at the Hotel Commodore in 1919. But what the meaning of Sir Thomas was I did not know, nor did I ask, for I had made up my mind, owing to the war that was then raging, to withdraw my book of travel and write another.

I then wrote "OUR POLICE GUARDIANS," the history of New York and its police force from the landing of Henry Hudson to the present day, and sold the second edition of the same, on sale at all booksellers at $3.00 per copy.

While I could have published my book of travel for $1,600.00 in 1916, it cost me nearly $3,500.00 to publish my "POLICE GUARDIANS" in 1925, so you can readily see what I could have saved, and to do this I was forced to pay the bill with the Liberty and Victory Bonds I had tried so hard to keep and by so doing, be helpful to my country.

I made one big mistake, and that was in being too patriotic, laying my business to one side and sailing to France with the American Legion, representing my two veteran sons, both of them married, and members of the force of boys in blue, America's first line of defense, the New York police, at the American Legion convention held in Paris, September 21st, 1927.

And after the convention, I traveled all of Europe and America, stopping over there one whole year, and when I returned I found that the type of my book had been broken up, or I may have been selling this work for all time among the rookie police, attending the Delehanty Institute of Civil Service learning on East 15th Street, Manhattan, by running a new edition each time a new class of policemen were ordered to school.

I certainly enjoyed the many historic countries visited, in both Europe and the Continent, and my reception by His Holiness, Pope Pius 11th, and my calling on Premier Mussolini, the next day, meeting the Holy Father on October 6th in the Vatican, and I wished to pay my respects to Signor Mussolini, who, by the way, had mailed his check for a copy of my police book, in the spring of 1927, for the Signor is a great admirer of New York and its police.

And my next happiness was my stopping with Father Hunt at "Casa Nova" in Jerusalem for two lovely weeks, visiting all the historic Biblical scenes, I having arrived from Constantinople, and landing in Heifa, stopping but a few days, visiting Nazareth, and then motoring to Jerusalem, and from this lovely "Holy City," visiting Bethlehem and its many holy places.

I was sorry to be leaving Jerusalem, but my mail and advances were not coming from home and I had to travel so that I could get back once more to civilization, entraining for Egypt, and seeing all that was to be seen there.   Then up the Nile to Africa, on my way to Bombay, India, to thank a bookseller who had mailed me an order for ten of my police books, that spoke so much of the life of Sir Thomas Lipton, and his duties as Honoray Police Chief, under the administration of that great social entertainer, Richard E. Enright, Police Commissioner of New York, because these people did much book-selling to the Lipton employees, on his famous tea plant in beautiful Ceylon.

I have no hesitation in saying that this book, "The Life of Tom Lipton," ought to be a good seller over there, or, in fact, in any corner of the globe, for good old Tom Lipton, he of the lion heart, was known everywhere, and his friends will be happy to know that an old friend of this great man is endeavoring to tell the sad story of his life and death.

Having left the beautiful, warm climate behind me in the Far East, a sad mistake, and having been told by an old seaman that the Riviera in Nice in the south of France, was a mighty fine place to spend my winter, I became one of a party of British soldiers carrying the mails in an aeroplane from Bombay to Palestine.   It did not take us long to get back to Alexandria.

Tired and weary and longing for dear old New York and my once happy home and family, I soon bought my ticket, and off with me to Trieste, Milan, and Nice, to hang out with the poorly advised, sick little rich men, who, when their doctors had taken all their money, advised them to go to the Riviera and there they soon would regain their health.   Waurra!   Waurra!

Why, for the four months that I was imprisoned there, for I could not leave because it was zero weather all around me, and very cold in Rome, Paris and London.   Yes, it was zero on the Riviera on January 1st, 1928, and a party of travelers, some from America, and some cattle dealers from Australia, and I had our photographs taken on the boardwalk.   But for sick men, well, I saw more funerals in Nice in the four months that I was there than at any other city, state or nation that I had ever been in, and the poor Counts of No Account were getting lousy for the want of a keeper, but I had to leave.

My extended passport was to expire on February 18th in dear old London town, so I lost no time in making Paris to say goodbye to my friends there, and I arrived at the Victoria Station in London, a poor, tired out old man, for crossing the Irish and French Channels is hell, I checked in at a nearby hotel, and rested up a lot, and wrote Sir Thomas, "I am here." I soon received a telegram:

"Congratulations on your arrival after your long travels you must come to Osidge when thoroughly rested up and tell me all about your own good self and my American friends that you left behind for this extended and I hope pleasant trip around the world.
"Yours faithfully,
"THOMAS J. LIPTON."

Well, believe me, I was a happy man to have left hungry France behind me and altogether honored by them as a member of the American Legion. I do not care now, nor do I desire to go back, unless to again meet and take luncheon with my good friends, among them Mark Severe of the American Consul staff, and good old Sparrow Robinson, sporting editor of the Paris "Tribune and Herald," and meet my old pals in the American bar; that is all, for any man or nation that will not pay their just debts is not worth visiting.

I then received a telegram from Sir Thomas: "Mr. Hickey, I want you here on Sunday. I will send my car to your hotel, so be ready." This confused me very much for I had to locate St. Patrick's Cathedral for Mass, for that I never miss, and I had not been to the Cathedral in Ashley Place since war time in 1914. I finished my breakfast, hurried to church and returned to the hotel to be told that a car was at the door waiting for me over an hour.

This surprised me very much, for I knew that the people in foreign countries are not early risers, and often one loses his train because of their tired feelings or tardiness, and after finishing several glasses of my favorite "Mild and Bitter," we were off on the double quick for Osidge, passing up through Hyde Park corner onto Southgate and Highgate, once the stamping ground of Dick Turpin and his bonny Black Bess.

It may be as well to state that Dick Turpin was a highwayman who, like Bold Brennan on the Moor, robbed the rich and gave to the poor, for when a young Irish nipper in London, I visited all such historical spots and, of course, was very glad to renew my visits. As a poor kid, I had to make these visits with "Shanks Mare," while at that time I was being taken to them in a beautiful motor car. Imagine my happiness when Sir Thomas and I met, and after a hurried lunch, filling the car with all the goody-goodies for the poor kiddies coming home from Sunday school, we were off to meet them and make them happy. My, but how this cockeyed world of ours has changed! Yes, the whole world is changing, even our own families are not as they use to be— loving and kind; even to the Gulf Stream, which is closing in on New

York more and more every year. Now it stands about two hundred miles off shore from this big New York Town, that nobody seems to love at all, even its own sons, they talk about her, the damned idiots, quite a lot. Now for the big story.

London, August 10th, 1930. This happened while the writer was in London in 1928, and besides reading about it, was told the story at a luncheon party of American tourists, who, of course, enjoyed the joke very much.

Of course, as with all other yacht clubs, the Royal Yacht Squadron, which is supposed to be one of the biggest yacht clubs in the world, and one of the most famous and exclusive. This week of which I write the officials were bursting over with rage and the many unprintable expressions, both nautical and otherwise, over what was meted out as most unusual conduct by one of America's greatest business men, and I speak of Mr. Gordon Selfridge, owner of one of the largest department stores in London, and right on the fashionable Oxford Street, among the upper ten, and where the lower five are given no invitation to visit. Royalty always holds a Cowes' week and the King and Queen and members of the royal family, when all is well, spends that week aboard their beautiful yacht *Victoria and Albert,* just as King George V has decided to spend a week in May next to assist in tuning up the *Shamrock V.*

The Royal Yacht is, of course, always moored at the Royal Buoy, but the unfortunate illness of His Majesty cast a dark shadow on all kinds of sport just then, so that the *Victoria and Albert* was out of commission and the Royal Buoy was not in use at the time.

Just that same week Mr. Selfridge and his family were in Cowes, and they were stopping on his yacht, the *Conqueror,* with a party that including his daughters and their husbands, and young Gordon Selfridge, Jr., went ashore and persuaded the Cowes harbor authorities to rent them the Royal Buoy, and it was hinted that the sum of $750 would be paid for the privilege, and who could blame these poor underpaid men to grab seven hundred and fifty dollars, easy money. Why, bless your soul, we have gunmen here and within a stone's throw of where I am writing this story, that would murder a whole family for $750 and the cop or coppers that got in their way, and there are cases where they have murdered for less money.

Yes, New York is a great city; one can buy anything, even the smallpox or an honorable judgeship, if you have the sugar; but there are things to date that you cannot buy, among them the 18th Amendment; yes, or the 16th Amendment, or a law permitting those hungry hypocrites to enforce that unAmerican enforcement of birth control, and so say we all.

Yes, sir, it was a terrible blow to the dyed-in-the-wool Britishers. Almost as big a blow as the story Sir Thomas liked to tell, that is how the former Mayor of Boston, Mass., imitated the King of England, by giving them the go-bye, ordering the captain of the Royal Launch to take him out to the Sir Thomas Lipton yacht, the *Erin,* on his visit to Sir Thomas in 1903.

Or even as bad as was this accidental statesman, Charles E. Hughes, as a Washington conference committee member on disarmament, he then holding the position of Secretary of State under Herby Hoover, in 1932, when he had the audacity to order another member of that same conference, no less a person than England's high admiral, Lord Beatty, and tell him of just what line of battleships England must scrap. Waurra! Waurra!

Of course, he had to do something for his vacation and a damn good time to try satisfy the minds of the people, that never wanted him as President and he and three others of his party were defeated for the high honor of Governor of New York, by a Bowery boy, Alfred E. Smith, who had served four terms, leaving his four Republican friends and opponents out in the cold.

What fools those mortals be! And all of this time King George V, having been told the story of the $750 for the use of the Royal Buoy, sat laughing to himself, and said: "My word, seven hundred and fifty dollars is a whole lot of money in these days of depression, and we still own the Buoy. Yes, the Buoy is still ours."

And when the pussy-footing aristocrats heard what the King had said, like old boy Bishop Cannon and his gang, sneaked back into their holes, for the King wanted no babish interference between his or any other nation. He was a peace, not a fight promoter, and that's that.

It is that kind of democratic spirit that has helped to make our two great English-speaking countries almost one, with that grand old bye-word of "All for one, and one for all" the slogan, and peace on every side.

Many other little stories of that kind could be told, such as the renting of the Royal Buoy, but they happen so frequently and our people are spending much time and money among their fellows of England with much more going to be spent by the Twenty-seventh Division of the American Legion visiting their war comrades in London next month, May, 1930, under the command of General John F. O'Ryan, Police Commissioner of New York, 1934. Little things that at one time were made big things attributed to the American freshness of our smart alecks, is overlooked and forgotten now, for they join and intermingle with our former trouble-makers, the Connecticut Yankees, of the past, who loved to go over on the other side and raise h——l. They wanted to be funny, but were they?

THE WILLARD AND DEMPSEY HEAVYWEIGHT
CHAMPIONSHIP—1919

PART II—CHAPTER III

Here we have the story of the Willard-Dempsey fight in 1919, and
while Sir Thomas was noted for his ability as an advertiser, I tried
to keep his name before the people whenever the opportunity presented.
That is how much I thought of the grand old sportsman.

Noticing that my good friend, the late Tex Rickard, with an eye
to business, was seeking to obtain the services of Lord Lonsdale, another one of dear old London's famous fight promoters, to act as the
third man in the ring, but the Lord could not be moved, and I then
substituted the name of my good friend, Sir Thomas. Now you have
heard that, suppose I go on with the story. To wit:

LONDON, E. C.,
19th June, 1919.

"Dear Mr. Hickey:

"Your kind letter of the 4th inst., has been received, I am exceedingly sorry
that our departure from New York was so unexpected and so quickly arranged
that there was no opportunity of seeing you before leaving your grand old city,
Little Old New York.

"Sir Thomas hopes to be back again in his foster home city, New York, in
a very short time. Many thanks for your courtesy in mailing to us the letter
sent to you by Mr. Rickard, which pleased Sir Thomas very much.

"Sir Thomas is very sorry, however, that he cannot be over on your side
at the time of the coming of that great advent; probably you will know that
we have a man over here named Joe Beckett, who is hoping to meet the winner
of this great bout of July 4th, 1919. And this was John Westwood's sad choice
for a champion to meet Jack Dempsey, Waurra Waurra, worse than Phil Scott.

"As you suppose, Mr. Crane has left the firm at Franklin Street, and was
succeeded by a Mr. Thomas E. Graham, who will always be glad to have you
call on him, so please do not be a stranger at the old landmark.

"Hoping this will find you in the best of condition, with all good wishes,

"Yours faithfully,

"JOHN WESTWOOD.

"P. S.: I am returning to you the letter mailed to you by Mr. Tex Rickard,
again we thank you.

"Mr. J. J. Hickey,
"Hotel St. Blaise, New York City."

In my book, "The History of Fistiana," it is recorded that Jess
Willard fought and defeated the then colored champion, Jack Johnson,
and won back the championship for the white race on April 5th, 1915.
I was then on the coast, stopping at the Cafe run by Jim and Jack
Jeffries, of Los Angeles.

Good-natured Jess Willard held the championship until there came from Salt Lake City, a Jack Dempsey, and he dared to fight our big champion, and the articles of agreement were signed and the fight took place in Toledo on July 4th, 1919. Jack Dempsey, a real champion, won on a knockout. My word, how happy Jim Jeffries was that day at the ticker calling off round by round.

Tex Rickard, the one man who, above all others, placed the noble art of self-defense on a much higher plane than ever before, only to be snatched from us in the height of his popularity, and our grand old champion, Jack Dempsey, a fighter and promoter of no mean ability, picked up where Tex Rickard left off and he made good, and while not our champion today, he is our hero, for a better fighter and a truer friend never before existed, and in spite of many handicaps, Jack is still going strong. Tex Rickard, the sporting wizard, was a great believer in advertising, and was ever ready to spend one hundred dollars to make two hundred; no fool at all, and that was why he was so desirous to have Lord Lonsdale, one of England's greatest sportsmen and lover of the noble art of self-defense, hit, stop and getaway, to be the third man in the ring.

And I, noticing the trouble he had in seeking the O.K. of Lonsdale, and having in mind my own good friend who could fill the bill, I wrote my friend, Tex Rickard, submitting to him the name of Sir Thomas Lipton, to be the referee of the coming battle, or third man in the ring.

Mr. Rickard answered that nothing would give him more pleasure than to have the great Irish sportsman, so highly respected by all, appointed for the position, but for the present the matter lies in the hands of a committee of three men who are working on the matter.

Tex Rickard's letter to me, read as follows:

"Mr. J. J. Hickey,
"244 East 20th Street, New York City.
"Dear John:
   "I was very much pleased to receive your letter, for I have not seen you since the Willard-Moran fight in the Old Madison Square Garden in 1916, and would like to meet you again for oldtime sake.
   "I like your suggestion for referee very much, and would delight in our having that grand old sportsman, Sir Thomas Lipton, in the ring July 4th, but I am sorry to say that the committee has already made their choice.
   "But, say, old scout, ask Sir Thomas if he and his party will honor us with his presence at the big show. I would appreciate it very much if he be my guest that day at the big fight of the century. Expecting that your good self will be a member of the Lipton party, and hoping to meet you July 4th next, and we can talk about old times in New York and Frisco.
                 "Your old friend,   "TEX."

I lost no time in mailing the invitation to Sir Thomas, and he was delighted, and would love to be present at the fight on July 4th, but could not leave London for at least two months.

"There is so much to be done at the office, for business is increasing so that we have to step lively, and stay around, and you know that I do not like that.

"However, you thank Mr. Rickard very kindly for me and say that I fully appreciate his generous offer, and I would be delighted to be at the ringside that memorable July day, for I greatly admire Dempsey's courage and I congratulate him on his nerve and wish him luck.

"Mr. Hickey, you please say to Mr. Rickard, that I want him to call on me when I get back to America in the Autumn, maybe we will meet in Hollywood on my regular trip Westward O, but surely in New York.

"Yours faithfully,

"THOMAS J. LIPTON."

Sir Thomas was a great lover of boxing, with a big warm heart, and kind word for all, he loved to sit and look at two men in prime condition, box, but he drew the line when he saw two small boys thrown into the ring; wee boys that should be home with their mothers. It is a pity to see them, many of them untrained, out looking for glory, or maybe a meal, who knows.

Often Sir Thomas and the writer would swap fight stories, for he was just starting to plug along in Glasgow, Scotland, a lad of ten, and I was born just a few months after the great international championship contest for the heavyweight title between John C. Heenan, "The Benica Boy," and the plucky little heavyweight champion of the British Isles, Tom Sayers, who simply was a middleweight, and like good old Charley Mitchell, England's best, and famous successor to Tom Sayers, fought at 155 pounds, and as that red top, Bob Fitzsimmons would say, "the bigger they come the harder they fall."

My dear old dad was present at that fight in Farnsborough, Kent, on April 17th, 1860, and I was born on August 6th, 1860, and a bit of a fighting blade at that, for I will at this age don the gloves in a friendly contest with the best of them. Today, of course, slugging and the strangle hold, and the rabbit punch, or big men jumping on the feet of the little men in a boxing contest is not allowed. No, sir.

I am proud to say that I have seen most all of the great fights that have taken place since seeing Tom Allen beat Charley Davies for the championship of the world in Shoreditch, London, in 1879, and fifty years ago after a good hard week's work, I would hand over my envelope to "Mary of Argyle," my good wife, then put on a clean jumper and off for the Bowery, dropping in at the principal boxing resorts, put on the gloves for a round or two, and was happy and willing to go back to work for another week. I knew all the men running these places and we called each other by our first names. Heavenly Father! how different were the men and times of those days to what they are in our day, life was then worth the living, now it is hell and damnation.

"CITY ROAD, LONDON, E. C.,
"21st November, 1919.

"Mr. J. J. Hickey,
"Hotel Elton, New York City.
"Dear Mr. Hickey:

"On my return to business after a prolonged illness I received your various letters and cuttings.

"As you will know by this time that Sir Thomas is on your side, and no doubt you have met him ere now.

"Unfortunately, I was not well enough to accompany him and consequently I am disappointed at not having the pleasure of meeting you as I hoped, but I expect, however, to be over on your side before the race for the "America's Cup," next summer, and then I will have the pleasure of meeting you.

"I am very much pleased to know of all the good news that you report and the fact of your two sons joining the colors, and I wish them all possible success in their careers in the Army and Navy of your Uncle Sam.

"Hoping this will find you well, and with renewed thanks for your kindness, in my behalf, I am,

"Yours faithfully,

"JOHN WESTWOOD."

It was on that visit that I gave Sir Thomas the $100 Victory Bond. I recall that he had with him a new secretary, a man that I had never seen on all previous occasions, or since, to my recollection, and our party at the Commodore that evening consisted of a Mr. Edward Pike, assistant manager to Mr. Sweeney of the Hotel Commodore, Sir Thomas and your humble servant.

Unfortunately, I have traveled so much my notes are at the moment mixed up, but will come to light some day, sooner or later.

But, what I cannot understand is why the new secretary did not make a note of the transaction, or maybe it was taken over by the Invisible Government, and mailed to John Westwood. Who knows? Or it may be that Miss Owens, John Westwood's clever assistant, in Hoboken, mailed it to her boss, Westwood.

So that there will be no misunderstanding about the length of time that I have had the pleasure and the honor of knowing Sir Thomas, and for all of these years enjoying the close personal friendship with the late grand old dean of the yachting world, I will do my best to supply you with his many letters to me; yes, even before John Westwood arrived on the job.

"196 CITY ROAD, LONDON, E. C.,
"9th of August, 1910.

"Mr. John J. Hickey,
"Parkville, Brooklyn, N. Y.
"Dear Sir:

"Your letter addressed to Sir Thomas Lipton is to hand, and I am directed by Sir Thomas to thank you for same, and to say that he is so very much pleased to hear from you and to know that you are well and have been promoted to the staff of the 'New York World,' a very responsible position I am sure, and Sir Thomas wishes to you every good luck.

"Sir Thomas desires me to state that he is always glad to hear from you and that your wife and children are enjoying good health, and your own good self prosperity.

"Yours faithfully,

"JOHN WESTWOOD."

I learned afterwards that Sir Thomas was then on his way to Ceylon, making his yearly visit to his tea plants and to check up on the past year, for this was most important, and Sir Thomas, until late years, would take much pleasure in going over these transactions himself personally.

But alas, old age and infirmities, coming on him, he had to give this up and you all know from these pages what followed, I am sad to relate.

I have many reasons to know just what I am talking about, for I, too, have had my sorrowful experience, that is, I, too, have been double-crossed by these miserable rats more than once and could tell you enough to set your blood boiling, for any decent person or charity can have the half of my dollar, but do not rob me, or if you do, you will have to take the responsibility, that is all.

About two years ago, on one of my usual visits to see Sir Thomas, I was received and held in the detention pen by John Westwood, until Sir Thomas came out of his room and he gave me hell. The old fellow, in a heated strain, said: "Mr. Hickey, I for years have been asking you to come and see me, either here in the hotel or over at my office in Hoboken, but you never come, and why?" Well, there was I looking in the face of Westwood, not knowing what answer to make my good friend. I grabbed my hat and was off.

But, that night I vowed vengeance on John Westwood, and all the way down Park Avenue I swore that come what may, Sir Thomas must know the truth, and I knew full well just what the truth was going to come to; that is, I would be blocked from ever seeing Sir Thomas, not only at the hotel, but at the factory, for the employees of this great factory were all under the wing of John Westwood; but come what may, it must and shall be done.

Two nights afterwards, I again called at the Biltmore to see Sir Thomas, and as usual I called up from the hotel office, and was told by John Westwood that Sir Thomas had company, and he made the mistake of sending his assistant, Mr. Waghorn, to see me to express his sorrow.

Mr. Waghorn, a somewhat decent fellow, said, "It is too bad, Mr. Hickey, when you come so far to see the 'Chief' and then do not see him. It is provoking, but, say, why don't you go over to the factory and see the Chief?" and that was just the opening that I was long waiting for, and I said, "Yes, Mr. Waghorn, how will I know when Sir Thomas is at the factory," and he said, "He is to be found there most every day, if no other business keeps him away. Why not go tomorrow, Mr. Hickey, he surely will be there and all alone?"

Sure enough, I was over in Hoboken, and after a long investigation from the officers on the twelfth floor, I was allowed to meet my friend, and again, when alone and sipping at our second cup of tea, Westwood not being there that day.

Sir Thomas and I were exchanging remarks until he again went at me about my not calling on him at all, and that was what I wanted, and I told Sir Thomas of my many visits, and having been told by John Westwood that Sir Thomas had company, or was dressing for dinner, or in conference. "Who told you that, Mr. Hickey?" and I repeated, "Mr. Westwood." Well, the grand old man got up from his chair and rang the bell bringing all his superintendents to him and he just roared out what he had been told. I then knowing that my presence would not be welcome in that factory any more, when John Westwood was given the news, I hurried back to my hotel and wrote Westwood the whole story.

And, in reply, I received a letter from John Westwood, stating: "My dear Mr. Hickey, I am very glad to hear from you again, for I am always glad to hear from an old friend.

"Any time that you wish to see Sir Thomas, just call me up and I will at once make an appointment," but again, in this he flunked, for just to try him out, I again visited the Biltmore and asked to see Sir Thomas, with the same old reply, but what could I do but try to catch Sir Thomas entering nights, and he would ask me up stairs and we would talk a lot, before he retired.

And I dare any living mother's son to charge me with ever in all of our long years of friendship, of having asked my good friend for a dollar.

But, when printing and binding was real cheap in 1916 and my first book ready for publication, I did write Sir Thomas, stating the facts, and asked if it would be possible for him to advance to my order and on my notes the loan of $1,600, to place my book before the public, and he to collect all its earnings with interest until his loan was paid. This, I feel sure, Sir Thomas never received, or did it get out of Westwood's hands.

So I had to plug along, and watch and wait and in 1925, it cost me some $3,700 dollars to print two thousand and bind the one, all of my own hard-earned savings, and from which I received good profits, at least enough to give me a trip with the American Legion to Paris in 1927 and permit me to travel all lands, including the Near and Far East, taking in all, one whole year.

But, I did send my money to Sir Thomas in the shape of American Liberty Bonds, and this is how it happened, to wit:

I, a member of the New York Police Veterans' Association, and in the election of officers for 1918, was elected first vice-president, and appointed chairman of their labor committee, and, thinking of my two motherless sons, busy overseas fighting for their country, I proposed that we, to help win the war, should have appointed a committee on Liberty Bonds and War Saving Stamps, but no committee was appointed but the job was saddled on my shoulders, and I was not a bit sorry, for I was better able to make good alone, and it proved so, for I had sold, in the name of our association, $175,000 worth of Liberty Bonds and War Saving Stamps among our members and the business men to whom I applied for employment of our members.

I, the writer, as chairman of the Liberty Bond Committee, would call at the office of the French Consul and ask them to have one of their French military men who had seen the rough side of things on the battlefields, to attend our meetings and tell their stories to the members and after every meeting the members came up with their dollars, like true blue heroes.

My only income being the small amount of $465 per year police pension, when it should have been $700 per year, for I had been injured in the line of duty on a number of occasions, and ordered before the Board of Surgeons, and ordered retirement on full pension.

But the Police Commissioner then in power, an old pensioner from the U. S. Army, drawing down a mighty fine pension, would not retire me on the half of the salary then paid, that of $700 per year, and because General Bingham, the Police Commissioner, did not see fit to give me what the law allowed, all the other lame ducks of Commissioners refused to increase my pension, and for eleven long years, with a wife and ten children to support, I had to do the best I could, by appealing to every commissioner for justice.

But they all turned a deaf ear, until Police Commissioner Richard E. Enright came into power in 1918, and he answered my long standing appeal, by submitting my case to the pension committee, who all agreed that I should have been granted full pension when retired, for one injured in the line of duty, besides holding a vested right in the pension, having paid a percentage of my salary for many years to keep the pension fund in existence.

The pension committee reported its findings to Police Commissioner Enright, who lost no time in signing the committee report, and I was from July 18th, 1918, paid my pension in full, $58.33, not much for a fellow to live on if he did not hustle, and believe me, I had to hustle, to make both ends meet, with my two oldest sons in the service, the third, Teddy, I placed in a Catholic institution after the passing away of his mother in 1912. He, too, asking to join the 69th Regiment to go to war.

"CITY ROAD, LONDON,
"January 17th, 1918.

"Mr. John J. Hickey,
"23 Duane Street, New York City.

"Dear Mr. Hickey:

"Very many thanks for your kind letter of the 17th ultimo, and your kind wishes for Christmas and the New Year.

"These I very highly appreciate and reciprocate most heartily, and I am looking forward to our little chats in the near future, that I am keeping constantly in mind.

"I note with interest what you tell me about your sons who are at the moment battling with the common enemy far overseas, and like you, I, too, hope and trust to Divine Providence and constant prayer that your sons will be spared to you and come through this terrible ordeal safe and sound for your Motherless sons deserve great credit, to think of it, both minors with a fighting spirit, answering their country's call,

"But for those abnormal times I would have been on your side before now and would have the pleasure of shaking the hand of my old friend, J. J. Hickey, once again. This, however, is I hope only a pleasure deferred for a short time, when happiness will again return to us all.

"I trust that this will find you fit and well, and I hope that 1918 will hold for both you and yours everything that is good and dear.

"With my very best wishes, I am

"Yours respectfully,

"THOMAS J. LIPTON."

"CITY ROAD, LONDON, E. C.,
"13th March, 1918.

"Mr. J. J. Hickey,
"23 Duane Street, New York City.

"Dear Mr. Hickey:

"I duly received your kind letters of the past, particularly that of the 15th ultimo, with enclosed cuttings which I have read with pleasure and interest. I am very grateful to you indeed for sending to me from time to time these very interesting writings, and I want you to know that I highly appreciate your kind thoughts of me.

"I have for a long time been in hopes that circumstances would give me a chance to get over to your side to again meet my dear friends, but they tell me that it is too dangerous to travel just now, and I have still to wait until all the danger is passed.

"Mr. Crane, however, has been visiting us here and if you call he will be delighted to tell you all the news concerning the circumstances and condition of things over here. So don't forget to drop in on Mr. Crane at his office on Franklin Street at your earliest convenience.

"I trust that this will find you fit and well. With kindest regards and best wishes, I am,

"Faithfully yours,

"THOMAS J. LIPTON."

"CITY ROAD, LONDON,
"20th June, 1918.

"Mr. John J. Hickey,
"23 Duane Street, New York City.

"Dear Mr. Hickey:

"Very many thanks for your kind letter of the 24th ultimo, enclosing the souvenir American Liberty Bond, for this I am very glad indeed to have in memory of America, and my great body of American friends whom I am longing to meet again. It is more than kind of you to think of me in this way and I can assure you that I very highly appreciate your kindness.

"I shall treasure this Liberty Bond, as a memento, first of all your own good self, and also of the most important event in the history of the world— the Union of the 'Stars and Stripes' and the 'Union Jack' united as brothers fighting for freedom's sake, and its preservation.

"Again let me thank you for your kind thought, and looking forward to the pleasure of meeting you and thanking you personally, for I appreciate your kind thoughts of me always. Trusting that this will find you fit and well.

"Yours faithfully,

"THOMAS J. LIPTON."

We met on his next visit, but not a word about the Liberty Bond. Why? This bond, No. 3,093,020, I had registered at the East 23rd Street Post Office.

This poem is most respectfully dedicated to the members of the Honor Legion of the Police Department of the City of New York, composed, written and copyrighted by Officer "787," John J. Hickey, retired, 1918.

Here's to the Honor Legion, and its members both noble and brave,
Who offered up their own sweet lives, in attempting some other to save.
Their deeds will reign Victorious, when they have passed and gone,
Leaving this world of sorrow, and loved ones behind to mourn.

While gazing on this noble band, on this beautiful January eve,
Watching them go through their various stunts, I certainly could not conceive,
What next will they do, or where will they stop, learning the tactics the enemy
    to drop.

The maneuvers of the Legion grand, is a credit to America our beloved land.
They are prepared to meet and defeat the foe, just as our forefather did
    years ago.

And woe be to the Hyphenated cuss, who with those heroes get into a muss,
There won't be much of them left to be seen, while our honored Legion will
    reign supreme.

Here's success to those heroes all, may they ever be ready at our country's call,
To fight our battles, this gallant band, either on sea, or on land.

May God's blessing go with them all, they have showed their mettle, and await
    the call,
To strike down the enemies of our beloved land, and learn them to thoroughly
    understand,
That we are a free and a peaceful land.

Here's to the promoters of this Legion grand who have banded together and
    promise to stand
In defense of America, our country game and true,
And prove to the world, that we are Red, White and Blue.
Here's to our Citizens, all faithful and true, that rallied to the assistance of
    heroes in blue,
Their kindly assistance, we never can forget, they stood by us manfully, and
    fhey are with us yet.

    Hark the drum, hark the drum, can't you hear our country calling?
Victory, Victory, our boys have returned, hark, hark the drum.

Strike up the band, here comes a sailor. All right, let the story travel. While chatting with Sir Thomas in Osidge, February, 1928, having spoken about my aeroplane contracts, he grabbed my arm, saying, "Mr. Hickey, you know that Graham White, my friend, asked me to take a ride with him in his machine. I did, but will never forget it, for all the time that White would say, 'Don't be afraid, Sir Thomas,' I was trembling from head to feet, and I declare to God, Mr. Hickey, I would sell *Shamrock I* for sixpence only to get back on solid ground. No, no, never again for Tom Lipton. That is the second time I was up in the air. No more for me," and he went on to tell of another adventure, when he was Colonel of the Glasgow Light Infantry and his horse threw him and ran away, very funny story.

"J. J. Hickey,   "CITY ROAD, LONDON, E. C.,
"Office of the 'Chronicle,'   "19th Dec., 1919.
"23, Duane Street, New York.

"Dear Mr. Hickey:

"Your letter of the 2nd inst., to hand and its contents duly noted. I was indeed sorry that I could not accompany Sir Thomas on the last occasion, but as I have already written, I hope to be over next year and to see then all of our good American friends.

"I am sorry to see on the day of writing you had not had any acknowledgment of your letter to the Prince of Wales, but feel sure that this will be duly attended to, as no doubt in the great rush it had not been found possible to answer all communications.

"Many thanks for your kind wishes for Christmas and the New Year. These, need hardly say, I most highly appreciate and very heartily reciprocate. I trust that 1920 will contain for you and yours all that is good.

"Yours faithfully,   "JOHN WESTWOOD."

In the above letter from Mr. Westwood in relation to the young Prince of Wales, this was answered two days later, and he, John Westwood, also mailed me the pictures and the account of the Georges Carpentier and Becket fight, that had just taken place in London.

"CITY ROAD, LONDON, E. C.,
"14th July, 1921.

"Dear Mr. Hickey:

"Your letters of the 1st and 4th, with accompanying cuttings, are to hand and we are very much interested in the Jersey City little matter, in fact your own letter is the best account that we have seen so far, and we quite agree with you, that had a different plan of action been followed the result might have been reversed, although Jack Dempsey, as you mentioned seems to be the very much stronger man.

"We have seen and read various other accounts of the fight from people that were present and have returned to London, and they all agree with you that Carpenter nearly did the trick in the second round.

"However, that is all over now and, as you say the newspaper will not be selling so freely.

"I am glad to hear that your hand is again well and that you are now looking forward to your annual holiday among the mountains, for that grand spot in Platte Clove, the Police Camp, that originated in the mind and the brain of Police Commissioner Enright, will again, put the old running pep into you and build you up strong for the coming year.

"I am glad to say that Sir Thomas is well, though as usual, working too hard.

"I do not yet know when he will be getting over to your side, but it pleases the Chief and makes him just feel like packing up right away, New York bound, and the more you tell him about his old friends, the more he is hurrying to make his getaway, but important business matters keep him from getting away, but he takes great pleasure in re-reading your letters before retiring, at midnight.

"However, one of these days we may surprise you by dropping in on you quite unexpectedly.

"I trust this will find you fit and well; with kind remembrances and with many thanks for all the trouble you have been taking all these long years, never tiring for an instant, even when on your holidays.

"Yours faithfully,

"Mr. J. J. Hickey,   "JOHN WESTWOOD.
"Hotel St. Blaise, 23rd Street, New York City."

THE COMING OF SIR THOMAS LIPTON IN 1923

Part II—Chapter IV

Next to the grand and glorious reception tendered to the late Admiral George Dewey, of the United States Navy, after his noble defeat of the big Spanish Armada, in 1899, came the reception accorded Sir Thomas Lipton on his early visit of 1923, by the Police Department of New York. Here is what the press had to write of same, to wit— Front page headlines galore.

"The sportsman arrives and announces that he will challenge with his *Shamrock V*.

"If the year ever comes when a ruddy faced sailor from England or Ireland fails to arrive here 'to lift America's Cup,' there will be deep sadness about the waters of New York harbor, and the ships' news reporters will not be feeling the same. But, Sir Thomas Lipton, of international yachting fame, looking even sturdier and healthier than ever before, despite his seventy-three years of youth, came in on the White Star liner *Cederic* yesterday with the smiling prediction that very shortly one of his *Shamrocks* is going to take the cup back to Ireland, where you can at least put something in it worth while. Sir Thomas will not challenge this year, he made that clear on landing. But next year he hoped that the official challenge will arrive for 1925, and to take Sir Thomas' word for it, 'there'll be something doing this year.'

"Sir Thomas came here this year on a flying trip to send his *Shamrock* metre back to her home in Ireland (she was then resting up in City Island) and would stay but three weeks. Captain William Manning, his chief skipper, also arrived here to sail her home across the broad Atlantic.

" 'Seventy years is a mighty long time to keep a cup away from home,' Sir Thomas said. 'Therefore, it seems right that the *Shamrock V*— that's my next yacht—should lift the cup and take it back home, for a few weeks at least.' And here the noted sportsman turned the talk to other things.

"For instance, he showed the marks of wear and tear resulting in his being chosen judge of a baby contest aboard the ship on her passage over.

"Twenty babies were brought up from the steerage to be passed on and this gallant old sportsman looked at the twenty mothers, and he no doubt said to himself, 'Heavenly Father! Why didn't I get married and have a baby.'

"But Sir Thomas, the wise old owl, having looked over and chatted with the twenty beautiful mothers, and knowing that he would be in their company a few days longer, took one look at the twenty babies and decided that he could not pick the winning baby. 'I wasn't taking any chances of having nineteen irate mothers on my back by making any choice, so I sent each baby a silver spoon, and called it a draw,' said the shrewd, diplomatic skipper.

"The serenade tendered to Sir Thomas down the bay on his arrival by the 100 members of the Police Department Band impressed him greatly.

" 'There are no better sportsmen in the world than the Americans,' said Sir Thomas. 'And the way that I am always received here is enough to cause me to visit New York oftener, even if I didn't want to take back the jolly old mug again.' Sir Thomas was staying at the Hotel Commodore, and will attend the yacht races and have a jolly old time with his hosts of friends in that historic old summer colony, Long Branch and Sandy Hook, attend several dinners that he has been invited to, among them his good friends of many years, our grand old friend and jurist, Mr. and Mrs. Morgan J. O'Brien, and pretty family, the one visit that he never passes over, for they love the company of each other very much." And every letter from Sir Thomas to yours truly the one prime question is, "Mr. Hickey, how is all of my dear old friends?"

Another reporter wrote his own story and this is what he stated:

"Sir Thomas Lipton, Bart, the veteran yachtsman, arrived yesterday from ould Ireland, brimming over with those grand old Irish smiles for which he is noted, and received a wonderful reception, the best that he had ever before received, making him very happy."

Another reporter wrote the following: "Sir Thomas Lipton, the famous Irish Baronet, and veteran international yachtsman, arrived here today, from old Ireland, beaming over with those grand old Irish smiles for which he is noted, and was received in royal style, for he was given one of the greatest receptions ever accorded to man, next to that given to Admiral George Dewey in 1899, after his wonderful victory over the Spanish Armada.

"Sir Thomas looked much better than in years, his moustache trimmed up and his long established polka dot tie, and his favorite little yachting cap cocked on one side, he looked the very picture of the late King Edward VII, then Prince of Wales, visiting us in 1860. But when Police Commissioner Richard E. Enright and his staff of millionaire one-dollar-a-year deputies, followed by Grover A. Whalen, chairman of the Mayor's committee for the reception of distinguished visitors, the fun commenced in earnest.

"The police band of one hundred performers playing 'The Wearing of the Green,' followed by the Police Department Glee Club of one hundred singers. Sir Thomas was taken from the steamer and received by the reception committee on that wonderful fighting machine, the police boat *Manhattan*. Every mother soul on board was happy, and a good time had by all."

"POLICE DEPARTMENT
"CITY OF NEW YORK, OFFICE OF THE COMMISSIONER

"September 23rd, 1923.

"Mr. John J. Hickey,
"Hotel Elton, City.
"My Dear John:
    "Your letter of the 13th inst. with enclosures that I have enjoyed the reading of, I am again returning to you forthwith, and I thank you very much for same.
    "I am glad to hear that you enjoyed the Police Field Days, many games in which we were forced to pack in so many events, giving the public the worth of their money and sending them home happy.
    "The second day's games was even better than the first, and the Police Relief Fund will be further enriched as a result.
    "Sir Thomas is to arrive here tomorrow, that is Sunday, and I am making all arrangements to give that grand old sportsman a right royal reception.
    "If you receive this notice in time, meet us at the Battery seawall, or Pier One at 12 noon, as I want you to go down the Bay on the *Macon*, with us with all best wishes,
                    "Sincerely,
                            "RICHARD E. ENRIGHT,
                            "Police Commissioner."

We met and sailed down the bay, and Sir Thomas was delighted at the wonderful reception, and the many fine people that were present. When I called on Sir Thomas at the Hotel Biltmore, he was still talking of the wonderful reception, that would do credit to King George V, or his son, the Prince of Wales.

This was a very fine reception and even to the last Sir Thomas would, in referring to his happy days spent in America, speak of the memorable reception, and my good friend Enright.

And all along since the Police Holy Name Communion Breakfast, held in the Hotel Commodore in 1919, when I gave Commissioner Enright the number of Sir Thomas' suite, and the Commissioner and his staff called on Sir Thomas and asked him down to the feast, that I had tried to do before giving the Police Commissioner the number of the suite. But Sir Thomas was a very bashful man, and tried to kill off all publicity, but that was something mighty hard to do, and for the long term of Richard E. Enright as our Police Commissioner, 1918 to 1926, this greeting to a grand old sportsman continued yearly and Sir Thomas never forgot a kind favor, and he grew to like Dick Enright, who, at the time, was one of New York's brightest stars.

A word about our millionaire police deputies, a body of good loyal men who had made their mark, and were patriotic enough to give their aid and comfort to our Police Commissioner when he needed all the help that he could get during the World's War. They rallied behind his banner, and they marched off to duty nightly with the flag of the good old U. S. A. tucked around their body, for they all were

Palais de Bruxelles.
le 1er mai 1919.

Monsieur,

La chaleureuse expression de vos sentiments de sympa-
thie pour Lui-même et pour la Belgique a beaucoup touché
le Roi.

Sa Majesté m'a chargé d'avoir l'honneur de vous trans-
mettre Ses vifs remerciements pour votre gracieuse attention et de vous féliciter du patriotisme dont vos fils ont
donné une si belle preuve.

Veuillez agréer, Monsieur, l'assurance de ma considé-
ration distinguée.

Le Chef du Cabinet du Roi,

Cte d'Arschot

A Monsieur
Monsieur John.J.HICKEY,
    &   &   &
   New-York.

"LINDSLEY' OWN"

Championship baseball team of the Police Athletic Association, 1905.
Lieutenant Charley Madigan, Manager

JOHN J. HICKEY

Veteran patrolman, champion long-distance runner of the New York Police Department, Past
President of the Police Athletic Association
of Greater New York, and prominent in police
and social clubs, numbers many eminent per-
sonages among his personal friends.

given dangerous jobs, and in the event of death they would be more easily recognized by the flag on their person.

It might be as well to have my readers know those men of whom I write, for they deserved the highest of respect and the able performance of duty should never be forgotten, and our children should be taught to know and to love these great men, that sacrificed their all for they were forced to give up all the comforts of home and loved ones to see to it that America and her allies would win the war. More power to them all, fast passing onward and upward, heaven their goal. Among them were William H. Todd, America's great ship builder, Dr. John H. Harriss, Col. Herman A. Metz, former Police Commissioners Rhinelander Waldo, Count George MacDonald and Douglas I. McKay, John Wanamaker, George Dougherty, and others who would report to Police Commissioner Enright's office nightly, receive their orders and with these two great American bankers, Edward and Randolph Guggenheim to the fore, they would all of them, report for duty along the docks.

But alas, the world will never know all the hardships that these good lovers of America's freedom endured, but they carried on, smiling in danger; real men, determined to see this damn thing through, and our country's enemies thrown into jail, and those good men having to be in court to prosecute, so you see they did not have much time to attend to their own business, but they were happy, for they could see victory just around the corner, and in spite of sad depression, these good men are enjoying the benefits of their arduous labor, and I hope will so continue to enjoy same.

But, the Police Commissioner was not at all unmindful of the sacrifices that these good men were ever willing to endure, for he had every man Jack of his official family on the job, including the chief surgeon, Patrick Murray, and his able assistant, Daniel J. Donovan, now chief; Dr. Charles E. Nammack; peace be to our dead honest John Daly, Inspector Ed. Mulrooney, who afterwards made such a wonderful career as Police Commissioner, as also did Grover A. Whalen in 1930, that good old-time policeman, Edward P. Mulrooney, driving the gunmen of New York to hell with a one-way ticket, and Grover Whalen having the Communists on their way to hell, also with a one-way ticket; but for the pussy-footing of Mayor Walker, they would be gone and forgotten before this, for Grover Whalen always made good, and he put the finishing touches on the reception to Sir Thomas in 1923 and 1930 in fine shape, for Grover Whalen was noted for his being an A-1 Major Domo, always doing something for humanity, constantly working for the people's aid and comfort, and he might have been elected Mayor of New York, and my friend, John P. O'Brien, still holding down his good job as Surrogate, elected by the people, only for an error of judgment, a mistake for which they are at the moment turning heaven and earth to unseat John Curry, and rightly so.

And, sad to relate, the Lord called our old Tammany leader, Mr. Charles F. Murphy to him, or John F. Hylan would have been re-elected to succeed himself, and we would not have the trouble we are having today electing, to my mind, fake leaders for such a noble organization.

But this was another big mistake of John Curry, to have Jimmy Walker succeed John F. Hylan, but there it was; Walker made Curry, and Curry made, and unmade James J. Walker. A darned sorrowful blow to the whole Walker family, for Jimmy Walker made a very fine Senate leader in Albany, and there he should have been left, but now he is an exile from home, and Mr. Curry is slated for a terrible beating, and we hope, taking his good dear friend, Max Steuer, in exile with him, for misery likes company always. Enough said.

Sir Thomas, the grand old sportsman, could never get over the wonderful sight and the many fine friends he met that day, many of them for the first time, but never lost sight of thereafter, for he often took delight ever afterwards to speak of that glorious day of his reception of 1923.

I called on the grand old chief the following night. He was stopping at the Biltmore hotel, and again he came from his own room into the detention pen, Room 618, and again he asked me why I did not call on him in his own room, that he had asked me so often to do, but it was the same old story—John Westwood did not want me to.

Sir Thomas drew his chair up close to mine and said, "Mr. Hickey, that friend of yours, Enright, is a wonderful man and must command a large salary." I answered, "Yes, Sir Thomas, Police Commissioner Enright is a wonderful man, and if you knew him as I have done since his entering the Police Department in 1897, appointed to the force by your old friend, Police Commissioner and President Theodore Roosevelt, you would say that Enright was a wonderful chap with a heart as big as 'Big Ben,' and all the salary he receives is seventy-five hundred dollars a year, that is all."

Sir Thomas arose from his chair amazed, saying, "Heavenly Father that man is worth at least twenty-five thousand dollars a year, in any business, I don't understand it at all." John Westwood, who of course was present, felt that his job was fast slipping, and became nervous, and I was willing and would be much happier if it had slipped, for Dick Enright would have made for him a far better secretary than did gruffy old John Westwood.

From the remarks made to me a little later when we were alone for a few moments, I feel and know that Sir Thomas would be delighted to have Enright on his personal staff, but when I wrote Mr. Enright of the conversation, he being a born policeman, loved his present job at the head of the force, and for once in his life he laid down on himself, and did not follow my lead.

I told Sir Thomas that in 1905, while General Bingham was Police

Commissioner, he did not like Enright, and said, "Damn it, that fellow is worth twenty thousand dollars a year in any other business," and after hopping around the room on his walking stick, said, "If that fellow don't soon get out of the Department he will own the whole damn business," and sure enough in 1918, Enright did own the whole damn Department, and kept it for eight years, a record that any man could be proud of, Enright appreciated his job highly.

"THE COMMODORE HOTEL, NEW YORK,
"8th of September, 1923.

"Mr. John J. Hickey,
"c/o Police Camp, Elka Park,
"Greene County, N. Y.
"Dear Mr. Hickey:
"Your very kind letter of good wishes is duly to hand and I am very pleased to hear from you.
"I looked for you on my arrival, and was sorry to miss you, and this for the first time in twenty years, but I am glad to know that you are well and that business at the Police Camp detained you.
"But I hope, however, to have a chat with you before we leave for home at the moment I cannot say when, but will advise you later.
"Hoping this will find you fit and well, and with all best wishes, I am,
"Yours respectfully,
"THOMAS J. LIPTON."

"LONDON, E. C.,
"29th May, 1925.

"Mr. John J. Hickey,
"Hotel Elton, 4th Avenue,
"New York.
"Dear Mr. Hickey:
"The copy of your book entitled 'OUR POLICE GUARDIAN' which you have been so kind as to send me, came duly to hand and I have perused it with the very greatest possible pleasure.
"It is a work most excellently produced, and is very instructive and entertaining and has afforded me some very delightful reading.
"I am also very glad to see the photographs of so many of my old friends that your book portrays, and, of course, being myself a member of the New York Police, who many thanks to your great Commissioner, I was appointed an Honorary Deputy Police Inspector, for which I was very grateful.
"I take a special interest in all that you have written, and particularly that fact of my being associated with New York's most prominent business men and foremost financiers also doing their bit as special Deputy Police Commissioners, at a dollar a day, I am told.
"You are certainly to be congratulated on the production of a first class history of the greatest Police Department in the world, and its great work of protecting the public, that you, your own self so ably and honorably served for many years.
"I hope to have the pleasure of meeting you soon.
"Yours sincerely,
"THOMAS J. LIPTON."

"Mr. John J. Hickey,   "LONDON, E. C.,
"Hotel Elton,   "23rd of Nov., 1925.
"New York City.
"Dear Mr. Hickey:
"Your further kind letter of the 11th inst., is to hand, I do not think that you can look for a visit this year, but probably in the early part of the New Year, Sir Thomas will be sailing westward.

"I am sorry to hear of your family loss and in this you have my sincere sympathy. I wish you the best of luck as a book publisher, and I hope that things are going better in this respect.

"With kindest regards and all good wishes,
"Yours faithfully,
"JOHN WESTWOOD."

"CITY ROAD, LONDON, E. C.,
"14th of April, 1924.

"My Dear Hickey:

"I was much pleased to receive your letters of the 17th and 19th ultimo, with the interesting enclosed cuttings, for which I thank you very much, for your past and present kind attention to me.

"I had just returned from the south of France, where I had been recuperating from a severe attack of influenza, and it was a very great pleasure for me to hear from my good old friends across the sea, and for this I thank you sincerely, for it has been very lonesome while away, and no word from them. I am glad to say, however, that my stay in France has greatly improved my health and on my way to my usual good form.

"I fully appreciate the many kind expressions contained in your many letters that are always so welcome and interesting, and I am looking forward with great pleasure to seeing my good old friend Hickey, on my next visit to the good old U.S.A. in a month or so, there to thank you personally.

"Meanwhile with my very best and kindest regards and good wishes, for you, I wish you a happy future, and always remembering your faithfulness to me. I am,
"Yours faithfully,
"THOMAS J. LIPTON.

"Mr. John J. Hickey,
"1025—40th Street,
"Brooklyn, N. Y."

"CITY ROAD, LONDON, E. C.,
"13th of May, 1924.

"My Dear Hickey:

"Very many thanks for your exceedingly kind letter of the 2nd and the pretty birthday card that I highly appreciate your kind thought and the good wishes which you have expressed.

"I hope that you are keeping as well as I would wish you, and that I shall have the pleasure of seeing you before long. With renewed thanks and kindest regards,
"Yours faithfully,
"THOMAS J. LIPTON.

"Mr. John J. Hickey,
"1025—40th Street,
"Brooklyn, N. Y."

OFFICE OF THE COMMISSIONER, POLICE DEPARTMENT,
CITY OF NEW YORK.
"October 18th, 1924.

"Mr. John J. Hickey,
"Hotel Elton,
"New York City.
"Dear John:

"Your letter of the 17th inst., with enclosures which I am returning to you forthwith.

"We are going down the bay to meet Sir Thomas, and if you will get in touch with me late Monday afternoon, I will then be in a position to inform you of our arrangements, and you must not fail to join us, on this trip out to sea to meet Sir Thomas, your old friend of many years.
"Sincerely yours,
"RICHARD E. ENRIGHT, Commissioner."

THE HOTEL BILTMORE, NEW YORK CITY.

"December 1st, 1924.

"Mr. John J. Hickey,
"Hotel Elton,
"New York City.
"Dear Mr. Hickey:

"We are again leaving for home on Saturday, and would be pleased to have you call up to the hotel to have a last chat with the big chief and myself, in case the excitement at the pier might prevent our not being able to have a talk, with your old friend, and shake hands.

"Sir Thomas is giving you his invitation to the Police Band Entertainment and Reception, taking place next week, and wishes you to be on the Grand Stand, and represent him while we are roaming over the high seas.

"Very truly yours,

"JOHN WESTWOOD."

SIR THOMAS LIPTON

INTERNATIONAL SPORTSMAN, CITIZEN OF EARTH AND SEA, AND GREATEST TEA AND COFFEE MERCHANT THE WORLD EVER KNEW.

By JOE MITCHELL CHAPPLE

When Sir Thomas Lipton appears in New York, or any other American city, wearing his nautical cap tilted jauntily to the starboard, he is hailed as "Sir Thomas" by the passersby as a "royal good fellow," exemplifying a type of red-blooded international sportsmanship and citizenship.

The career of Sir Thomas is one of the outstanding biographic thrillers of the century. A wee lad of fourteen arrived at Castle Garden in New York from Glasgow, Scotland, over fifty years ago with only a few coppers left. On the voyage over, he wrote letters for his fellow passengers and paid his first week's board in New York City by writing.

Later he went to New Orleans and grew to love the Southland. On his return to Great Britain he was not long in applying the enterprise he learned as an errand boy in America. Having saved his every penny while in America, he opened a little grocery store in his natal city of Glasgow, thereby laying the corner stone of his vast fortunes.

At the early age of nineteen, Sir Thomas was proprietor of this single grocery store; ten years later a millionaire. This decade is an object lesson of what pluck and practical perseverance can achieve.

When the door of opportunity opened—Tom Lipton was ready. A syndicate owning large tea plantations in far off Ceylon had failed, owing to the prejudice existing in the British Isles against Ceylon Tea.

Opportunity again saw bonny young Tom Lipton on the job, watching and waiting and when his time had come, he said to himself, "Now, Tom Lipton, up guards and at them, for we must be going," and he went,

He had made up his mind that it was time to start, and he courageously "bid in" on a failure. "At that time," said Sir Thomas, "I didn't know a tea bush from a fig tree, but it seemed to me that they had not understood selling tea to the public who were drinking tea."

"I felt that I understood how to sell goods to the people of my locality, and that people were people the world over."

And in a reminiscent mood, Sir Thomas continued.

"I had received only a meagre education, but I knew how to work."

"I had so much to do in that little Scotch grocery store that I made myself a bed under the counter and literally 'slept with my business.' "

"There is no fun like work." There was a soft Irish light in the eyes of Sir Thomas, as he continued pointing out to me a picture on the table that he always carries with him: "The inspiration of my life was my fond and loving mother." The one thing I built up my business for was because I had promised mother that some day I would buy her a carriage and pair."

"She always encouraged me." "Every day of my life while she lived I either telegraphed or cabled her and was ever under her influence." "Perhaps that is the reason that I never married?"

"I have the same ambitious dreams now as I had in those days as a boy in my little grocery store, with only one little wee helper, and now I employ eight thousand helpers in the Island of Ceylon alone, my tea gardens."

Sir Thomas Lipton has been known as the world's greatest tea merchant and has the largest selling plant in the world, and brand of tea in the world. In his ambition to win the international yachting Cup, Sir Thomas is still persistent and doesn't mind spending a million or two for the sport of trying four times. Sir Thomas has stimulated amicable international relations through his sportsmanlike qualities.

A tall man with Irish twinkling eyes, a grey mustache and goatee, with slightly stooped shoulders, he has a mannerism that seems to be friendly with a smile and a gentle pat on the shoulder for all he meets.

A cosmopolite, he is just as much at home in one part of the world as another.

The greatest of honors and decorations have been showered upon him from the former crowned heads of Europe in every country that he has travelled, for his charming Irish speech and pleasing personality is know and respected the world over.

Referring to them, unfolding his tall form when rising, he said, "The highest decorations of them all was the hearty greeting of my friends in America and the whole world over."

When visiting New York, Sir Thomas is given the freedom of the big city by his friends and he delights to be the guest of Police Commissioner Richard E. Enright, either at the Police field days or at the Police camp, a prize fight or a baseball game, greatly admiring the beautiful Police camp purchased by Commissioner Enright and his cabinet of New York's millionaire deputies, with a salary of a dollar a year and doing great work and mighty important service during the late great World War.

And in conclusion, Sir Thomas delights to sit in the company of "Joan" Mrs. Richard E. Enright, and her many companions at all times.

This was a mighty fine interview and I happened to be present when our good old friend Joe Mitchell Chapelle, interviewed Sir Thomas at his hotel.

And one of the grandest evenings in the life of Sir Thomas, among his vast number of friends, among whom were such notables as Police Commissioner Enright and wife, Col. Walter Scott, Barron Collier, and Count George MacDonald.

One of the greatest happenings in the life of Sir Thomas, was the one big event of 1923, that was the presentation of the Freedom of Glasgow, his natal city, to the grand old Duke, the 2nd day of October, 1923, by the Mayor and other officials of Glasgow, Scotland.

It was a proud day for Sir Thomas, to think back a few years, when as a poor kid he romped and played around her streets, very often hungry, and today after making good in other lands, this poor Irish kid, returns home a multi-millionaire, and God knows, Scotland wanted money badly, and they got it aplenty, and they were proud of their natal son, and he, Sir Thomas, was also proud of his natal mother, so they broke even.

Of course, you all know the early life of Tom Lipton, if not, you will read it in another chapter of this book, so it is no use of repeating, and we will go along with the story.

I was more than surprised to receive a telegram making the announcement of Sir Thomas, receiving this honor right from the City Hall of Glasgow, where the services were taking place, and I too, was a happy man that day, and myself and a few friends certainly celebrated that great event right here in little old New York, yes we danced the Highland fling, and toasted bonny Prince Charlie, and our good old friend Sir Thomas, winding up in the wee small hours singing: "Good Save Ireland" and "The Wearing of the Green." Oh, Boy.

But it took our great Police Commissioner Richard E. Enright, to show the love of every New Yorker, for Dick Enright had ordered his the first line of defense of New York, the Army and Navy of the New York Police Department, the Police Band and all the Deputies and Special Deputy Police Commissioners were there in a body to welcome to his American home that grand old warrior, and when the band played, "When Tommy comes marching home again, hurrah," traveling at a high rate of speed and every man jack of us aboard the *S. S. Macon,* with a big bumper to drink the health of Sir Thomas, who that day was honored by Dick Enright, when he appointed Sir Thomas a Special Deputy Chief of Police of New York.

My, how proud was Sir Thomas that day, for while he had won for himself the honor and glory of every land, he prized his honor more than all.

It was a pleasure to know that these two famous sporting men, Sir Thomas J. Lipton, Bart, and Sir James Bell were chosen for this high honor, both of them poor boys who had faced the world and made good, one of whom we have the honor of knowing personally, that is Sir Thomas Lipton, for the kiddies of every land have heard the story of Tom Lipton's career, but of Sir James Bell, we have only read.

The great body of representative officials, both of royalty and the aristocracy of Europe that assembled that day in grand old St. Andrew's big auditorium will long be remembered, particularly by those that had the good fortune of having been invited to this great ceremony.

Sir Thomas Lipton was as happy that day as the young groom that was leading his pretty bride to the alter of God, there to be united in wedlock, and so well he might be, for this was a day of all days, a day never before celebrated in all Europe.

Many interests, particularly that of industrial and commercial, were represented in that vast audience, for they were all interested, and were quick to recognize the day that they were there to celebrate.

Before the hour of opening, those present were entertained with a long programme of music, rendered by that great artist, Mr. Herbert Walton of the great Glasgow Cathedral, and his assistants.

When the Judges and Magistrates assembled in their robes and chains of office, all eyes were turned towards the entrance for the coming of the Lord Provost (Sir Thomas Paxton, Bart) and his staff, and the rostrum on either side was lined with men of note, both of the army and navy, that went to make a beautiful picture to be hung in the gallery of the gallant Scots for all time. The grand gathering was entertained in an opening prayer and the two men so highly honored that they were escorted to the dias by the Lord Mayor and his aides, and were received with thunderous applause that could be heard in far off Bonnie Dundee.

The programme was a long and very interesting ceremony and after Sir Thomas Lipton, and Sir James Bell, were invested with the oath of office and jewels, they were each called upon to address the vast assemblage, and just as we, the friends of Sir Thomas well know, that Sir Thomas was born to work, yes to do great things, by dint of hard work, and not an orator, of or for the pulpit, but nevertheless he did himself proud on that grand occasion for his every word was received with great applause.

It was explained by the Town Clerk in wig and gown, who read off the abstracts from the minutes of the Corporation of Glasgow, Sir John Lindsey, —that the reason of the presentation to Sir James Bell, also a native of the city of Glasgow, was because of his life's work in the services of the city, he having held every position of note even to that of Lord Lieutenant, and also for his spirited effort to win the America's Cup; and as an expression of the great esteem in which he is deservedly held by the good citizens of all Glasgow.

My readers may remember that this good man, Sir James Bell, sent his challenge for the America's Cup through the Royal Clyde Yacht Club, to the New York Yacht Club, in 1886, and he built and sailed the *Thistle,* against *Volunteer* and after making a spirited fight was defeated by General Paine of Boston, Mass., and his *Volunteer.* Both Sir James Bell, and Lord Dunraven who also challenged for the America's Cup, are now in their happy home for which they departed this life—one in 1926 and the other in 1928, peace be to them all.

Sir Thomas is still fighting, and his fondest dreams, the nearest of which in your heart is the America's Cup, may be realized.

Sir Thomas Lipton was then escorted to the dais and presented with his honors a part of which was the Freedom of the City of Glasgow.

(Sir John Lindsey) the Town Clerk, explained from the records of the Corporation of Glasgow, that the freedom of the city were bestowed on Sir Thomas Lipton, in acknowledgment of the exemplary and patriotic services which he had rendered to the country, particularly through the great World's War, also to the Corporation and the whole community by his repeated and generous gifts for the benefit of the poor.

And for his kindness in aiding his fellow citizens in the saddest hour of need, when unemployed; Sir Thomas for months drove the wolf from their doors, a kindness that shall never be forgotten, and in recognition of his many services to mankind the world over, and in further recognition of the credit and renown which came from both far and near, he has brought to his native city by his devotion and success and his own very pleasing personality and honesty, bringing with them all much trade and commerce.

Also for the great part played by him to make permanent the friendships and respects of every other land with that of his own in particular, that of the British-American friendship, and to his determination as a sportsman to regain for his country the America's Cup, and also as an expression of the high respect and admiration in which Sir Thomas Lipton, is held universally, for his all 'round good fellowship, and liberality to the needy.

"Oor Ain Folk"

The subscription of the Burgess Roll followed, after which the Lord Provost, addressed the two recipients.

He referred to the two gentlemen as of "Oor ain folk"—worthy citizens of Glasgow who had both shed lustre upon our commercial traditions and who were types of men who had done much to build up Glasgow's reputation all over the world. By adding the names of these two gentlemen to the honorary Burgess Roll we are only augmenting and increasing its importance as a notable document in the history of our great city. (Much applause shaking the very foundations of old St. Andrews).

It was fitting that side by side with eminent politicians, philosophers, scientists, explorers, soldiers, and sailors and men of letters, we should have the good names of our princes of industry.

Career of Supreme Usefulness.

The Lord Provost touched upon the various good deeds of both gentlemen and how hard they strived to make dear old Glasgow, what she is today, a great city and on a footing with any city in the world.

He said that the good work of both men, their honesty of purpose and all 'round good fellowship made many friends for their natal city, and long after they have past and gone, the good names of Sir Thomas Lipton and Sir James Bell, will be referred to by the boys and girls of Bonnie Scotland.

Both, Sir Thomas and Sir James were called upon to address the great assemblage and each made a very suitable reply, with continued applause and welcome remarks, their addresses were received by all present with a vote of thanks. Then the grand march to the Guild Hall where a great dinner was prepared of which all enjoyed to their hearts content followed by speeches, musical selections and songs of Bonnie Scotland, and after many hours of celebration it was voted one of the greatest days in the history of that beautiful land of the *Thistle,* that the men and women loved so well, reminded of the childhood days rambling through its lochs and dells, winding up this great celebration, with that glorious Scotch Bonnie Prince Charley.

"Unhook the west port and let us go free, to fight under the banner of Bonnie Dundee."

Just as I was about to close writing this beautiful story on the lives of these two great men, sons of Bonnie Scotland, they that helped to do so much for their poor kinsmen and women, I received a dispatch from Belfast, Ireland, dated June the 19th, 1930.

Stating that Sir Thomas Lipton was ill, and confined to bed, and forbidden to leave the house to witness his pretty yacht *Shamrock V,* defeat her competitors then racing on Bangor Bay.

That was to be expected, Sir Thomas who has just passed his eightieth birthday, has been working hard both night and day, to help tune up *Shamrock V* so that besides her beating everything on the coast of the British Isles, will be in good shape to tackle America's best, on September 13th next, and believe me that it will take a whole lot of sickness to keep Sir Thomas from being an eye witness in watching *Shamrock V* clean up all before her off Newport, Rhode Island, and we will trust in Providence, even if we do fetch up in beautiful Boston, the land of beef and beans, good Mayors, the choice of Ireland's sons and daughters, I speak of the Hon. John F. Fitzgerald and the followers, a man that has done so much for that grand old city of tea tax haters and alleged desperate foulers of both man and yacht for we can never forget *Puritan-V-Genesta* in 1885.

MY MEETING WITH HIS EMINENCE, P. CARDINAL O'DONNELL, PRIMATE OF ALL IRELAND, WHILE ATTENDING THE EUCHARISTIC CONGRESS IN CHICAGO, ILL., JUNE, 1926, AND AGAIN ON HIS RETURN TO NEW YORK, AND WHAT FOLLOWED

PART II—CHAPTER V

While taking part in the Eucharistic Congress in Chicago, June, 1926, among others I had the honor and the pleasure of meeting, that grand old gentleman, Cardinal O'Donnell of fond and loving memory, may the Heavens be his bed today, and for all time.

We met again later on at the Lexington Hotel, Park Avenue, New York, and I promised to mail to him a copy of my book "OUR POLICE GUARDIANS." This I did all right, and here is the dear old Cardinal's signature to, wit:—

"CARDINAL'S RESIDENCE,
"COUNTY OF ARMAGH, IRELAND.
"November 15th, 1926.

"Many thanks for your Police book. I am,
"P. CARDINAL O'DONNELL."

This good man was taken ill and died shortly after, forwarding this receipt, may the good Lord have mercy on his soul.—AUTHOR.

Before leaving New York, the Cardinal said that I should visit him and become his guest at his residence on my next visit to Ireland, with the American Legion, 1927-1928—but my having stayed so long in France, I had no time left to make this mission at that time, but expected to fill the engagement at the Grand Eucharistic Congress held in Dublin, Ireland, in 1932, but death had overtaken him before this great festival arrived.

My several questions calling for an answer, you will notice was not answered, particularly those asking what had become of the two Liberty Bonds of America, one of the 3rd issue and the other a Victory Bond, handed to Sir Thomas one evening in the Hotel Commodore in 1919.

I made these presents to Sir Thomas, thinking that I would receive two British Bonds in return, and I am sure such would be the case if Sir Thomas himself had handled them.

God knows that a man living on an income of $58.33 monthly pension, can't be expected to give his millionaire friends a $150, good American dollars, unless others are returned to take their place, a hands across the sea policy, to show patriotism towards America and her principal allies, our brothers of the British Isles.

112

Think now that Sir Thomas is dead, these bonds should revert back to the sender, and not given to those that forget their work and all that they are paid for. That is all.

Waiting for the John Westwood answer reminds me of the fellow that went to the post office to buy a stamp, and he waited and waited while the girl in charge was dolling up, powdering her nose, and chewing gum, and when she was ready, she strolled out and says, "Well what do you want?"

Answer, when I came in, it was to buy a new George Washington stamp, but I have since thought that I had better make application for an old age pension.

"July 27th, 1929.

"Dear Mr. Hickey:

"Your letter of the 18th inst., with enclosures just to hand, and very much appreciated. My only wish is that we hadn't the time to read them as they should be read and carefully understood.

"With regard to Sir Thomas's next visit to the little old U.S.A., nothing has yet been settled, and it will probably not be before September, so that this will give you time to take and enjoy your vacation at the Police Camp, your summer home up in the Catskills.

"With kindest regards and best wishes,

"Yours faithfully,

"JOHN WESTWOOD."

(A true copy)
R. CONSOLATO GENERALE D'ITALIA,
No. 5323 February 25th, 1927.
Pos. Gab.
Hickey, J. J.

"Mr. John J. Hickey,
"Hotel Elton,
"365—Fourth Ave.,
"New York City.

"Dear Sir:

"I have been requested by His Excellency, Premier Mussolini, to forward to you herewith, inclosed check for $2.00 covering the fee for the book "OUR POLICE GUARDIANS" which you sent him and which he greatly appreciated.

"Very truly yours,

"ROYAL CONSUL GENERALE OF ITALY."

"I forthwith answered the very fine letter, stating to the Premier, thanking him very much for his kindness in acknowledging my work, I thank you very much for both the letter and check, but the check was of minor importance.

"Trusting to have the honor of paying my respects to your Excellency after the Convention of the American Legion, of which I am a member, in Paris, God willing I will entrain for Rome, there to pay homage to Our Holy Father, Pope Pius XI, on October 6th, and present my card at your office, October 7th, both of 1927.

"Again thanking your Excellency, and trusting that this letter will find you in the best of good health and all supreme, I beg to remain, as ever,

"Yours faithfully,

"JOHN J. HICKEY,

"Author, Hotel Elton,
"New York City."

I followed this programme out to the letter, but owing to the matter that some day sooner or later will come to light, I could not meet Mr. Mussolini having been chiseled out of my stopovers in Rome, by a selfish clerk in the office of the "Italian State Railways, 2-Semptere Street, Paris." Simply because I did not pay him 600 Francs, for what I received for 350 Francs.

I purchased my tickets from the Lloyd Trestino Steamship Company office near the "Opera" in Paris, September and October, 1927, no doubt you may get this information from them, relating to this dirty piece of chiselling, for even though one do purchase his tickets from a steamship, they must also go through the hands of these clerks employed in the Italian States Railway Company, and they may do as they please, with all stopovers that should not be. It seemed that the clerk in Lloyd Trestino's was afraid of this red headed rat, so he sent me to him and I saw him.

Here is a copy of the letter received from Jack Dempsey, while stopping at the Hotel Belmont in New York City in July, 1927, to wit :—

"Mr. John J. Hickey,   "Hotel Belmont, City,
"Hotel Elton,   "July 28th, 1927.
"365—Fourth Ave.,
"New York City.
"Dear Mr. Hickey:
   "This is to acknowledge receipt of your letter containing your good wishes, for which please accept my heartiest thanks.
   "It certainly has been a great source of pleasure to me to know that I have so many well wishers all over the country, among them your very dear old friend and greatest sportsman, Sir Thomas Lipton.
   "We spent a few very enjoyable evenings in Hollywood, on several occasions for the folks there think very much of Sir Thomas, for they swear by Sir Thomas and his great sportsmanship, we are to meet again next year out on the coast. Trusting that this will find you well,
                         "Sincerely yours,
                                        "JACK DEMPSEY."

I answered this on August 6th, 1927, just before I was to leave for the American Legion Congress in Paris, September 21st, 1927, I leaving with the pathfinding division on the *President Harding,* October 9th, 1927.

In this letter I informed Jack Dempsey of my plans, and the request of Sir Thomas, that I bring Jack Dempsey to Osidge, when I arrived in the grand old city of London in the spring of 1928.

Stating that I hoped to meet him in London, and for both of us to make a call on Sir Thomas at his beautiful home at Osidge, as per request of the great sportsman himself.

We were to meet at the Hotel Savoy but I, taken sick, was forced to do the best I could to get back to home in dear old New York, supposedly to die, sailing from Southampton, July 2nd, 1928, on the *S.S. George Washington,* landing in New York July 10th more dead than alive.

Jack Dempsey's defeat by Referee Barry's long count in Chicago upset our friend Jack, so that he was not able to go to London, and Sir Thomas was very much disappointed, but through no fault of mine, but by the actions of his own secretary, John Westwood.

But I was in hopes to have Jack Dempsey and myself call on Sir Thomas when next he came to the U. S. A., but things went topsy-turvy with us all and the visit was never made good. I am sad to relate for this would have cheered him very much to see Jack Dempsey and Jack Hickey again.

Sir Thomas was of a human heart for, while he delighted to see two of our heavyweight champions, well trained, in the ring, he was never satisfied when called upon to sit and watch the smaller champions fight, and he often sent John Westwood into the dressing room to stake the loser of a bout, and leave for his hotel forthwith, disgusted. What a shame that such a noble character met with such a sad end, among the people that he loved so well.

But let me let you in on an inside story. It was not so much to see our old champions, Jack Dempsey and Tom Mix, it was to mix up with the pretty girls that he visited Hollywood, as often as possible, and often in our quiet chats, Sir Thomas would speak of Colleen Moore, Norma Shearer, and the then Mrs. Jack Dempsey, nee Loretta Taylor, but he certainly was stuck on his first love, and often spoke of Colleen Moore, and the kindness of all.

One night when we were both in good spirits and alone, I ventured to say: "Sir Thomas, it is too bad that you did not take one of those pretty girls as your secretary or adopted daughter, and not be up against grunts. They would fill you up with cheer." His answer was: "Mr. Hickey, I wish I had."

THE END OF THE ROAD

Having visited France as a member of the American Legion in September, 1927, and after spending several months in and around Paris, the convention over, and adjourned for this session, I broke away and visited every country of Europe and the Continent.

Going as far as the Near and Far East, into Africa and India, on both business and pleasure bent, and having been advised to spend my winter on the Riviera in Nice, France, and the winter closing in, I hurried there, to hang out with a lot of broken-down millionaires, and Counts of no account, with the weather cold and down to zero most of the time. Yes, on New Year's Day of 1928, a party of Americans and your humble servant were photographed with the American flag very much to the fore. This, too, on the grand promenade of the Riviera, but oh, how my heart longed for home. I hold this photo.

And having to make a call on my friends in gay Paree, and be in London by February 15th when my passport expired, I made my happy getaway from the famous rich man's paradise for I was very well satisfied to get back to home and loved ones, but I could not do that until I had spent some time as a guest of Sir Thomas Lipton, the world's famous international yachtsman, at his beautiful home, "Osidge," in the suburbs of London, England.

I had spent, all told, three months at the Riviera, and every day when visiting the beautiful Notre Dame Cathedral, I would sure meet a funeral of some poor unfortunate that had gone there to help regain his health, so that I was all the time thinking to myself, was I going to be the next victim.

And, of course, I felt mighty blue, for it was impossible to leave Nice for the weather reports daily were zero in Rome, Paris, and in fact, every one of the cities that I wanted to revisit before crossing the dangerous old English Channel, for I knew that I would never want to visit these places again. Once is enough for this old New York copper, believe me.

But, on one of my last visits to Notre Dame, I saw the streets lined with people on Avenue Victoria, on all sides, and my conclusions were that it was another case of a poor little rich man passing on.

But nothing daunted; I entered the beautiful edifice to pray, and was so much pleased to see a marriage ceremony that I even forgot my prayers and after the ceremony and the kisses and congratulations were bestowed, I was soon to be found in the nearest cafe, and drinking good health and happiness to the bride and groom.

And while, as a New York bobby, I on several occasions just missed the gun of a burglar, and escaped being shot, leaving my children to mourn my loss.

And while I never wanted to be whole-shot, I had no objections to my being half-shot, on many joyous occasions, and this was one of them, for to me it appeared that this happy episode had changed my luck, and I then called for another brandy and soda, and later on when I ran into the few of my American friends left in Nice, we had a few more.

From that day on I became a new man, and drank no more until I had met my good friends, Mark Severe, Vice-Consul at the American Embassy in Paris, and Sparrow Robinson of New York, then holding the position of sporting editor of the Paris "Herald-Tribune," meeting several times to have lunch together, and a little old bottle of rich wine with every meal. Oh, boy, when I thought of looking to get back to my own country, as dry as a traveler passing over the burning plains of Egypt, I kind of got afraid.

And when King George, who was at the time dangerously ill, was advised to go to the Riviera to pick up, I wrote Buckingham Palace my experience.

My extended passport was to expire in London, February 18th, 1928, and after spending four long dreary months on the so-called "Riviera," I longed for home, but was not unmindful of the promise I made Sir Thomas, that I, in spite of my feelings should spend a week with him at "Osidge," I had to be on my way, and travel six hundred miles to "Gay Paree" to bid my dear good friends good bye, Sir Thomas soon to see. Having to give myself time to look the ground over on my way, not ever thinking of going there again.

"Cannes" being my first stop, and thinking back to the dear old days spent in Cannes by the late King Edward VII, and our dear old friend Tom Lipton, and having looked the pretty little seaport over pretty well, I hurried home to sleep as I thought in clover, but alas that was not to be, I could not sleep, thinking of the past and all I saw that day, the beautiful statue of H.R.H. Prince Albert in yachting uniform, and our dear old friend Sir Thomas. The young Prince of Wales, the future King Edward VII, looked mighty fine.

Prince of Wales, later King Edward VII, I knew that H.R.H. and Sir Thomas often skipped off and spent a few days there, and out of respect I hated to leave Cannes, but it had to be, so I got on my way, to beautiful "Marseilles," and for the first time in a year I imagined I was back in New York, so much shipping, and with the grand churches both old and new and with other holy places built away on top of the mountains, with a moat built around, so that in case of trouble they would be prepared. My, but I loved that holy country very much for its grand old buildings, but my principal object there was to locate and visit the graves of Bishop Lazarus and that of Bishop Pon's of "Cimez" of whom I heard so much about making a pretty little story.

Visiting "Cimez" was one of my regular hobbies while lingering in Nice the mercury was down to zero, that was Rome, Paris, London and Berlin, in every city and country around me, I had to stay in spite of myself. My next stop was "Avignon," the former home of the Popes, now of Rome, a very pretty mountainous country, but I was tired of getting on and off trains and climbing high mountains, and I stayed on the train until I reached the city of Frog eaters, Paris, visited my friends; Mark Severe, American Vice Consul, and old boy Sparrow Robinson of New York, Sporting Editor of the Paris *Herald-Tribune,* and after several luncheons, I said goodbye but I had to visit beautiful Notre Dame, and my old hangouts of the Latin quarter where I lived for four months. But my stomach was in a mood to rebel, for what to eat I could not tell, and then boy, how you long for dear old New York and her ham and eggs, wheat, and buckwheat cakes in the morning, but of course, they went without wine, while in Paris what you order is an order for wine and I tell you boys it was fine.

To keep our records straight, it may be as well to know that when the writer of this work arrived in London, February, 1928, and after our big Convention, September 20th, 1927—broke away from his friends and comrades to visit every land, and having visited and obtained all the information of any particular use and arriving in London, putting up at an hotel not far from the Victoria station, for I was so tired after crossing the English channel.

I was very much surprised to receive the following telegram from Sir Thomas through his secretary, that read as follows—to wit:—

Dear Mr. Hickey, we were looking for you, please call up Palmers Green this P.M., Sir Thomas wants you to join him at Osidge.

I certainly was surprised, and when I did report to Sir Thomas on his beautiful estate at Osidge, he gave me one wonderful time, one that I shall never forget, one that might better suit a man of his class and station, but from the heart of this good man, he chose no class or society, all Sir Thomas wanted is an old friend, rich or poor, it makes no difference to him, he will make you happy, and you in turn will delight in his company for he will keep you ever on the move, he is going all the time.

We have heard and seen the Dan O'Leary's, and old man Weston, but none of them has a darned thing on Sir Thomas Lipton, for he can walk as fast as he can talk, and believe me Sir Thomas is a great talker, that is when he is among his friends, for he never was carried away with functions.

Often Sir Thomas has told the writer, that he loves his friends, both new and old, but he tires of dinners and functions, "I would rather that I was sitting down in my room with an old friend like yourself, Mr. Hickey, or Mr. and Mrs. Morgan J. O'Brien, and such fine people, that one would delight to spend the evening with, either at home or abroad.

"But, alas it is to be, I must meet my society friends, among them many members of the Royal families of Europe, who are constantly inviting me to visit them, and I love to grant their constant requests, but Heavenly Father, I did not know that I was going to live so long, and I am simply played out, I need rest, and concentration, for I have a long walk to Heaven, when Gabriel blows his horn."

MY FIRST VISIT TO OSIDGE, SIR THOMAS THEN O.K.

Part III—Chapter I

I spent a very happy day riding over the moors, and the highways and byways of old Highgate, with Sir Thomas, after his having supplied the wants of the poor kiddies for miles around, coming from both far and near to attend Sunday school, and then meet Sir Thomas, receive their presents and play ball along the roadway homeward bound, a bunch of happy youngsters.

After lunch, Sir Thomas would order Shamrock to prepare the billiard tables, so that he could give Mr. Hickey and Dr. Goodheart a few lessons in his famous old system of how to hit and pocket the ball, that he himself was a past master of, for he was very much carried away with billiards.

At 11 P.M., he would ask if Mr. Hickey was going to stay all night, if not, my car is ready to take you to your hotel, and I looking forward to one good long rest and sleep next day, would say good night, Sir Thomas, Cheerio and over the highways away we go, and when the lights of London town came into view, I would dismiss my driver, partake of a glass or two of mild and bitter together, and send the lad home happy, for it was a long old drive to my lodgings, and he had been going all day.

But as a matter of fact, the moment that I arrived at Hyde Park Corner I had to dismount, and walk around the memorable spots of Tyburn tree, and think back to the 15th century, and the many judicial murders that were being committed day after day, and for the poor souls, I would kneel and pray.

Feeling that I had done my duty to both the dead and the living, down through the beautiful "Green" park, I would go with the Kings' palace dead to the outside world, arriving at Westminster Bridge, just as Big Ben is striking twelve, for I cannot forget my old Police life, I love to do the last tour, from Midnight to 6 A.M. on patrol, and so it will ever be, I suppose, for I loved to patrol dear old Park Row, meeting my many newspaper friends after their strenuous hours of labor were at an end, and the news of the day was being circulated the world over. I often found myself patrolling old Fleet Street and taking a wee drop in the old "Chesire Cheese" after hours, the house of call for the newspaper men of London, and meeting some old timer and exchanging reminiscences of both London and New York, day by day.

Returning to the old homestead tired but happy, for it is a pleasure to one that has worked so hard through life, to say he can go to bed when he likes and get up when he likes, and free from petticoat government, and I would have to tell Sir Thomas something about all of his American friends, for this made him happy. I certainly was happy to be able to supply the old fellows wants in this urgent case, for like all of us old folks, we want to know all the latest news and among others on my travels, I told him the following story.

I recall that Mayor Walker was on his way to visit Germany at this time, what he was visiting there for I know not, nor was it my business, but I did not think it proper for his ship, the *S.S. Berengaria,* to pass our good American steamer, the *President Harding,* and not give us a salute, and we but a short distance away.

We were the forerunners of the American Legion, going to Paris, France to prepare the way for the Legion Convention, and the Veterans on our steamer was not at all pleased, that was August 13th, 1927, we had left New York, August 9th, 1927, and the *Berengaria* several days later.

I also remember my visiting the Mayor at his Hotel in France, later I, like all others, three thousand miles away from home delights to meet old friends from home, but even though I had been introduced to Mayor Walker on several occasions, prior to this, he gave me a cool reception, why, I know not, and Senator Barney Downing, a boyhood friend, I could not see at all.

And if I am rightly informed, the Vets got back at the Mayor, for I was told that he requested 20 tickets for the reviewing stand in Paris, and all they would allow him was three invitations, so they got hunk on his failing to salute our ship that passed in the night, but it happened to be a very fine afternoon when they passed us, and without a salute, Why?

But all things do not run true to form, and often makes one wish that he was never born, we all have our troubles, and God knows, Sir Thomas had his woes and troubles, not so bad if they come to one in youth, but when we are attacked in old age, as was this grand old sport, betrayed by the very men that he was paying a large salary, that was too much to stand for, so he at once broke down, and we all know what followed, more is the pity.

This grand old sportsman worried himself to death, in his dear old heart, knowing full well that he was being betrayed by some person or persons in his own employ, and nothing on earth can make me believe different after the many private conversations and whisperings to me, when alone, for then he talked freely, to the contrary notwithstanding. Westwood, knew all this.

I was not long in Osidge when I knew all was not well, for Sir Thomas was a changed man, while he did not show it openly, for Tom Lipton, was that kind of a man, that would not give vent to his feelings, but this laid very heavy on his mind, to only whisper something to his friend Hickey, was a happy relief.

Sir Thomas confided much in me, and so too did his assistant secretary, Mr. Waghorn, and from them I learned an awful lot, enough to drive the old man into a lunatic asylum, my presence there was poison in the Westwood eye and soon you will read how cowardly he behaved later, after begging me to visit him, against my wishes for somehow, I suspected his dirty work.

In one of those hurried whispers of conversation Sir Thomas said, "Mr. Hickey, I don't know what happened to my boat, but something was wrong with her and of that I am sure," this was after dinner and we were playing billiards, and alone, the only chance that he ever had to talk freely.

Shamrock, his servant would step into the big hall to set the balls, and no doubt if I had asked Shamrock, why Mr. Westwood was so nervous that day while Sir Thomas and his party were at lunch, he Westwood, waiting to give old man Hickey a buggy ride, my God when I think of it, I, that as a New York Policeman would face the murderer, without a fear, and then to stand for such nonsense from a dirty contemptible rascal like Westwood.

That is what grieves me more than anything else, for I didn't have a chance to ask anybody questions, all that I could do was to walk, walk, walk around the beautiful London parks to keep the life in my body, and when I had been examined by a doctor in the Charing Cross Hospital and found out that I could safely make the trip home, I lost no time in journeying on to Southampton, there to leave on the steamer *George Washington,* New York bound.

I remember having called on Sir Thomas, several nights before he was to be presented with the Loving Cup by Mayor Walker, it turned out to be one of those evenings that Lord Westwood did not want me to meet my dear old friend, and I was forced to park in the reception room No. 618, the rest of this story you will read further on in these pages. Sir Thomas came out and told me that they said he must make a speech, and I said, no, it's too much for you. The point that touches me more than any other, is the fact of his dying alone, one of his secretaries at his home in Finsbury, and the other God knows where, when they should have been with him and hear his last words, if the old gent was able to speak at all, what excuse have they to offer if any, is what I want to find out, so that we will be better able to place the blame upon the one on whom it should be blamed upon, and to my mind, that would be his secretary, John Westwood, and none other. But this is how I feel about that, to my mind, Sir Thomas was not suffering from chills, but from the worry and thoughts of soon meeting his many good old American friends, and this in the face of one of the worst beatings he ever before received, after all the ballyhoo about *Shamrock V,* that's why.

But it was no use, his life was fast ebbing away and he alone, My God, who would expect such treatment, from those that you have supported for so many years, so that the grand old man asked God to take him and he did.

I have trashed this whole matter out in my brains, morning, noon and night and the only conclusion arrived at is that he was shamefully abused and ill-treated by his own servants, and in this I am backed up by many.

A day of reckoning will come and then we will know all, God willing that the writer of this biography is given an extension of life, as it were.

"OSIDGE, SOUTHGATE, LONDON.
"23rd of March, 1928.

"Mr. J. J. Hickey, Dennis House,
"Denbigh Street, Westminster, S.W.I.
"Dear Mr. Hickey:
"I am very glad to get your letter just to hand, as I have been wondering for a long time where you were and how you were getting along, as I should like very much to see you again, and the Chief would also like to hear your story of travels in Europe, the Near and Far East and other of the many lands visited by you in 1927-1928.
"I will get in touch with you next week so we can mutually agree on the date that you will come out to Osidge, but in any case don't leave London until we meet. I am glad to say the Chief is well and in fine condition; trusting that he will so remain. Hoping this will find you well,
"Yours respectfully,
"JOHN WESTWOOD."

I could not imagine what was on John Westwood's mind, for I had seen Sir Thomas before, so I did not go out to see John Westwood until June, and it came near being my last, Waurra, Waurra.

"OSIDGE, SOUTHGATE, MIDDLESEX, LONDON.
"29th of March, 1928.

"Mr. J. J. Hickey,
"45 Denbigh Street, Westminster, London, S.W.I.
"Dear Mr. Hickey:
"Your letter of the 28th inst. is to hand and I do not think that you can do any better than to follow the policy that you yourself suggests in relation to His Majesty's Secretary. It is not a matter in which special influence could be utilized. I presume that you have heard of the sad news of Sir Charles Russell, England's famous Barrister at law, and a very close friend of the Chief for many years.
"Our good friend, Mr. Russell, will be buried from St. Patrick's Cathedral, Ashley Place, and Sir Thomas and I hope to meet you there, and we will, no doubt, have time for a good chat after the funeral. With all best wishes,
"Yours faithfully,
"JOHN WESTWOOD."

The first paragraph of this letter relates to my having sent by mail to his Majesty King George V, a copy of my work, "Our Police Guardians" which speaks of the King and his noble son, the Prince of Wales, visiting the battlefields of Flanders during the world's war, and how close they both came to being shot by the guns of the enemy, and other matter.

I waited for several weeks, and I dropped in to have a chat with Lord Stampfordham, the King's private secretary, a very fine old gentleman, who was taken ill, and after several weeks he passed on. In 1930, Lord Stampfordham told me that King George was very much pleased with the book, but that he has made it a practice to except no presents from any but his own subjects, but if you can get a letter from the American Consul, the King no doubt would receive your book.

But what could I do, a poor sick man, in a strange land, unknown and of course, uncared for, thanks to the dirty work of John Westwood, at the time, that is fate, I lost a wonderful opportunity, but through no fault of my own, for if King George had to have taken the book, I could have run an English edition of my work, and may have sold many books, but that's the luck of the Irish, happy and doing great things today, and unhappy tomorrow and why?

Sir Charles Russell, like his grand old father, was known as one of England's greatest Barristers at law, I knew them both, both friends of Ireland, and we the Irish of England, honored and respected all friends of the old sod, may the good Lord have mercy on the dead. I knew them as a boy in London.

At Sir Thomas' request, I happened to be visiting Osidge in 1928, when the ingrates that he took under his wing had made them a part of the Lipton Limited, got together to overthrow him and demand his resignation as President of that world's renowned tea corporation. Yes, Sir Thomas felt that keenly, but did not let that bring on a broken heart, not at all man, he had received worse hard blows than that, and he soon pulled himself together and forgot the dirty work of these ingrates, for the world knows that Sir Thomas was not worthy of such a mean trick, being served on him, and so sudden.

But as a matter of fact, the pioneer in all such cases gets the worst of the deal, and Tom Lipton, was no exception, but he bore it manfully as in all his other defeats, for he was a good soldier, and friend.

What bothered Sir Thomas most was the fact that he was forced to close the six hundred stores that he had opened in London and her suburbs, not because he was compelled to, but because he would not give his enemies the pleasure of enjoying the large incomes accumulated from these stores.

Prior to this unfortunate turn in affairs, it was a pleasure when roaming around old London town, to drop in, to have a wee cup of Tom Lipton's Ceylon tea, with pastry and meats of every description, sandwiches galore was ever at your hand, to help break up the monotony, and to jack up your Sullivan rubber heels for another long stroll, out Clapham Common way.

The heart of Sir Thomas became deeply dejected when he had to give the order to close up all of these shops, thereby throwing out of employment the many thousands of young men and young women, that he had engaged in both Ireland and Scotland, years before, but what could he do otherwise, the darn thing was forced upon him, and he had to act, and true to form Sir Thomas Lipton, acted, and soon the Lipton Limited began to slide down hill.

But under the able direction of the successor chosen to take the work of Sir Thomas, over on himself and his very able assistants, namely, Commodore Taylor, Duncan F. Neill, Mr. Shannon and Mr. O'Neill. Lord Inverforth, will succeed, in making the Lipton Trust, a lasting memorial to that grand old sportsman, philanthropist and friend, that will live for ages, yes, long after his enemies have gone to the devil knows where, the good name of Lipton will live on. At least so it appears in March and April of 1934.

I shall never forget that sad memorable day that Sir Thomas was called upon to attend a meeting of the Lipton Limited, that this grand old businessman himself established, and had thrown open to many of Englands aristocracy, always looking to unseat the London grocer. Our dear Chief suffered very much, thinking of the sin of ingratitude, by the rats.

Sir Thomas had requested that I should visit Osidge and have a chat, and when with tears in his eyes he told me the sad story, my heart bled for my dear old friend, for he had worked hard to build up this corporation.

But like many other such profitable establishments, a clique got together to oust their maker and like many others they bit the hand that fed them, and now that Sir Thomas has gone, so too will the Lipton Limited and the gang that thought they knew it all, in ousting Tom Lipton the man.

Sir Thomas felt this blow keenly, for while he was giving up his connections with this organization, he still maintained his Sir Thomas Lipton Incorporation of America and Canada, and while Tom Lipton lived, so too would this once great institution, but the passing of Sir Thomas, will prove to be a death blow, and the invisible committee of the past will be thrown out of a job, with no sympathy from the real good friends of Sir Thomas.

But it was not of the Lipton Limited that Sir Thomas was thinking, it was of the many poor girls and boys that he brought over from Ireland and Scotland to run the more than 600 tea and lunch rooms and provision stores that he himself had personally fitted up, and did not intend leaving them doing business to enrich his defamers of the Lipton Limited.

This grand old Chieftain, with tears in his eyes called his employees together and having told his intentions and why he was closing up these stores he gave each a big bonus and a trip back to their homes, what more could any man do under the circumstances, let me ask?

That to my mind was the beginning of the end, to think that he was to give up his long connection with the firm that he himself established, and to close up his stores and put the poor employees out of work, bothered him as much as did the blowing up of the *Erin* or any other of his troubles, and he had many in his last days on earth.

But that did not bring about the breaking of Sir Thomas Lipton's heart, not at all, for his intentions were, some day to become a resident of our own beautiful country, the land that he loved more than any other, and the people that gave him a heartier welcome and a squarer deal than any other.

I shall never forget his sorrowful words and expressions at dinner that evening, for he said, "Mr. Hickey, did you ever know it to fail, these men who in many cases grew wealthy under my directorship, wanted the whole hog or none, and now when I have grown to be an old man, they push me out.

"Heavenly Father, I only have a few more years to live, and they could just as well awaited to my last, no, no, they thought that I was too popular and spending their money on yachts and pleasure, but as true as God is my judge, never a dollar of theirs was spent by me, but all out of my own bank account."

But before leaving that evening, after dinner, Dr. Goodheart and myself played billiards, and drank our tea, and we had Sir Thomas cheered up so that he remarked in a happy cheerful manner, "To the devil with them, I will make my future home among my American friends, and be happy forever after."

It will be mighty hard for me to forget the sad remarks at dinner that evening in Osidge what with the sorrowful countenance and remarks he bore, and made, that will forever linger in this dear old Irish heart that I am proud to possess.

"An insult to Pat, like a sharp sting is felt, a smile the next moment would
   make your heart melt.
He would give his last loaf to the good natured elf;
For that is the style in old Ireland."

Sir Thomas was forced to tears, and he was not alone either, when he said, "Mr. Hickey, did you ever knew it to fail, these men who in many cases grew wealthy under my directorship, came to the conclusion that Sir Thomas was too popular for them, who had supposed was spending their money on his yacht racing, was to walk the plank, they wanted the whole hog or none, and now that I have grown to be a poor old gray headed man, they push me out?

"Heavenly Father, I only have a few years to live, and they could just as well awaited until my end, and then reorganize, and allow me to die happy and contented among my friends, and leave for a long, long cruise on board my beautiful yacht, *Shamrock V* and go sailing on.

"I can conscientiously say that not a penny but my own money was ever spent by me for all of my boats and the races that followed, but the many friendships that I have made, increased the profits of the Lipton Limited and its many industries tenfold.

"But there, it is no use worrying, I love America and the many friends that I have made, and some day we may wind up in that beautiful Police Camp that Mr. Enright built for the Police of New York, for I am sure the boys would give us a hearty welcome.

"Or perhaps build a castle in the beautiful Catskill mountains where you are noted as a mountain climber, and we could spend the rest of our days in peace and happiness, 'don't you think that a good idea Mr. Hickey?' "

"CITY ROAD, LONDON, E. C.,
"13th of March, 1918.

"Mr. John J. Hickey,
"Office of the Police 'Chronicle',
"23 Duane Street, New York City.
"Dear Mr. Hickey:

"I have duly received your many kind letters of the past, particularly that of the 15th ultimo and the vast amount of good news that they always contain, and for which I thank you very much.

"I have been hoping for a long time to get over to New York, but it is utterly impossible under the present circumstances, but living in hopes that some day, I will be sailing over to see you and my many good friends for whom I hold the very highest regards.

"I trust that this will find you fit and well, and with my kindest regards and best wishes to all, I am,

"Yours faithfully,

"THOMAS J. LIPTON."

Oh, how I love to think back to those dark days of war time when one's soul was not his own, and while the enemy was busy trying to blow up London and its people, my letters to Sir Thomas would cheer him up, knowing that he had good friends and a refuge in good old New York, that some day he was hoping to see and spend many nights and days in their company.

I like mankind love to sing the old songs, and read over the old letters of good old friends, particularly this, the last letter that I had the honor of receiving from Sir Thomas, and I will always keep it among my fondest and dearest possessions, to wit:—

This letter was written aboard the *S. S. Leviathan,* and on the stationary of the United States Lines, at sea.

"December, 1928.

"Mr. John J. Hickey,
"Hotel Elton, Fourth Avenue,
"New York City,
"Dear Mr. Hickey:

"Please accept my sincere thanks for the lovely flowers sent me by you to help make my voyage a pleasant one. You always seem to use good judgment when the opportunity comes your way, as in this and many other like occasions, all of which I appreciate very much, the good word or a kindness from an old friend, always so pleasing and refreshing, particularly when in pain, as I am at this moment.

"I have also received your manuscript, namely, the 'Auto-Biography of Sir Thomas J. Lipton,' and I look forward to pleasant memories while perusing its pages, that I am sure are ably written.

"I am making good progress though slow, but I hope to be fairly well by the time we reach London, there to rest up in Osidge, and in thinking back to dear old New York and my many friends, I will always have in mind the good name of that old scout and endearing friend, Hickey.

"I wish that you would come and stay with me in Osidge, it would be to me so pleasing to have an old New York friend stopping with me, come over and on arrival, I will have my car in waiting to bring yourself and luggage out to Osidge, please don't forget that your presence will bring back to me so many fond recollections of your country and my many friends there.

"With my sincere thanks for your kind thought, and the very best of good wishes for your future, I am,

"Sincerely yours,

"THOMAS J. LIPTON."

I had not yet met John Westwood, and by his actions he seemed very much put out about my being alone with Sir Thomas, and it would have been better for me if I never met Mr. Westwood, for I did not know what was before me.

Mr. Westwood called me up to go meet him at Osidge the following Sunday, but this I could not do, for I was to join the Cardinal Bourne parade from Newgate Jail, to Tyburn Tree, walking over the same ground as did the early martyrs of our faith, when ordered to be executed for their love and devotion and adherence to the "Faith of Our Fathers."

Again, later in the week he called me up, and I had to promise him that I would be at Osidge on Wednesday, but it would be after lunch, but that was not satisfactory to him, for reasons best known to himself, he wanted me to be present at lunch with Sir Thomas, Duncan Neill, and Doc Goodheart, and this proved almost to be my last lunch on this earth, and why?

While Sir Thomas and Mr. Neill were busy talking over business matters, Doctor Goodheart and I were eating, drinking and talking, but, when I saw Johnny Westwood so troublesome, appearing at the door beckoning me to hurry, I was not at all pleased, and when Shamrock would appear with more coffee, he would say in an undertone, Mr. Hickey, Mr. Westwood has the car at the door waiting for you, I found that I had to go with him, in spite of myself and when I said, Goodbye to Sir Thomas, he said, "What's your hurry Mr. Hickey, you just arrived and now you want to get away again, I want you to go driving with me later on, so be sure and come back."

When the car had started, I asked Mr. Westwood, why on earth all this hurry, he said, "I want to make the bank on Villiers Street Strand before 3," arriving at the bank, we got out and bade each other goodbye, and I made for the Thames embankment to sit and rest, when lo and behold, I at once became deathly sick, and I fell to the ground a changed man.

A number of good fellows ran to my assistance, and wanted to call a policeman, but this I asked them not to do, I would soon be alright, but I was far from being, or getting alright, and it took me two hours to crawl back to my lodgings, a very sick man, weak and distressed like a man with the palsy, unknown and forsaken three thousand miles from home, a damn sorry plight, and one that I shall never forget, how my poor old heart longed to be back home in dear old New York, and away from that murdering set, and soon I found myself singing that grand old song so dear to the hearts of all American tourists when far from home and motherland, to wit:—

"Take me back to New York Town, New York Town, New York Town,
That's where I want to be, with the friends so dear to me.
Coney Island down the bay, or the gentle breeze of Far Rockaway,
Herald Square, I don't care, any where, New York Town, take me there."

I suffered for many days, leaving the hotel after breakfast to sit and ponder over my illness, afraid to have a Doctor, for fear of my loved ones at home getting worried, so day after day, after my regular visit to Mass at St. Patrick's, Ashley place, I would sit alone watching the many beautiful swans in the lake at St. James Park, facing Buckingham Palace, oh, boy, how I did pray to the Lord to restore me back to health so I could get back home, for I was afraid to take a chance, suffering as I did.

They say that "misery loves company" be that as it may, King George, of England was suffering from a similar dose, and his Doctors would send out bulletins every hour, and I would drag myself over to the gates of Buckingham Palace to get the news, not knowing if King George, or King John, were to be the first to kick in. But we both pulled through, thank God, and are well able to hold our own today, although it was a mighty narrow squeeze for both of us, but the King had five or more Doctors and all I had was my own doctor, Doc Hickey, whom I would consult, and talk with, but even the Hickeys don't want to be neglected and alone with themselves too much.

I wandered into Charing Cross Hospital one afternoon, and I was received quite royally, and when I explained my case to the doctors, I was given a thorough overhauling, and when I told them that I must go home, and if they thought that I could stand the hardships of a sea trip, they said, "Yes, you are sound in every form, and with the assistance of this medicine you may safely make the trip homeward," and it did not take me long to get my baggage packed and on my way to Southampton, and board the *S. S. George Washington,* and soon thank Heaven, was homeward bound, arriving in New York a mighty sick man, and while there were 27 Hickeys to see me off, there was not one to meet me on my return, for they knew not what had happened to me, but a call to Police Headquarters soon brought my sons to the Hoboken docks and I was driven home to the Hotel Elton, a much happier man.

"OSIDGE, LONDON.
"18th June, 1928.

"Mr. John J. Hickey,
21 Denbigh Street, Westminster, London, S.W.I.

"Dear Mr. Hickey:

"I have just received your very kind letter of the 16th inst., and I am greatly obliged to you for your hearty congratulations on *Shamrock's* victory. I am also very much pleased that you were an eye-witness of the race; from the end of the long pier that extends so far out in the sea at Harwich. I missed you in the morning.

"You certainly must have been elated watching the race for so many hours, with your heart's delight, *Shamrock,* in the lead every inch of the big, ugly route on that barren English coast, fighting against seven yachts, with King George V of England at the tiller of *Britannia* last, nearly a mile in the rear, but it was a fine race all the way, and I am happy.

"Don't forget to run out to Osidge in a day or two so we can talk it over, over a cup of tea. I will be looking for you. Hoping you are keeping fit and well, with all best wishes, I am,

"Yours faithfully,

"THOMAS J. LIPTON."

I had promised Sir Thomas that I would be at the start and take that race with him, but my train was late leaving the Victoria Station, and when I arrived at the starting point they were ready to leave, and I missed one grand historical event through the laxiness of the railway.

"MIDDLESEX, LONDON, E.C.
"9th of March, 1929.

"Mr. John J. Hickey,
"Hotel Elton, 4th Avenue,
"New York City.

"Dear Mr. Hickey:

"Your letter of the 1st inst. is to hand with enclosures for which we thank you very much for we have found them very interesting, Sir Thomas learning from them of a question that he was very much interested in, and again we thank you very much.

"I am sorry to say that Sir Thomas is still suffering great pain and is not at all well, that is, as we would like to see him, but he keeps up with that never-say-die spirit.

"Sir Thomas was resting up at the Riviera in Nice, France, and was summoned home on urgent business, but hopes to return to the South of France again just as soon as business will permit, for a few weeks at least, and if all is well return to London, and I think prepare for another trip to your great city of New York, and, of course, look for his old friend, J. J. Hickey.

"Many thanks for the cuttings that I, too, enjoyed very much. You will please excuse the brevity of this letter as we are right now in the middle of some very important business matters with our every moment fully occupied. As you are aware, Sir Thomas is a hard worker, and so must all around him be when the occasion requires it.

In any case, I expect to sail with Sir Thomas and, therefore, am looking forward to meeting you in New York, or at the pier at least.

"In haste, with our kindest regards and best wishes,

"Yours faithfully,

"JOHN WESTWOOD.

"*P. S.*—I have just discovered your typewritten matter on the Auto-biography of Sir Thomas, but there has not been a moment that I could have submitted it to him owing to the Chief's illness, but it can be dealt with later on if you are still disposed to use it.   I find it most interesting myself."

The following letter received from Sir Thomas explains itself and one that I shall never forget for what followed after, on his arrival from his yearly visit to the coast of California, suffering great pain and I am pleased to say I helped to dispel a whole lot.

PALMER HOUSE, CHICAGO, ILLINOIS

Part III—Chapter II

"Mr. John J. Hickey,
"Hotel Elton, 4th Avenue,
"New York City.

"PALMER HOUSE, CHICAGO, ILL.
"November 28th, 1928.

"Dear Mr. Hickey:

"I have just received your letter of the 21st, and I am leaving here tomorrow for New York, and will be at the Hotel Biltmore where I hope to meet my good friend Hickey in a few days, or as soon as time may permit. The clippings that you sent me I find mighty interesting, particularly that relating to Hickey introducing athletics to the men of the New York Police Department; also the cuttings you sent regarding the yachting age, and the one relating to Mayor Thompson of Chicago, whom I learn, has been running into great troubles, and for which I am sorry.

"The paragraph regarding the Empress Eugenie, I have also read with much interest, but am somewhat surprised that my name does not appear in connection with it, as for years she would not go any place without my being with her. I am very grateful to you for the trouble you have taken sending me all of these interesting cuttings.

"As I have indicated, I will be in New York Friday, and looking forward to meeting you at the hotel soon. I had a very interesting time during my visits to Omaha, San Francisco, Los Angeles, etc. With my best wishes,
"Yours faithfully, "THOMAS J. LIPTON."

I, having given Sir Thomas time to rest up, visited him at the Biltmore, but as on all like occasions, I was asked by John Westwood to take off my hat and coat and make myself at home in the same old "Detention Pen," Room 618.

I asked to see Sir Thomas, but John Westwood said he had friends, but as a matter of fact the grand old fellow was alone worrying his head off and after an hour or more had passed, Sir Thomas walked into Room 618, and when he saw me he got mighty angry, asking me how long I had been there and why I had not visited his room.

I answered Sir Thomas, "I am sorry, but you appear to be angry. Are you in pain?" "Yes," he answered, "I am in hellish pain, come with me," and he walked me towards the bath room. I suppose he thought that Westwood had told me that he was suffering much pain, but John Westwood never said a word about it, so that I was very much surprised to be taken to a bath room. Having closed the door, Sir Thomas let go his suspenders and he said: "Pull down my shirt, Mr. Hickey." Having done as he requested, I was shocked, and said: "Why, Sir Thomas, I don't wonder at your being angry. You must be in great pain."

"Yes, I am," said Sir Thomas. "What do you think of it?" I, to make him feel better than he was, said: "Well, Sir Thomas, I don't think anything of it, for it is something that comes to all travelers, sometime or other; a foreign rash that comes from unsanitary bedding that all travelers fear. But 'Cherio,' Sir Thomas, there is nothing to it, and will pass away in a few days. I have had this same thing after my visiting the exhibitions of San Diego, San Francisco and Los Angeles, California, in February, 1915."

"Is that your opinion, Mr. Hickey?" almost shouted Sir Thomas, brightening up at my remarks. "What do you do for it, Mr. Hickey? I have four well paid doctors, and they don't tell me a damn thing."

I answered, "Sir Thomas, in the first place I would call no doctors, for I could not fee them, and in the second place, I don't think them needed. I would ask one of my daughters or sons to stop into the hotel on their way home from business and lather my back with vaseline."

"What is that you say, Mr. Hickey, vaseline?" "Why, yes, Sir Thomas," I answered, "Well, that is mighty strange," said Sir Thomas, "that's only what the damn doctors are doing," and we both had a good laugh, and he buttoned up and we sat until midnight talking over it, he feeling in high glee.

I kept him in roars of laughter telling him of us poor men's ills and the simple remedies we are forced to resort to, to save a dollar, and in a fit of high glee, he said, "I am so glad that you came, for you have cheered me a whole lot. Good night, and don't be so long away. I thank you very much for this visit, but why don't you come over to the factory to see me? You, on a number of occasions, promised you would, but you don't come."

This same thing happened on several other occasions. I called a short time later and was taken into Westwood's own room, 614, and anchored in there until it came time to leave, and I asked Westwood if I could not see Sir Thomas, if only for a minute. "I will see," he said, and left the room, returning, he said, "Yes, you may see him but for a minute only."

Again, I found Sir Thomas suffering great pain from a foreign growth in his toe; it kind of overlapped the other, and he was raising cain with his valets, who were fixing him up for bed, and again I got a bawling out. "Where have you been that you could not come in to see me, and I again waiting for you, suffering great pain. Come, what do you think of this? 'Get out of here,'" he shouted to the two poor English valets.

I again used the self same salve, and Westwood says, "Your minute is up," and I had to go, but not before Sir Thomas had again given me hell for not visiting him at the factory, and why, simply because Westwood did not want me to, that was all, for when I made up my mind to call at the factory, I was looked upon as an interloper by his watchmen, having to tell them why I was there, and on whose request, but I got to Sir Thomas's office after a damn long wait, thanks to the invisible committee.

*Many thanks for
your birthday greetings.*

GENERAL PERSHING

John J. Pershing

This card came to me from the General, in reply to a letter that I had forwarded to him on his birthday, Sept. 14, 1918.

And in December I also forwarded to the General a card of Christmas greeting, and stating that all America was proud of him, and to return to home and motherland to become our President, when our present beloved President chose to lay down the reins of office.

And on my application for the General's autograph, this card followed.

J. J. HICKEY.

RICHARD E. ENRIGHT
Former Lieutenant

Promoted from the ranks by Mayor John F. Hylan, serving two terms of four years as Police Commissioner of this great city.

SIR THOMAS LIPTON IN BOSTON, MASS., 1927

In this I was helped very much by Mr. Waghorn, assistant secretary, from whom I learned more in one hour than I learned from Westwood in twenty years, and I have a whole lot to thank Mr. Waghorn for, but the jig was up and after being taken to Sir Thomas by a Mr. Fields, whom I told that I would never go there again after his treatment, for I made up my mind to be honest with Sir Thomas, and I told him the reason why I never visited him at the factory. Well, Heavenly Father! Sir Thomas flew into a rage, and instead of his taking that as a warning, he rang a bell and had all of his floor superintendents appear forthwith, and he made the mistake of telling them my story, saying, "My God, Mr. Hickey told me the reason that he never visited me at the factory was because his presence was so often denied me by Mr. Westwood," and, of course, the invisible committee had the phones going forthwith acquainting their superior, Mr. Westwood, their boss, of all that had taken place and Sir Thomas, after saying, "My God, I never knew that a secretary of mine would dare deny me to my friends," grabbed his coat and made for the Biltmore Hotel.

It was then that Cashier Fields took me to his office and left me, he going home. Why did this gent do this, or what was on his mind? I want to know.

I lost no time in getting back to my hotel, for I knew full well what was happening at the Biltmore, and so that Westwood would prevent my seeing Sir Thomas, when I called I wrote to Westwood, telling him of all that took place at the factory that afternoon, and to my surprise I received an answer to my letter—a copy of which I am enclosing, the principal of the letter I keep for future reference.

"BILTMORE HOTEL.
"October 23rd, 1928.

"Mr. J. J. Hickey,
"Hotel Elton, 4th Avenue,
"New York City.
"Dear Mr. Hickey:

"Yours of the 22nd at hand. I am sorry if there has been any misunderstanding or neglect in connection with making an appointment for you to see Sir Thomas, or in my dealing with your manuscript.

"I rather expected to hear from you but apparently the mistake has been mine. If you will telephone me as to when you are free to call, I shall arrange for you to see Sir Thomas.
"With all best wishes,

"JOHN WESTWOOD."

Just to try him out, I called on Sir Thomas a few nights after, and the same old story, Sir Thomas is very busy, and on hearing that he was attending a dinner party, I hid myself in an out-of-the-way spot until he returned, and when he saw me, he asked why I was not up in his room instead of in the lobby of the hotel? Asking me up to his room, we chatted there for an hour, he saying, "Don't be away long,

Mr. Hickey, and when you get here come right into my room, good night."

This whole damn business is and always was very distasteful to me, for I am bitterly opposed to such stuff, but you want to and must hear the truth, and Mr. Waghorn is still in the flesh, and can or will bear me out, for it was getting on my nerves, particularly so, when he would leave the room for a few moments and on returning, slip an envelope across the table to me, saying, "Mr. Hickey, Sir Thomas sent this to you with his compliments.

A damn lie, for if Sir Thomas knew that I was a prisoner in room 618, he would be out giving me hell for not going to his room, and of course the same old story. I returned the envelope forthwith without opening or even knowing how much was in it, nor did I care, for I said, you please go give the envelope back for all the money in the United States Treasury cannot buy my friendship for Sir Thomas Lipton, grabbing my hat, good night.

My God, how I stood for this yellow dog's insults so long, I don't know, for this was not the first or the second time that same episode occurred.

I had for years suspected him, for I was given many reasons, that Sir Thomas knew nothing about it, but let it slide on account of Westwood being a busy man, but I never dreamed that he would resort to slip a pill into my cup of coffee or tea, as was done in June, 1928, at Osidge, London. For as true as that God is my judge, that is what happened, for I never before felt as I did then.

It will be a sorry day, the day I find the evidence that I am looking for, connected with the yacht racing of September, 1930, and the breaking of my old friend's heart, and I will not attempt to deny that I have already submitted my thoughts in this matter to Scotland Yard, so they as friends of Tom Lipton, and as fellow policemen, cause an investigation, unknowingly to the rest of the world. But no doubt, the fact of Westwood being British and I an American, I never received an answer.

There is no doubt that our writers following the Cup racing could tell a good story relating to what they saw or what they heard—but will they? Some day they may tell all they know, let us hope so.

I felt mighty sorry for Sir Thomas, for he took this very much to heart, but it was not my doing, my story had to be told, and maybe it would have been different if my story had been told years before, Sir Thomas then would have known more of what he was up against, and stop it.

And when Sir Thomas had called his managers and cashier, Mr. Fields to his office and said, "Why, gentlemen, Mr. Hickey has just told me that he often came to this factory and to my hotel but could not see me—that is terrible, why I am astonished to think that my secretary would ever dare keep my friends calling on me, and not being able to see me."

Sir Thomas had gone and Mr. Fields asked me to go into the office of his secretary, and he would be back, but never showed up and after waiting one hour and hearing nothing but quietness, I thought it time to go, but I have often since then thought it so strange, I often wondered what were his thoughts that evening, but I swallowed it all, for I did not want to hurt the feelings of my dear old friend any more. It was a mighty strange thing to do, I wonder, did he think that I would have stayed there until late and have their night watchman shoot me down as a burglar? No one would ever know a thing about it, for many such things have been done along the waters' edge of both New York and New Jersey, just drop the victim overboard and that would be the finish of this strange but perfectly true story.

But, I beat them to it, for I am quite sure that they got me out of the first office so that they would be free to call up John Westwood, so he would know the whole story before Sir Thomas arrived at the Biltmore Hotel, for that is how the invisible government worked their points, I saw their actions many times, but did not want to interfere, I was quite sure that this gang had a quiet little racket among themselves, God help our dear old friend, Sir Thomas, for he was their rich prey.

If this man John Westwood, had done his full duty, Sir Thomas would not be worried about a million dollar suit for breach of promise, and rushed out of his room under cover after midnight when he should be in bed sleeping to board a steamer for home, that was to sail in the wee small hours that morning, when the rascal of a so-called Russian Princess and her lawyer, Nathan Burkan the fixer and others were still sleeping, with Sir Thomas locked in his room, and not even his dearest friends could bid him goodbye.

For the information and guidance of my readers, I herewith publish a copy of a letter received from a very prominent lawyer and yachtsman friend of Sir Thomas for many years, this is but one of many, to prove to you that I am not alone in my way of thinking and writing this biography, to wit:—

"New York, October 9th, 1931.

"Mr. John J. Hickey, Hotel Elton, City.

"Dear Captain Hickey:

"I am in receipt of your very kind letter of the 5th inst. bearing upon the death of our good friend, Sir Thomas Lipton.

"As you intimate, he was the only one of his class, and the best of sportsmen that lived from the days of the Romans, and he certainly kept things going as long as he could, and it was only on account of the very severe depression and personal distress which may insue during the winter that he refrained from issuing another challenge.

"He certainly was entitled to win and I am not so sure that his many failures in capturing the cup, gained for him more respect and esteem than though he had won and have taken the cup with him, many years ago.

"I am sure that all of his personal friends feel as you do about him and it is certainly a shame he could not have lived through one more race when, under the new rules and conditions, his chances would have been better and we would all then hope and do everything possible, to see him win, but as you say, it now cannot be.

"Trusting that you are personally well, and with all good wishes, I am,
"Respectfully yours,
"JOHN DOE."

I fully appreciate the worth of such letters, for they go far to substantiate my findings in this whole matter, but as you will agree with me it would not be fair or honorable for me to mention names, at this time, but I know of no other man on earth today, better able to tell the sorrowful story than this gentleman that wrote the above letter.

There are other letters, but it serves no purpose to publish them here, I will keep them forever secret and unless appealed to, all of such letters and names of the senders are my dearest personal belongings. Here is a case of John Westwood's second offense, so that you will know this man better.

On a number of occasions while hooked up with John Westwood in his reception Room 618, Biltmore Hotel, with Sir Thomas sitting alone in Room 622, Westwood would excuse himself and leave the room, as if going into the room occupied by Sir Thomas, and sally forth with an envelope, saying, "Mr. Hickey, Sir Thomas sent this out to you with his good wishes."

Knowing the man that I was dealing with, I answered, "Did Sir Thomas send that to me." Money, I suppose? Well Mr. Westwood, you will please return this envelope to Sir Thomas, and thank him, but all the money in the bank of America could not buy my friendship for Sir Thomas Lipton, and you, it seems do not know the man that you have been writing to all of these years, good night, grabbing my hat, I beat it, for all that I got from Westwood was a grunt, just as one would get from Tom Lipton's orphans, years ago.

From that night on I began to get suspicious of John Westwood, and I watched him very closely, and you know no doubt that when you get the sharp eye of a New York Bobby on you, one had better pack up and get out, for sooner or later you are pinched, and taken down-town for the line-up.

I was not then aware of all the persecution, grunts and snarls that my dear old friends was handed; morning, noon and night. I saw several things happen that I did not like, for instance, while stopping with Sir Thomas at Osidge, Westwood beckoned me into his room, and while there I overheard an argument between John Westwood and Mr. Waghorn about gas bills, but not wanting to interfere, I withdrew, leaving them to fight it out alone.

It was after my conversation with Counsellor, Mr. .... that I first learned of the treatment accorded Sir Thomas, of course the force they used to have him make a speech at the City Hall, when being presented with the American People's Loving Cup, had me guessing, I was amazed of the conversation with our dear old friends, oldest of American friends convinced me that all was not well, but lousy, I would like you to know all the Commodore told me, but not having met John Westwood since, I have not had a chance to tell him just what I always knew and that he was a louse and a rat to use that dear old man of an employer in such a vile manner and although I have not had a chance to speak out personally, my book will tell it all, and under the circumstances, one can't go far enough in his denouncing of a man of the Westwood character, and his actions.

But while Sir Thomas may be sleeping, the Lord never sleeps, for that would be impossible, when there are murderous looking hounds running around, but the day of reckoning will come to us all, and there won't be many of us in humor to celebrate the day of judgment, the Lord be praised, and Tom Lipton avenged, for murder must and will win out. Imagine the sufferings of Sir Thomas when he said to his friend, "I don't know what I am going to do with my secretary, for he is very nasty and gruffly when he answers me," my friend at once said, "Sir Thomas, I will speak to Mr. Westwood about his actions," No don't, Mr. Thomas, it will make things worse for me. Mr. Thomas did alright.

Who can blame me for writing and talking in such strain, when I had discovered long before this time that my dear old friend Sir Thomas, was being trifled with, yes, sold out, and by them drawing down big salaries from the Lipton payrolls.

But, there was never a chance for me to have Sir Thomas know of all that I had seen and heard, for if I wrote him, Westwood got the letter, and if I called on Sir Thomas at the Hotel, he was denied me, so what was I to do, but watch and wait.

"Like the cunning old Owl that lived in an Oak, the more he heard the less he spoke, the less he spoke the more he heard.

So I played the part of that foxy old bird."

Appointing myself as it were, a minister without portfolio, and that from away back in 1920, when Sir Thomas asked me when leaving here to write him personally, for he then began to smell a rat.

But it is no use, these secretaries are the whole shooting match, for it is the same all over, they are in touch with the heads of the factories, or workshops, and they are responsible to none but this same secretary, who in turn tells his employer just what he feels like telling him.

And if the employer decides to visit the works, and have a look over the books and conditions, the secretary runs to the telephone and calls up the factory and all is in fine shape when the employer gets there, and not knowing the real facts, returns to his hotel smiling.

And so it goes on, unless one wants to make a rowdy of himself and on calling, break right into the old friends room, but then, you have his secretary to deal with, no more letters or telephone calls answered, or will you be admitted if going to the hotel, or notified away in advance that the boss is leaving on such and such a day, and for what purpose.

However, Sir Thomas is resting in the palace of his makers today, for he lived a right royal saintly life, but his enemies and traducers, were in "all that is good and pious," are they going to wind up, God forbid that I should be their judge, that is in the hands of our Devine Lord.

I am publishing these little things and without fear of contradiction for I hold 100 letters to bear me out, many of whom you will read copies of in this book, nor will I stop until I learn the truth about how, and why, Sir Thomas J. Lipton, and his pretty little *Shamrock V* did not win the American Cup, or even get a look in, in September, 1930.

Also the facts regarding his death, and many other questions that I am not making public at this time.

Now folks let us try and be happy, and drive dull care away, by jumping on the band wagon and shout for the N.R.A. and by so doing forget our troubles to help out our President, Franklin D. Roosevelt, that Devine Providence blessed us with, Hurrah, Hurrah, Hurrah, we are winning.

Do you know folks, that a few years ago at the St. Patrick's dinner, the eve of St. Patrick's Day in the morning, one of the grandest men of that day in the person of the late Cardinal Lough Primate of all Ireland, was in turn called upon to speak, and this is what he said, to wit :—

"Gentlemen, all of my speeches is given in my sermons in Church, I will tell you a funny story that I am sure will be pleasing to you all. One night while I was hearing confessions at home, a woman came to the confession and her lady friend too and after receiving absolution, she joined her friend, and when asked how she made out, said, 'Alright, but he is the homeliest looking devil I ever saw,' her friend answered, 'My God, you can't go to communion, after your remarks about the poor priest,' well what I am going to do, is go back and tell him what you said about him, she went back to the confessional, and told me that she had only just left the confessional and how she said that you are the homeliest looking devil of a man I ever saw, I said, tut, tut, be off with you woman dear, you are not so good looking yourself," and that is just what we will be telling the knockers of the N.R.A. someday—you are full of soup and not so good looking yourself.

But alas, my chances have gone forever, mores the pity, as for Westwood, I have no desire to see him again either dead or alive, for he has played Sir Thomas, his employer and his friends false, with his rubber stamp diplomacy, and canny Scotch actions.

I have written to him, asking to explain this or that story told me, for instance, his writing me to say that he was leaving for New York, October 2nd, and to look for him October 9th on board the *S. S. Leviathan,* and I, like the damn fool, I was running around town first to get permission to board the steamer at her pier, and secondly, telephoning all over Long Island trying to locate Miss Owens, to see if she could give me any information concerning the movements of Mr. Westwood.

Tired out and sick at heart with the papers stating that Sir Thomas had passed away, on the very day that he and his party were to leave for God's own country, New York, and all the time four doctors were in attendance on Sir Thomas, supposed to be suffering for the past two weeks with a chill, received while out riding, if that isn't taking a fellow for a ride, than I don't know what is.

And after Church on Sunday, October 3rd, 1931, sick at heart, unable to sleep all night as a last resort, I visited the Hotel Biltmore, and asked to see the genial Manager, Mr. Roarke, my good friend, and having explained my mission, he said, "Yes Mr. Hickey, they held a reservation, that since the death of Sir Thomas, has been cancelled," and then I took myself into confidence and I more than once asked myself, how do you reconcile this and that, until I was near being a fit subject for the observation Ward in Bellevue Hospital.

The very thought of it, Sir Thomas supposedly ill for two weeks, with four first class doctors attending him, and yet they could not grant his last request, and that was, "Send for Sir Harry Lauder, and Sir Harry, only a hop step and a jump away over in Scotland," was unable to reach the death bed side until long after Sir Thomas had passed away, why?

Well, here is the answer, yes they had booked to sail on the *Leviathan,* for Sir Thomas was not suffering from any chills, he was suffering from what I stated in my first chapter, a broken heart, and the excitement of getting ready to sail, and the thought of what brought about this broken heart, Sir Thomas was unable to stand the strain and flopped.

That to my detective mind is the story pure and simple, and no one can ever change it, at least, none of the suspects, that the writer has in mind, and in conclusion, no doubt when this work gets before the public Westwood will run to cover and answer my questions.

"OSIDGE, MIDDLESEX,
"August, 1928.

"Dear Mr. Hickey:

"I am glad to have your letter of 23rd ultimo; and to know that you have got back to God's own country, but am sorry to hear, however, that you have been in the wars and an accident occurred, but hope you are now O.K.

"We deferred sending the 'History of Monaghan' until we knew that you were really back, and it is going out in the next mail to the Hotel Elton, so please keep an eye out for it, Mr. Hickey.

"*Shamrock V*, you will be glad to know, has had a very successful season so far. Out of seven yachts in her class and eighteen starts, *Shamrock V* has won 8 firsts, 3 seconds and 2 thirds, and in one race and in a good position was forced to give up to recover a man that had fallen overboard.

"*Britannia* has also done well with 6 firsts, 3 seconds and 1 third; so you can see there has not been much left for the rest of the seven.

"Sir Thomas has also received your very kind letter addressed to himself, with the most interesting cuttings and has asked me to convey to you his sincere thanks and he sends you his best wishes, he also asked me to return the letter you received from Mayor Walker's Secretary, dated the 11th of May, 1927, which he has read with both interest and pleasure.

"I am attaching this letter hereto. With kindest regards and best wishes, both from Sir Thomas and myself,

"Yours faithfully,

"JOHN WESTWOOD."

Letters of like character were received by me: November 5th, 1920; April 7th, 1921; May 2nd, 1921, which reads as follows:

"LONDON, E. C.,
"May 2nd, 1921.

"Mr. John J. Hickey,
"244 East 20th Street,
"New York City.

"Dear Mr. Hickey:

"Your various letters and cuttings all safely received and much appreciated. The only cutting I cannot find and the one that you call my particular attention to is that referring to the Hope Fishing Club Dinner, at which Commodore Enright spoke so highly of Sir Thomas. I was very much interested to know what you wrote on the subject and perhaps if you can still find the cutting, or a duplicate of same, kindly send it along.

"I was sorry to note that your son was compelled to undergo an operation and hope this was successful and is now restored to his usual good health or on the way to complete convalescence.

"I also note some of the editorials, but am quite certain that the solid common sense of both nations will prevent anything like real trouble. If you should be able to read the book called 'A Straight Deal' or 'Ancient Grudge' by Owen Wister, you will find it well worthy of your perusal in this connection.

"I return herewith your records of the different champions of the cinder path, of which you, yourself was a champion long distance runner, holding the championship won in 1905, for 13 years, retiring the undefeated mile champion of the Police Department of New York.

"The record made by W. G. George at Lille Bridge in 1886, stood for many years, that of 12¾, until along comes your American champion N. S. Taber lapping off 1/20th from George's time—1/20th part of a second is mighty close clocking, I should say.

"Please do not bother about anything political but sport, I take great delight in reading and you have kept some mighty fine records, if time would permit our going over them, as we would like.

"Hoping that this will find you well, and with all best wishes,

"Yours respectfully,

"JOHN WESTWOOD."

I am proud to say at this time, that my son Tim, whom Mr. Westwood inquired about is well today, while I am making a true copy of this interesting letter. Tim. Hickey is a member of the championship team of the New York Police Department of hand ball fame.

Often in our little chats, Sir Thomas would introduce reminiscences and stories about his boyhood and his playmates after school, and how they called out, "Hey, Tom Lipton, come and get some games for them to play."

"Do you know, Mr. Hickey, that I often wish that I could again be called Tom Lipton, for big names and riches don't bring happiness, and my heart will ever harken to my former happy days, and my wee boys and girls playmates."

That was the character and the makeup of this wonderful Irish Scotch multi-millionaire, never at ease unless when doing something for humanity, handing out alms to the needy, and making some poor family happy.

And while these happy memories will always live in my heart the loss of Sir Thomas was a very sad blow to me, for I miss his many beautiful letters to me reminding me that he would meet me soon, either in New York or London, and hoping to find me fit and well, and ever ready for a long chat about old friends and old times, but alas them days have gone forever.

Oh yes, the hand of death will sooner or later be laid on the shoulders of us all, never till my dying day, will I forget to think and pray, for my dear old friend, so far, far, away. Of course, you folks have either heard or read of "Mary Helen," the charitable queen of 1875, Tom Lipton took her place.

Noted as A, No. 1 story teller and always ready to entertain a party of friends, telling of his travels of more than fifty years ago, the dark nights and days when his good old friend Tom Edison, the wizard was busy working on his wonderful inventions to blaze up and down Fifth Avenue, throwing its beautiful rays of today on the worlds highest building, the Empire State and other such wonderful additions to little old New York.

And my, how we poor policemen thanked God for relieving us on patrol under the dark old gas lamp, doing duty along such streets as Cherry Street, James Street, Roosevelt Street, and other holes and corners of the lower East side, always on the alert for a burglar, or some other vicious character to hop out on you in the wee small hours, often on an empty stomach.

This was long before the Telephone, or Radio, and the moving pictures, the Aeroplanes and Skyscrapers, when we would delight to attend a lecture by some explorer, by which he picked up for himself a fine living.

Here we are today, we have the Lions and Tigers, brought right before us, and there is no need of a lecturer, more's the pity, and Tom Lipton, dead.

"OSIDGE, SOUTHGATE, LONDON,
"August 15th, 1928.

"Mr. John J. Hickey,
"New York City,
"Dear Mr. Hickey:

"Sir Thomas has duly received your kind letters and the two letters that you have received from your old friend Police Commissioner and former President of the United States, and he is very much pleased and thankful to you for having mailed them to him.

"Sir Thomas greatly appreciates the reading of these letters, and he is hoping that they will be safely returned to you, for as you say, you are donating them to the 'Roosevelt' Home Association of New York, a mighty fine thought of yours, for there they will please the old friends of your former President and soldier, and they will be given the care that we are unable to give them.

"Sir Thomas greatly admired President Theodore Roosevelt for his upright manly methods, and a real 100 per cent American, a jovial way when meeting one whom he had never met before, and it delighted me, the great welcome that he gave our party and myself when dining with him, September, 1903.

"Yes, Sir Thomas often speaks of Mr. Roosevelt, and he likes to tell a funny story that had President Roosevelt laughing heartily, after the dinner, September, 1903.

"Sir Thomas also requests me to thank you for the beautiful birthday card you sent him just to hand and to thank you for your everlasting kind remembrances of him, particularly at this time every year, for the past long number of years, you had never slipped up one year to my knowledge.

"Trusting to find you well and in good shape, with all kind wishes, I am,
"Yours faithfully,
"John Westwood."

"HOTEL BILTMORE, N. Y. C.
"September 24th, 1928.

"Mr. John J. Hickey,
"Hotel Elton, New York City.
"Dear Mr. Hickey:

"Sir Thomas has just received your very kind letter of the 22nd, and will be pleased to see the proof of the story that you have written for your book, namely the Lipton 'Ones' of 1760 and 1770, that he longs to both hear and read about.

"Give me a ring tomorrow and I will appoint a time when you are ready to join Sir Thomas and be alone, as he is very anxious to see these stories in print, and they will make a great setting for your proposed autobiography when complete.

"Trusting that this will find you fit and well, and with best wishes,
"Yours faithfully,
"John Westwood."

It goes without saying that I lost no time in submitting this manuscript to Sir Thomas, and next evening found me at the Biltmore, and satisfying the mind of this grand old scout, who was highly pleased and his last words to me on leaving was, "Mr. Hickey, that is just as I wanted, you keep right on with your story, and when complete let me know, won't you?"

"I am very anxious to see this story in book form, and I want the first copy of this work of my good friend Hickey, good night."

"HOTEL BILTMORE, N. Y. C.
"December 5th, 1928.

"Dear Mr. Hickey:

"Very many thanks for your letter of the 4th inst., which I have read with much interest as well as the inclosures from Miss Mary Childs Nerney, secretary to Mr. Thomas A. Edison, which I am returning forthwith.

"This I think will be a very interesting interview, and would like to be within hearing of same, your history of Mr. Edison, and old timers, in and around New York, dating back to 1880, and the many instances that necessitated your many meetings in those early days.

"Please excuse haste as we are just getting ready to sail homeward.

"With kind regards and best wishes,

"Yours respectfully,

"JOHN WESTWOOD,

"Mr. J. J. Hickey, Hotel Elton,
"26th Street and 4th Ave., N. Y. C."

I will explain, dear readers the reason of this letter to your entire satisfaction, I hope, to wit:—

One of the late Thomas A. Edison's sons, I was given to understand, undertook to compile the autobiography of his talented father, the wizard, and I, knowing so much of Thomas A. Edison from the day I landed here in 1881, until many years after when I joined the force with my night post on Fulton Street at Pearl, when I often met Mr. Edison on his way after a hard night's work to get a cup of coffee, and fly back to the old United States Hotel, Pearl and Fulton Streets, to get a few hours sleep.

My information they thought to be good, so I was invited to meet this fine young lady, and be interviewed by her, giving all the facts in my possession which I was happy to be able to do.

I suppose like myself, with the autobiography of Sir Thomas, now turned into the life and times of Sir Thomas, young Mr. Edison is progressing with his work, and I wish him every success, for it is far from being an easy contract.

To think of it, these two wonderful men, now dead, and almost forgotten, that is by some, who don't know that they are alive themselves.

"OSIDGE, SOUTHGATE,
"MIDDLESEX, LONDON,
"December 15th, 1928.

"Dear Mr. Hickey:

"Your letter of the 6th inst. is duly to hand, and I am advised by Sir Thomas to express his great appreciation of your kind thought. It was a great pleasure for him to receive the beautiful flowers, which you were good enough to send to the *Leviathan,* which helped to cheer up his sitting room during the trip homeward.

"I am sorry to have to tell you that Sir Thomas has been suffering pretty badly from Neuritis since he left New York, and even now is suffering great pain. He is, however, progressing slowly and we hope that in the course of a week or so he may be pretty well recovered.

"Sir Thomas desires me to send to you his best wishes for Christmas and the New Year, which he hopes will be very happy and prosperous.

"With kind regards and all good wishes,

"Yours faithfully,

"JOHN WESTWOOD.

"Mr. J. J. Hickey, Hotel Elton,
"4th Avenue, New York City."

"OSIDGE, SOUTHGATE,
"LONDON, ENGLAND,
"May 6th, 1929.

"Mr. John J. Hickey, Hotel Elton,
"4th Avenue, New York City.
"Dear Mr. Hickey:

"Your letter of the 16th ultimo addressed to Sir Thomas, with the many enclosures came duly to hand, and again we appreciate your kind thoughts, very much so for all of your pure American news to both Sir Thomas and myself are very cheering at all times.

"Sir Thomas has recently returned from France, that is the 'Riviera' the spot that you spent your winter of 1927-1928.

"With mercury down to the zero mark and you and your American and Australian friends with your overcoats on your arms, having your photos taken on the Promenade on New Years day, and every time that we look at your photographs we have to laugh, at its being taken under such circumstances.

"But the weather man in Nice was not so kind to Sir Thomas, and he was mighty glad to be back in his own home, after all, in spite of the fact that the weather here was most disagreeable, nevertheless it is his home, and one may travel the world over and over, but there is no place like home, and now Sir Thomas appears to be more cheerful. His one constant worry is when he will be able to visit his American friends again, for his first love little olde New York appeals to him always, not counting his many friends of the Empire city of the U. S. A.

"The thoughts of meeting you among his good old friends is mighty cheering, and he asks me to convey to you his very best wishes and kindest thought of a happy future, and in which I join Sir Thomas, always.

"Yours respectfully,

"JOHN WESTWOOD."

You will notice in another part of this work, my remarks about the big mistake that is made in a doctor, advising his patients to go for the summer at this so-called health resort, at the moment when they were advising his Majesty King George of England to go to rest up, but I notice the King did not go there, to associate with the crooks of the world, Counts and Counts of no account, one big bunch of get-rich-quick men of every conceivable creed and nation, with the undertakers becoming millionaires. I had written to the Privy Council my experience, all winter on the Riviera, that was enough I guess.

"OSIDGE, SOUTHGATE,
"LONDON, ENGLAND,
"May 10th, 1929.

"Mr. John J. Hickey, Hotel Elton,
"4th Avenue, New York City.
"Dear Mr. Hickey:

"Your very kind letters are duly to hand, as is also your lovely birthday card, for all of which I thank you very much and most highly appreciate your many kindnesses to me at all times.

"It is so very good to have you thinking of me all the time, and mailing to me weekly, cheering news about my many friends over there, never for a single moment do you, or have you forgotten to write me and cheer me up in my advancing years, this I will never forget, both in season and out of season, my old friend Hickey is on the job. 'In summer or winter, in rain, snow or hale, here comes Mr. Hickey, with his arms full of mail.'

"With all kind wishes, trusting that you are keeping fit and well, I am,

"Yours sincerely,

"THOMAS J. LIPTON."

"OSIDGE, SOUTHGATE,
"LONDON, ENGLAND,
"May 15th, 1929.

"Mr. John J. Hickey, Hotel Elton,
"4th Avenue, New York City.
"Dear Mr. Hickey:

"Your very kind letter of the 7th inst. is at hand, also the many enclosures it contains that we enjoy so much always, please excuse briefness an emergency call to answer.

"Yours respectfully,

"JOHN WESTWOOD."

Sir Thomas Lipton, had often been misquoted in interviews, and to be on the safe side while busy writing up his autobiography, I dropped in to the Biltmore Hotel and submitted those that I thought were phony, and he having passed on them they were destroyed, for above all things the grand old sportsman, tried hard to avoid mistakes.

The following Sunday, August 17th, 1930, I again called on Sir Thomas, at his hotel, and I was very much pleased at his appearance, he had slept well and promising to abandon the poorhouse story altogether, and after breakfast he took a very fine long drive, taking his dinner at the New York Club House on Travers Island, he arrived later looking and feeling one hundred per cent better, than on yesterday, thank Heaven.

Knowing that he had the appointment with Mayor Walker at the City Hall next day, he retired early, rising like a lark in the morning, he was mighty soon on his way to 14th Street, Hoboken, his factory, cleaning up and off to the big show at 4 p.m. in the Mayor's Office.

Mayor Walker also had several other delegations calling on him and he shook their hands and spoke his kindly words of praise, out in the vestibule of the City Hall, and sent them away mighty happy, as you know Jimmy Walker, was a noted past master at that part of his busy day.

It did not take the Mayor long to get Sir Thomas going, and he himself lost no time in setting the ball of wisecracks going, having seen to it that all present, that is the Lipton party, of which I was a member, were at once seated, the fun commenced.

With the late Sir Thomas Lipton, and our late Mayor, the Hon. James J. Walker, face to face, the whole party were happy, for when two men of such popularity meet, silence is Golden.

Mayor Walker, among other things said, "Sir Thomas, you having traveled the world, may I ask how many languages do you speak," "Four came the Fargo Express reply", what are they please asked the Mayor. "English, Irish, Scotch, and American, answered Sir Thomas."

That's all Sir Thomas, asked the Mayor, and to my mind if one can speak those four he is doing well, but that surprised me very much for Jimmy Walker has travelled some, but if he had travelled more, then he would soon find out that the fellow to travel will have a very hard road ahead if he cannot speak either French, German, or Italian, I know, only too well.

Again Mayor Walker, called the attention of Sir Thomas to a certain race course, and how he met Sir Thomas, who in turn was given an introduction to all of Sir Thomas's friends, among them was the late Lord Dewar, and Sir Thomas chuckled with glee.

Sir Thomas facing the scratch said: "Mr. Walker, do you know that Lord Dewar, supported two committees, one to look out for the wants of the other while in jail," and that brought about a great laugh. Mayor Walker enjoyed this very much.

And after enjoying a good laugh, Mayor Walker turned around to his cabinet and says, "perhaps that would be a capital thing for me to do, to appoint two committees among the heads of Departments, to watch over the one in jail, the second committee would try hard to keep out, and take care of their friends inside the jail."

And would it surprise you to know, that former Judge Seabury forced Mayor Walker to resign his job as Mayor, less than one year from that date, when all was happiness and sunshine, and in two short years Sir Thomas after a sudden death, went to "blighty" and to add to this, Sam Seabury, makes Mayor La Guardia Mayor of New York, some history, my word.

(RETURNING HOMEWARD AFTER MY WORLD'S TRAVELS OF 1927-1928)

Part III—Chapter III

I was visited at the hotel by a female reporter, connected with the N. Y. "Sun", same being published in the "Sun" in the Fall of 1928, and this is what was written, to wit:—"Back from his world's travels, Ex-Policeman J. J. Hickey, lets in light on foreign lands."

Mr. Hickey, was charmed by "Jerusalem" where he had stopped two weeks, but did not like Ireland under the conditions then prevailing, and why, well it happened that at that time, President Cosgrove, of the Irish Free State, was defeated for re-election, by Mr. De Valera.

"A little disillusioned since he has travelled the world" and looked foreign countries in the face, John J. Hickey, a retired New York Policeman, and founder of Police track and field Athletics in the department some forty years ago, is back in his room at the Hotel Elton, (the old Putnam House), Fourth Avenue and Twenty-sixth Street, a stopping place of the American and English champions of the past, among them the famous Boston Strong Boy, the late John Lawrence Sullivan, America's Idol, of his day.

Charley Rowell and Jimmy Michaels, and many more that are too numerous to mention, that gave us old timers plenty of amusement in the past, in the old Madison Square Garden, that stood on the site of the New York Life building, often nights laying in bed I could hear the wild fans like at the Northwest corner of 26th Street and Fourth Avenue.

The Hotel Elton stands on the North East Side of the avenue. God bless them good old days, when New York was New York, and its men and women real humans, faithful until death.

"I found Mr. Hickey, busily engaged when I called on him, at his typewriter writing to the Private Secretary to King George V of England, Lord Stampfordham, in answer to a letter just received from London, in relation to his advising that King George V should not go to the Riviera for his convalescence under the mistaken notion that it was warm there.

"For the King would have been mistaken finding the Riviera cold and uncomfortable," said Mr. Hickey.

"I made the greatest mistake in my life when I undertook to winter at the Riviera instead of my staying either in Egypt, or India, where the sun was always shining and always warm and pleasant, instead of going to the Riviera, for I was frozen, and could not keep warm, but a fellow may try anything once, but never again.

"Another startling reaction to his world's travels for an Irishman, and a former 'Fenian' at that, is Mr. Hickey's conclusion that he prefers Jerusalem to Ireland as a place of residence—under the present circumstances," he explained hastily. My happy stay in Jerusalem fulfilled a life-long desire to walk over the same ground as did our Lord and Saviour.

"The grass is growing over the farms in Ireland, for the young men have migrated to America, and in many cases paid the passage of their girl friends, leaving the old folks to attend to the farming and its upkeep, but God help them, they are too old for that now.

"Since the young folks have left them, there is nothing left for the old folks to do but sell their farms, and their holdings, and there are plenty of men and women British agents looking for bargains daily, for they want to grab Ireland, and if the people of Ireland do not stop their bickering, we will soon find Ireland, only in name.

"I had great hopes, in Mr. Cosgrove's administration, that Ireland would be Ireland once again, for he was then doing some great work along the famous old river 'Shannon,' but alas, not getting the support that he was entitled to, and then defeated for re-election, destroyed all prospects of a grand and glorious happy and prosperous 'Emerald Isle.' "

Much could be said or written of the different episodes in Ireland's history of the past, of which I was a party to in my boyhood days and after, ever ready to do or die in the cause of Ireland's freedom, one of which my readers might like to read, as follows:

I recall the sad days of 1867, when three gallant heroes, Allen, Larken, and O'Brien, the Manchester Martyrs, were hanged for the accidental killing of Sergeant Britt, while they were trying to set free several of their companions, from the patrol wagon, taking them to jail, murder was far from their minds. We, the Irish of London marched with bands and banners to protest to the Crown, but was denied admission into Hyde Park, protected by the Life Guards from Whitehall, and we were ordered to move on, or suffer the consequences, did we quit? Why bless your heart no, you never knew of a decent Irishman quitting, not at all man, not at all.

But they reckoned without their host, for you may just as well try pumping the East River into the North River, to ask an Irishman to change his mind once it is made up, and the bloody battle commenced in earnest, we kids digging up the stones from the street, giving them to our Fathers and Mothers to fire at the Life Guards, and we won, the soldiers being called off, they knew they were doing wrong, keeping us out of Hyde Park.

We were fighting for Ireland's freedom, and now that we have

Freedom that we have been fighting for for over eight hundred years, Ireland is, I am sorry to say, worse off than ever, our farmers starving, and why?

Well, the Cosgrove party proved themselves, and Ireland was in a fair way of final recovery until defeated by the whims of the foolish Irish, oh yes, in many cases, by armed threats of the opposition party, the De Valera party, and what is the consequence? Well, let us pray for prosperity once more and if left to themselves will make Ireland happy and beautiful once again.

But this other element under the old Republican leadership, of Mr. De Valera is not helping Ireland at all, but holding her back for we Tourists hate to visit Ireland with this faction fight still going on, even as much as we love the old land. The employees on the railways are still silent or darned impolite, they confiscate your luggage, and before you get through with the paying of your bills you will find a big increase, in your expenses.

In contrast to this dismal picture Mr. Hickey found Jerusalem a beautiful place, and stopping at "Casa Nova" a welcoming home for all creeds and nationalities, run as a hotel, under the supervision of the Reverend Father Godfrey P. Hunt, a former World's War Army Chaplain, and now the Director of the Monastery of St. Saviour, a very fine building situated in old Jerusalem, the ground our Lord and Savior Jesus Christ walked over following the way of the cross, and praying in the Garden of "Gethsemane," the Mount of Olives, the graves of Margaret and Mary, St. Joseph and St. Lazarus, then on the road to old "Jerico" and the River Jordan, and the Dead Sea.

The next day visiting "Bethlehem" a Pilgrim seven mile walk, and next day visiting Nazareth, Tiberas, Hebron, and Galilee, Damaskus, and all those lovely biblical scenes, so dear to the heart of we of the Christian faith, of "Our Fathers" with the many bells ringing, calling us travellers to Church morning, noon and night, my what a happy life to live, in one's old days.

My, what a beautiful country the "Holy Lands, Jerusalem", I love you.

But, after all we of the Irish race don't own the world, although we have always done our bit, coming down through the ages from the days of the American Revolution, down to the last battle of the great world's war, always ready to die fighting for the protection of our beloved country.

But we must not forget that there is what is known as a Hebrew race, yes the Jewish race, who have been picking up and laying down, in every nation of the world, since time immemorial, and they do not own a country since, unless you might say America, and they are fast copping, dear old Columbia.

But like the Irish, they too have been fighting for a home and motherland, and when promised a National Home by an old English Faker at the time of the great World's War, when our allies were getting beaten right and left, then Balfour, was giving away everything for nothing to win this terrible war, but all that the old fool did was to kid the Jew along, and they are as far from a Jewish National Home in Jerusalem today as they were five hundred years ago, for the Arab won't permit such a building, and mark you, these Arabs are a great people, and must be reckoned with, at all times.

And from the writer's experience in the Holy Lands in 1927, I would know and have right along proposed that the Jews of Palestine, with their Arabian brothers and sisters, be left alone, leave them to themselves, and you will find that sooner or later everything will work its way rightly.

But if the American or English Jew is going to continue their drives, drives, and more drives, to continue agitating the minds of the Arabian, by sending this money, or maybe 10 per cent of it to beautify as they say, the Holy Lands, that the Arabs don't want, or either will they stand for, then they are themselves responsible and they alone, remember my words. I have many good friends who are of the Hebrew race, I have voted for them, so don't misunderstand me.

The trouble with the Jew is that he wants to claim everything worth while, and this in every country the world over, until the people get wise to them, and again they get their walking papers, and are told (scram) to get out.

You cannot blame them for that, if they can get away with it—we don't want any cursed Hitler or Ku Klux stuff here, so be yourselves.

This same thing is now cursing America, the four million Jews in America today, the two million in New York in particular, are grabbing off everything, yes, actually demanding positions as being theirs, simply because Tammany Hall gave them their first recognition, but our bum leaders are to blame for this.

If visiting the Holy Lands and you follow my advice you will save both time and money, and annoyances, that none of us want, hotel runners and other nuisances. The Port of Haifa, has been rebuilt, and one may first visit Jerusalem, and after seeing all there, find a party that is going to Haifa, but they won't leave unless they have a full car. You can have a car at any old time, night or day, and very reasonable at that.

This lovely visit will prolong one's life, far better than any doctor could try to prescribe, and if you feel sick and not up to the mark, just open up and have a good drink of brandy, very cheap and always handy, but do not go the way I went, I would advise you to go from Rome to Trieste, to Jaffa if possible, cut out the long ride to Alexander to Quantera and onto Jerusalem.

In London, Mr. Hickey called on his good friend Sir Thomas Lipton, and spent many happy days motoring around that beautiful country, full of history and romance, out on the Golf Links and evenings at Billiards.

What could one wish better than that sort of a life, and when it comes to yachting time, go and take a ride in *Shamrock, Metre* 23 or *Shamrock IV* and now *Shamrock V*. Why I was the happiest man in all Christendom, and next summer, God willing, I will return for the kind of pleasure we all love to enjoy, and that is the company of a dear good friend, for they are not many under this cockeyed spirit of modernism of 1928.

It was a pleasure to me to be sitting at the side of Sir Thomas Lipton every Sunday afternoon meeting the poor children coming home from Sunday school and giving each a box of candy and a pair of good warm gloves, and all the time this grand old charitable heart smiling to his heart's content, for he knew that he was doing the work of God.

Officer 787—Mr. Hickey's old number in the Police Department, held the amateur championship long distance running for thirteen years, and the beautiful gold medal worth $500, emblematic of the one-mile championship won three times and is now in the possession of and owned by John J. Hickey.

Whatever else he found on the borders of the seven seas, Mr. Hickey was happy that he would soon be returning to little old New York, for there was no other city either finer or happier today on God's foot stool.

Mr. Hickey, who had taken notice of all cities visited, was sure that the New York Police ranked the best and "Finest" in the whole world, and that the traffic system was the best and most scientific to be seen anywhere.

Dear friends and readers, that was line for line of the interview given, and I thank and appreciate the "Sun's" doing me the honor of such an interview, of which I am a reader for the past fifty years, and hope to remain so.

I thoroughly enjoyed seeing King George V, and Queen Mary, smiling, saluting and bowing to his people, the commoners, a sermon made me feel so happy for this wonderful change, for when I was a poor kid in London, just like the aristocratic American slobs of today, if they saw a crowd of poor people lining the sidewalks they would call a Cop to drive them away.

Not so today, for King George cannot get too close to his people for he loves them all, and they in turn love their King, long may he reign, and ever ready to attend to the wants of his people, and they in turn rally around their good King, and then there will not be any troubles or misunderstandings, not at all man, not at all, between the King and his people.

That is why I wrote King George, man to man, for I hold the highest of respect for King George V or any other good ruler that is ever ready to go among his poor subjects and help them, just as their sons are doing today, the Prince of Wales for instance, or the Duke and Duchess of York, one fond loving couple without any doldrums on them.

I have met them all for the past sixty long years, and when I first met the Duchess of York, I was so carried away with her beautiful smiles going out to all, attending a meeting at No. 10 Downing Street, June, 1928, I thought back to the time when others of like station, frowned on the people, and turned them away in dismay, my word, what a difference, thank Heaven.

And in conclusion let me say right here that I did not ask for the interview, or do I ever want another, of course it was very kind of the editor who sent her, I thank them both very much for it was darned good advertising for the Hickey Publishing Company, the cheapest that ever I got in all my time in this cockeyed world.

And about my letter to His Majesty, King George V of England, I have no apologies to offer, or to make, for I would do the same thing tomorrow under like circumstances, and I am sure it gave the King a laugh, even though he was mighty sick to think of an American coming three thousand miles to advise and console him in sickness, good night. Laugh and grow fat.

Be that as it may, it is a well known fact that His Imperial Majesty, King George of England did not go to the Riviera to recuperate, but was more than pleased to stay right in his own Dominions and today after his successful season of yachting, is back into his old form, fit and well.

I hold these letters and the copy of my work of "Our Police Guardians" that I sent to the King, among my most dearest possessions, and for the few short years that I expect to be with you, will always respect and admire them, but I fear that after I am gone, they will like myself, be forgotten, but who cares?

And in conclusion, I again wish to thank the editor of the "Sun", for having ordered this good lady to call for this interview, but would like Miss Watt, or any other person, to inform me of their coming, so that I will be prepared for them, and avoid all bungling and confusing of my remarks.

That was a very fine long article for an interview, to say the least and if you have ever had a woman call on you unknowingly, to interview you, then you know just what you are up against.

With much other matter on your mind and a short time to do your talking, one finds it very hard to concentrate his thoughts, and woman-like, it was garbled some, and this fair young lady's meal ticket was secure, for that day at least. And about my warning King George V against the Riveria, I just looked upon that as a part of my duty, for we are both married men, and I should not forget that I was at one time one of his subjects Great Britain and Ireland prior to 1921.

IN CONCLUSION, DEAR READERS JUST A WORD ABOUT THE HOLY CITY, OF FOND AND LOVING MEMORY, ONE CITY ABOVE ALL OTHERS THAT ONE WOULD NOT THINK WAS CURSED WITH GRAFTERS AND RACK-ETEERS, HEAVEN BE PRAISED, BUT IT IS.

"Jerusalem" my happy home, how do I sigh for you, yes Jerusalem, I love you and my one object in life is to return in Casa Nova, a modest priced hotel, for all denominations, with wine at every meal, and something that cannot be beat, go where you will.

I sailed from Brindisi, Italy, to Greece, Constantinople, and along up to Haifa, and after seeing all there was to be seen there, I motored to Nazareth, and having seen all of the good things of God, I motored into the Holy City at midnight, 150 miles from Haifa, my fellow passengers, all Arabs, numbering seven and the driver a fast going young Arab.

Yes, his top speed was from 85 to 90 miles per hour, on a beautiful road, built by England in the late war, and this along the ledge of a deep mountainside at a depth of 1,000 feet, my thoughts were at what part of this mountain were they going to drop me over, but I found that I was for once in my life riding in good honest company, Arab or no Arab, I found them O.K. and I have met many savages in my days, for they all come to New York sooner or later, the grafters haven, and racketeers playground.

But these can be found in every city, and God help you if you are foolish enough to blunder and get into their hands, my first experience of that character was when I, being sent to the Italian State Railroads' office, No. 4, Septere Street, and asked them to draw me up an itinerary of travel as I should have to go in my long passage to Bombay, and all way stations, they asked for twice as much as did the Lloyd Trestino Steamship and Railroad Company, and because I did not pay them what they asked, they cut off my stopovers, and I was placed under arrest in Rome.

A word to the wise—buy all travelling tickets through the American Express Company or the Cooks Agency, and stay away from these red headed damn thieves, for if I ever run across the red headed rat that tried to rob me in New York, I will throw him over the Battery sea wall. I would know him out of a million, for rascals of that character disgraces the humane work of Premier Signor Benito Mussolini, and his good government party.

A word to the wise, just carry with you only what you need, one suitcase, so that you can carry it yourself and to the devil with these thieving red caps or blue caps, they are all from the one school of grafters, so have nothing whatever to do with them, or you too will have reasons to be sorry.

God willing, I hope to go over all of that ground again, cutting out the spots that are not fair to a stranger, and my past experience will save me a lot of money, for instead of my traveling to Brindisi, twelve solid hours on an empty stomach, for the business people are darned lazy, and to catch an early train you have to leave without a cup of coffee.

The cutting off of my stopovers made it hard on me, for I would delight to stop a week or two in Rome, four or five days in Naples, and then entrain for Brindisi, to board the *S. S. Cleopatra,* a lovely trip up through the Dardanelles to Constantinople, they made it so that I would have to stay four days in Brindisi, putting up at a first class hotel, paying out my little money, when I could have left Naples the night before the arrival of the *Cleopatra* and take a cab from the railway depot to the steamer, I would then be saving much and could have seen more of beautiful Naples.

So beware, you wouldbe travelers, "for he that will not profit by his own past experience, turns his best schoolmaster out of doors," and one may try anything once, as Steve Brodie did when he jumped the Brooklyn Bridge.

And now that the bugle is blowing, all lights out go to bed, I will say good night, but remember what I've said, and you will be happy, Cheerio.

THE MEETING OF COUNT GEORGE MacDONALD, AT THE DINNER OF THE N. Y. Y. C., TENDERED TO SIR THOMAS J. LIPTON, OCTOBER, 1929, AND THE STORY TOLD

PART III—CHAPTER IV

The story in question was told to Sir Thomas, by Count MacDonald, and told the writer by Sir Thomas, that same night, and often afterwards, and I am sure will please my readers very much, at least I hope it will.

One of the happiest nights that Sir Thomas ever spent in America, was the night of the dinner tendered to the grand old sportsman, by the members of the New York Yacht Club, in October, 1929, on one of his semi-yearly visits, and he being one of the five Honorary members, made so by that great yachtsman and world's banker, the late Pierpont Morgan, of the house of Morgan, yes the pioneer of the Morgan family, who thought so much of Tom Lipton.

This dinner turned out to be one of the greatest ever given in this grand old city of ours for it represented the cream of New York Society, there being representatives from most every trade and calling, bankers and brokers, and leaders in politics and athletics, and lovers of yachting and boxing, a gathering that would lighten the heart of every true blue sport.

There were many sons and grandsons of the famous old yachtsmen of the past, among them the Hon. Morgan J. O'Brien, and J. Pierpont Morgan, and many others too numerous to mention, at this time, but a jolly old crowd that it would be mighty hard to get together again, for grim death has taken a few of them, and our former Mayor James J. Walker, now in exile, who at the time was the most talked of man in America, barring Tom Lipton, but Lipton has gone west, and Walker is living in the South, oh yes, the South of France, among the frog eaters, no no, not the South of America, among the rats of Ku Kluxers, and by the way, Jimmy is now a reporter at the conference on the economists of the world, an American lesson on economy.

I often think what a big man Jimmy Walker would be today, had he have stayed on his job, and attended to the wants of his people by cutting out these jaunts around the world, first to Germany and again making himself very conspicuous by his visit to the Golden Gate, there to tell Governor Rolph, of California, how to run his government, and order the freedom of one of his subjects that was tried and found guilty of having thrown a bomb in among his fellow citizens, on parade, killing many.

And all of this time, Mayor Walker, was blind to the fact that former Judge Seabury was out to get him and put him out of his job, Waurra, Waurra.

If he had studied economy, by attending to his business and leaving the wisemen and get-rich-quick fellows, off his staff and out of his mind, but alas, Sam Seabury, wanted his pound of flesh, and he followed James J. by night and by day, until he found that he had the goods on Mr. Walker, and forced his resignation, but that alone won't carry Judge Seabury to Heaven or glory?

When the dinner was over and the cigars handed around, the speechmaking commenced, and the ball set rolling for a glorious night, and this is how it started, President Kennelly, presented Sir Thomas with a plaque, and made a few appropriate remarks, then sat down calling on Sir Thomas to make his bow, and we all knew just how he started, and finished, a man of a few words, full of interesting meaning, and he sat down among the plaudits of all present, after thanking them all for the honor bestowed, he told them that he was preparing to have another try at the America's Cup, and he was going to try mighty hard to win her this time, I thank you Gentlemen, No, No, not for the Cup, but for the honor of being permitted to address you all.

And by the way, that is the only thing that Sir Thomas ever asked our American people for the Cup, but those world renowned yachtsmen both old and young, would say, nay, nay, Sir Thomas, we love that old Mug too well to give her away, and if you must get her, then you will have to fight.

Oh yes, the grand old Veteran fought and fought hard, but just as he was fighting hard to win, there were others fighting just as hard to defeat that grand old Irish Baronet and his pretty little Shamrocks, 1, 2-3-4-and-5, and if we could but get a line to Heaven, I would bet the Empire State Building against the Chicago Fair, that Sir Thomas was working on his plans for building a Shamrock VI, and still go sailing on.

I can't help repeating but it was a glorious night, with over twelve hundred persons sitting down to dinner, among them John Curry, Leader of Tammany Hall, and a maker of Judges over night, and of course our wisecracking clothing model of a Mayor, the Hon. James J. Walker was sitting beside his Chief, no doubt thinking to himself, "Who's Looney Now" or will you love me in December as you used to love me in May, of whom was he speaking?

General Herman A. Metz, Big Jim Farley, and Gene Tunney were swapping many funny stories, with Judge O'Brien, Commodore Taylor and other game old Liptonians of New York City, sportsmen all. Oh, boy, sports and yachting magnates, Harold Vanderbilt and his party singing "Hail Columbia" and it turned out afterwards that Miss Columbia heard his prayer, and saw to it that he won the America's Cup, and therefore became America's champion and, the people's idol.

But there was one man at that dinner that Sir Thomas got mighty interested in, and that was George MacDonald, a former special Deputy Police Commissioner under the Enright Administration, and a Count of the Papal See.

Sir Thomas took a great liking to Count George, and the remarkable thing he was doing, or about to do, for he, Sir Thomas, was amazed to hear the big Count's story, and he kept it foremost in mind until he arrived home to the Biltmore Hotel, and meeting me there I had to go up to his room until he told me the story.

Sir Thomas said Mr. Hickey, "I met a man at the dinner whom I did not know, and he told me that he was paying $125,000 a month for four months for a steam yacht, to take himself and his distinguished party, for a long trip."

But while Sir Thomas did not know Count George MacDonald, I did, and I knew all about the story, several weeks ahead, but I was not in a position to tell my story at that time, and we postponed same for another meeting, but poor old Tom Lipton, could not get that story of rash spending out of his head, until he again meets his old friend Hickey.

We met again about a week later and when I told Sir Thomas the story as it was told to me by a prominent official in the knowing, he gasped to think of it, to wit—That Commissioner Count MacDonald, like himself was a self made man, very charitable to both Church and State, and a devout Catholic, and very much thought of among the high officials of the Church, both in America and Rome, Italy, visiting the Vatican yearly to pay his respects to his Holiness Pope Pius XI, who for his charity and devoutness, honored Mr. MacDonald, by bestowing on him the title of "Count George MacDonald," an office that is so highly prized by the faithful.

I also stated to Sir Thomas, that Count MacDonald, was a Special Deputy Police Commissioner of New York in the Enright Administration, of which he himself held the proud position of Honorary Chief of Police, but they never met, for in war time, each of these good men who had loaned their names to our then Commissioner of Police, Richard E. Enright, and were assigned to some quarter of the city by both night, and day, and all for a dollar a year.

We, the members of the Catholic Church of New York were proud of our fine specimen of a Catholic Big Brother, who by dint of good judgment and sagacity during the World's War, raised himself from a poor young fellow, to be honored and respected by all who have had the good fortune of knowing, this great big good hearted God-loving follower of Jesus Christ, who always takes care of those that takes care of himself, or at least makes an attempt, to live the life of a good Catholic Big Brother.

It may not be out of place to state that the title of "Count" of the Papal Household, has been bestowed on a very few Americans to date, only such men as our former Jurists who proved themselves before the world of their love of Church and Country, have been recognized by the Holy Father.

Men of the type of the Hon. Victor J. Dowling, Morgan J. O'Brien, Daniel F. Cohalan, and the Hon. Alfred E. Talley, and last but not the least Count George MacDonald, all of these gentlemen of fond and loving memory, I am proud to say are friends of the Author of this work.

But going back to yachting, we must remember that the preparing of the yachts, for racing is no joke, but hard work and little rest, for the owners, designers and the members of the racing committee, are constantly on the go, for there are so many things to attend to, always. This includes both countries, America and England, each of them trying to put one over on the other, but in a friendly strain, and somehow or other, they manage to greet each other with a well known Hello, how are you, goodbye, friendly enemies, that's all, and this because Tom Lipton wants the America's Cup, and the members of the New York Yacht Club, and their champion say "no, no, Sir Thomas, we love you and respect you to the highest, but don't ask for, nor will you ever get that old mug back, we have had it too long, and we would be lost without it, and when we look back to the yachting days of 1851, and our dear old American champion, of that day, the *America,* we look at that cup and say, 'Thou shall not pass'."

THE STORY OF WHAT COUNT GEORGE MacDONALD TOLD SIR THOMAS

Sir Thomas, I have a business and pleasure trip, and about to charter one of the finest American steam yachts afloat, at a cost of $125,000 per month for four months, and we will thoroughly enjoy every minute of our time sailing through the beautiful Mediterranean Sea, accomplishing all that we are desiring of accomplishing. I perchance may be repeating in this and other stories and episodes, but I want my readers to know, if possible.

What is money to men that have millions like these two men that I now speak of, and write about, well not so much, and it would be better for the world if there were more war millionaires and others that would open up their bank accounts and give business something to do, by the employment of man power to fill the contracts given, by these unselfish men.

Yes, pleasure and business sometimes comes high, but what's the difference, when one accomplishes all that he goes after, and that is what Count George MacDonald, has done, at least I hope so, for Count MacDonald, ran into another son of little old New York in Naples, none other than His Eminence Patrick Cardinal Hayes, of this great big city, and State, of New York.

What better company would one want to ask for when on a particular business trip? for what the one could not put over, the other one could and did, I feel sure, for either one of these two great men never failed.

However, you just take my tip, watch the papers and you will then read of the immense success of Count George MacDonald, in his voyage through the Mediterranean Sea, Naples, Florence, and all the other many beautiful scenes that one meets with out that way, that I the writer enjoyed so much in 1927-1928, with last but not least an audience with His Holiness the Pope, Pius XIth, of Holy and fond loving memory, sitting quietly in the chair of St. Peter, is now what is known as the Vatican Free State surrounded by his many faithful followers, and Princes of the Church, dear friends, that one blessed little episode alone is worth all the big outlay, and money was well spent, and if it was not, then it is none of your business, or mine, for a "faint heart, never won a fair lady." And after my reception by His Holiness, I called on Signor Mussolini, Oh boy!

And in conclusion, let us take off our hats to those two great noblemen, a credit to any country, and the people thereof, namely Count George MacDonald, and Sir Thomas Lipton, the uncrowned king of Irish sportsmanship, and one that never weakens, loved and respected by all good peoples the world over, and that means much coming as it does, so let us rejoice.

Following the big dinner at the New York A. C., Sir Thomas bade goodbye to New York to make his usual yearly visit to Canada, to look his factories over and to check up, thinking to get a much needed rest, but that was not to be, for Sir Thomas was kept jumping all around while there.

He was met at the railway depot by Government officials and invited to a dinner in his honor the next evening, and it was one dinner after another, the short time that Sir Thomas stayed in Canada, making the same very confident speeches of his expected good luck in winning the blooming mug in September, 1930, for he has great hopes in his new yacht to be named *Shamrock V,* for again he believes with Brian O' Linn, that there is luck in odd numbers, this being his fifth time trying to win the cup.

If all is well at home, Sir Thomas will return to New York about October 23rd, and shortly after, sail for Golden West, for he loves the beautiful sunshine of Southern California, and his many friends in Hollywood and all over the country, and after a brief stay in the

Golden West, he will visit San Francisco, and all towns on his way back to Chicago, in all of these cities to look his factories over and to check up on the past years business, for Sir Thomas mixes business with pleasure, and is very well satisfied to get back to Osidge, his country home outside of London, a little before Christmas, to feed the poor families every year.

And sure enough, if he did not visit Mayor Bill Thompson of Chicago yearly, King George V would sure lose his throne and Sir Thomas would be held responsible, and while there, he sure will meet his friend the former heavyweight champion, Jack Dempsey, now turned fight promoter and in his new profession is also very successful, for you can't keep a good man down, and that goes for all good men in every line of endeavor.

But the next year will not be long passing and P. P. Providence permitting we are all spared to visit Newport while the next yacht races for the America's Cup is taking place, we may all be surprised at what may happen for no one can tell, and confidence means an awful lot in any contest so that we must all of us be prepared for the best or worst of it.

Sir Thomas, never tired in speaking of that happy episode, I may repeat one of the happiest evenings spent by Sir Thomas, was at the dinner given in honor of this great yachtsman, by the way, one of their five living honorary members by the New York Yacht Club, in October, 1929.

Sir Thomas never tired speaking of this and the other receptions tendered to him by former Police Commissioner, Richard E. Enright, in 1923, and that given by Police Commissioner Grover A. Whalen, and his staff in 1930.

But an episode presented itself at the dinner that Sir Thomas, never forgot, and in our few moments together both in New York and London, the grand old Chief would love to speak of, for what he learned that evening amazed him, for he was told a very remarkable story, if what he thought was the height of extravagance, to say the least.

I, in my humble way will do my best to tell the story as told to me by that grand old happy warrior, who never once thought of his own extravagance, for he always looked upon that as a charitable act, for every dollar spent by him, brought joy and happiness in many American and British homes.

Sir Thomas J. Lipton, Dean of the yachting world, known the world over as a true blue humanitarian, spending his millions either in charity or the building of yachts, known as *Shamrocks I, II, III, IV* and *V*, for he was forever trying to win the America's Cup, but in this, the poor man failed.

And without fear of contradiction, this grand old Irish Baronet, has spent nigh ten millions of dollars, to accomplish that end, and in so doing looked upon his extravagance as a charity, offering up same as penance, a happy and a wholesome thought, that he was admired for, by his many friends.

It made no difference either in victory or defeat, he would be seen with that beautiful Irish smile and Scotch brogue, always happy and contented, for what was money to him, and he would sail away by saying, "Goodbye folks, I will return again some day, and take that old Mug along with me, I hope."

Others build and sail yachts, and many borrow yachts, than why not Sir Thomas spend his money as he sees fit? That is none of our business, but by all that is good and pious, when told the story in question, the poor old fellow could not get over his amazement, Sir Thomas not knowing at the time, the Hon. Count, George MacDonald, of the Papal Household of Rome, Italy.

These two good men had previously been members of the Enright staff but had never met, their hours of duty being so different, and old age, kept Sir Thomas from remembering faces, that he was always noted for in younger days, but he was delighted to meet the Count that evening, yes a pleasure.

THE DEED OF GIFT OF JULY 8th, 1857

THE HISTORY OF SAME

PART III—CHAPTER V

The syndicate represented by Mr. Schuyler, were a body of grand old New York yachtsmen of that day, the men that made yachting what it is today, just as George W. Matsell, at that same time made the New York Police Department what it is today. By his laying of a solid foundation.

This grand old body of men were all members of the New York Yacht Club and it was their intention to make the N. Y. Y. C. the trustees of the cup, but for the time being only.

So along about July 8th, 1857 a letter received turning over the cup that was known to all at that time as the "Queen's Cup", this letter containing certain conditions, a list of questions and answers that are offered to all trustees under the circumstances, and the deal was closed.

But strange to say, that on the letter of July 8th, 1857, offering the cup, the name of Commodore Stephens, who had just passed away, and who was always at the head of the list, was absent, and the name of two other men was substituted, supposedly to represent the grand old Commodore.

And another noticeable thing about this letter and its signatures, and that is, that the name of Col. Alexander Hamilton, a part owner, whose signature was not attached to the letter at all, Why? The Colonel was then in the flesh, and should not have been ignored, this should be explained by someone in authority, sooner or later.

Another former owner whose name was not on the letter of presentation of the cup to the N. Y. Y. C. was that of Hamilton Wilkes, he had died in France some five years before, but there surely must have been some relatives of this patriotic good citizen living somewhere in America.

And that is as much as I can now remember or write about the "Queen's Cup," that 100-guinea cup that was presented by the Royal Yacht Squadron of England in 1851, and so goes the story of that valuable cup of silver, with an opening on both ends, that we must all take a peep at if on public exhibition, as per promise during the coming races.

After this wonderful trophy had been received by the members of the New York Yacht Club, they met from time to time to amend the conditions on which it was entrusted to the members of the N. Y. Y. C. as trustees and they still keep on amending these same conditions, building a stone wall around it with their new amendments from time to time, yes, ever since 1882, have these same trustees been breaking faith by amending the sportsman-like conditions of George Schuyler, and what is now known as his deed of gift, but not his, but theirs, and the world knows that.

And let me inform you of the fact, that when the yachting public really understood all about this amending of the conditions in 1882, and 1887, they were not at all pleased, for many of our own people placed all sorts of constructions on the provisions of these deeds of gift, and one of the most visionary being that of Mr. Thomas Lawson, the Copper King, who in 1901 declared that the America's Cup belonged to the American people, meaning those in the little old U. S. A. and that any American citizen had a right to defend it.

And that has been the author's contention for the past fifty years, yes, of course we must stand by these parts of the conditions, relating to that part of them that says but one American yacht shall be chosen to defend.

But it will not be any surprise to me if it is all over but the shouting right now, the America's Cup will soon be finding a new home and then perhaps a new deed of gift, or perhaps not, but whatever the finish may be the deed of gift that has been fluttered to the breeze for nearly fifty years, will be like Kaiser Wilhelm's word and treaties, simply a scrap of paper that one may light his pipe with.

And should it come to pass that the cup is doomed to stay here longer then perhaps these good gentlemen forming the Board of Trustees, then we may deem it fit and proper to call a meeting of the whole and amend the present conditions so as to live, and let live, by giving our challengers a better run for their money, and not be so arbitrary, don't be amending the rules just when you think that it will be so much easier for our yachts, and so much harder for the other fellow, let us play the game fair and on the square, even if we never get the cup back again, we must not forget that we are Americans, with the one flag, and freedom to all, for ever, and ever.

There is much that I could add here, but for the present that is not to be, for I am trying to give you a little information on all of these interesting stories of past history, but would love to present full stories.

It may yet come to pass that this very valuable cup will again be put away and almost forgotten about, but I for one believe that it should be kept intact and preserved, for its old time history.

Do you know that at one time it was thought that the cup should be cut into many pieces so that it could be distributed among the living relatives of its former owners, in the shape of medals enclosed in silk.

But long before that, the Stephens brothers, that was Commodore John C. and Edwin A. Stephens, of the famous Stephens battery in Hoboken, the men that built the *Merrimac* to fight and defeat the *Monitor* during the great American Civil War, to destroy the Blockade, and Col. James A. Hamilton, son of the great Alexander Hamilton, who was killed in a duel by Aaron Burr, the very man that financed the project or syndicate that built the *America,* met in the Stephen's home.

The Queen's or America's Cup was housed at that time in the Stephens' mansion, and the conversation arose as to what should be done with the cup, and one suggestion was that it be hammered into medals, each to be enclosed in silver-lined boxes and distributed among its six owners of the *America.*

They had already each received a substantial dividend on their original investment, and be it remembered that this pretty yacht, *America,* produced by Mr. Steers, was the only cup race yacht that ever did produce, or showed a profit. But *America* was far different to all other yachts, for the great work that she had done, in sailing over the ocean and swiftly out-sailing of fourteen yachts of England's famous production, she was worth her weight in gold. But the different suggestions put forth at that meeting bore no fruit, and so the matter rested until 1857, when it was discovered that a George L. Schuyler, had called upon George Steers, and offered to him quite a sum of money for the exchange of *America.*

And after many meetings and consultations, the offer of Mr. Schuyler was accepted, and at a bargain day price for George Schuyler, saved the syndicate that he represented over $10,000, not so bad for one day's work?

For many years Sir Thomas Lipton had been appealing to the official committee of the New York Yacht Club to modify their rulings in the deed of gift. But nothing was ever done about this, until after the series of races in 1920, it was found to be absolutely necessary or else Sir Thomas would be compelled to withdraw his challenge.

Sir Thomas then took a long lay-off, hoping that some other man, syndicate or nation would issue a challenge for the America's Cup, but nothing was done about a new challenge, because all the world knew how heavily Sir Thomas Lipton and his *Shamrocks* were handicapped.

And after waiting ten years or more, and not wanting to let the grand old sport die out, Sir Thomas forwarded another letter and it being written in plain English, stating to that honorable body, his many reasons for asking for these changes and all that he was asking was a square deal.

This request brought some good results to wit:—The good men of the racing committee of the N. Y. Y. C. met and concluded that

THE LATE JOHN E. REDMOND, ESQ.
IRELAND'S FAMOUS LEADER

AUGHAVANAGH,
AUGHRIM,
CO. WICKLOW.

Private.

January 6th, 1915.

Dear Mr. Hickey,-

       I am much obliged for your letter of the
22nd December, which reached me in due course, and which I have
read with great interest.   In Ireland, the people are united
almost as one man in support of the Irish Party and its attitude
in regard to the war, and I have felt all along that the Party
could count upon the continued and unwavering support of the
overwhelming majority of the Irish in America.   Your letter is
most encouraging, and I am delighted to know that you are
taking an active part in counteracting the machinations of
the enemies of Ireland in the United States.

       With best regards, Believe me,

                        Very truly yours,

                        J R Redmond

Hon. John J. Hickey, ——

SIR THOMAS LIPTON
in Hollywood on His Yearly Visits

DEPUTY CHIEF INSPECTOR
MATHEW J. McGRATH
World's Champion

JOHN J. HICKEY, *Past Regent*
Chairman of Games Committee

something must be done, for they all admired Sir Thomas Lipton, they admired him as a clean, honest sportsman, and a man among men, the result.

This great sport loving body of America's noblest sons, none of them living today, peace be to them all, decided that in the event of a new challenge being issued, Sir Thomas Lipton would be within his rights to have his sloop towed by her convoy in the time of danger, by storms, or high seas.

And on January 11th, 1927, Sir Thomas requested the officials of the Royal Ulster Yacht Club to issue another challenge, same to be forwarded to the New York Yacht Club forthwith, again stating his former request for the changes most desirable, that is to assist in protecting the officers and crew when on the high seas. This challenge was received and acted on by the officials, and it was agreed to permit *Shamrock* being towed in the event of storm, and *Shamrock V* was being towed a part of the way.

We are all aware of the dangers to a frail little skimming dish like *Shamrock V* in being towed in the storms of the ocean, for the danger of her being strained, and maybe spring a leak, for we often hear of the Queen of ocean travel the good old *S. S. Leviathan* has had sorrowful experience for Father Neptune, holds no briefs for age or beauty, and the *Mauretania,* once the Queen of ocean travel, had to take the long count, and she too was forced out of commission, and while still afloat, she will never be the old reliable ocean beauty that she was, and the *Leviathan* has gone to keep her company, for misery likes company, that is if one is a real man, or woman, and not one that grunts and snarls at his betters, you understand?

So for God's sake, be men, and think of these great cardinal principles of "Virtue, Mercy and Charity," all for one and one for all.

Give good old Tom Lipton a better break, for he deserves a better deal today, we all know this grand old Irish Baronet, but when he is gone and yachting stays alive we will have to deal with strangers.

And here is where the question of Mercy presents itself, and the grand old sportsmen of the world are hoping that something will be done, and done mighty soon, if our great racing officials of whom all America is, and always will be proud, must show mercy to their fellow men.

It must be remembered that a racing sloop is not built to be dragged through the seas, but is built to speed through them, and not pulled through them and avoid all dangers of being strained.

The yachting world, for several years has been looking forward to a change in design of our future cup racers, our experts in particular have been working very hard to bring this about.

We want real racing craft, even if we have to go back to the schooner design, again making it safer and saner than racing these skeletonized towering sloops, built and sent here to race our fastest, and best, but often after, not worth a damn in European competition.

But that great American boast of fair play never seemed to enter here. Year after year Sir Thomas Lipton has been protesting against certain clauses in the moth-eaten old deed of gift, but these protests have always been presented in a friendly way, far be it from Tom Lipton, that he would lower himself and lose his thousands of good American friends, no, no, it took many years to make them, and whatever may be the result by the eternal light of Heaven, he is not going to lose them, cup or no cup.

And in conclusion, on behalf of my many readers, I most respectfully petition these eminent gentlemen that comprise the makeup of the New York Yacht Club racing committee, to get together and devise some Godly means to bring about better results for all future racing, we surely are not afraid of Tom Lipton and his pretty sloops, are we? Then be fair, gentlemen, for while we have a Tom Lipton with us today, we don't know the moment he is called away.

"Mr. J. J. Hickey,   "OSIDGE, SOUTHGATE, LONDON,
"St. Denis Hotel,   "March, 1928.
"Westminster, London, S.W.I.
"Dear Mr. Hickey,

"I hope this will find you well, sorry I have not seen you since you arrived from France, but hope to soon, you must come out to Osidge again, say tomorrow, for lunch, as I missed you on your last visits, but under no conditions, leave London until we meet.

"Trusting to find you well and enjoying London O.K., with all best wishes I beg to remain,

"Yours faithfully,

"JOHN WESTWOOD."

"OSIDGE, SOUTHGATE,
"MIDDLESEX, LONDON,
"March 27th, 1930.

"Mr. J. J. Hickey,
"Hotel Elton, 4th Ave.,
"New York City.
"Dear Mr. Hickey,

"Again I write you to say that on behalf of Sir Thomas and myself, I thank you most kindly, for every letter that you mail brings to us sweet tidings of good cheer.

"What you say in the letter just received, your American yachts are also making good headway, and that is charming news to Sir Thomas, for he wants to tackle the best that the little old U. S. A. can produce, so if defeated, *Shamrock V* will not be disgraced.

"To quote the words of Sir Thomas to wit, 'What, if we are defeated another defeat won't drive me out of the field, for there is no disgrace after I and *Shamrock V*, do all we can to win, for I spend my money, and my Shamrocks spend their speed giving all that is into her.'

"I hope that this will find you well, and back into your good old fighting form, and if you have any doubts about it, go put the gloves on with your big Italian slugging friend, Carnera.

"With all best wishes, kindest regards and many thanks.

"Yours faithfully,

"JOHN WESTWOOD."

"OSIDGE, SOUTHGATE,
"MIDDLESEX, LONDON,
"May 2nd, 1930.

"Mr. J. J. Hickey,
"Hotel Elton, 4th Ave.,
"New York City.
"Dear Mr. Hickey,

"Since writing you last, I have had an opportunity of looking through your typewritten manuscript and have greatly enjoyed its perusal.

'You certainly have a wonderful gift of expression and I am greatly obliged to you for giving me the privilege of reading over your manuscript, and I look upon it as a great favor.

"I am returning it to you herewith, as I should not like it to get into the wrong hands, or go astray.

"With kind regards and best wishes.

"Yours faithfully,

"JOHN WESTWOOD."

THIS IS GOOD NEWS, BUT (TOO LATE) ALAS—TOO LATE

Part IV—Chapter I

New York City, February 1, 1930.—The following statement was given out for publication to wit:—At a special meeting of the members of the New York Yacht Club held last week, the new racing rules were adopted.

They are of particular interest and importance in that the right-of-way rules contained in them are identical with the right-of-way rules adopted by the International Yacht Racing Union at its conference held in London, England, last November and attended by representatives of the New York Yacht Club and the North American Yacht Racing Union.

There are but few differences between the remaining rules adopted and those formerly in force in the New York Yacht Club, the chief ones being: (1) A new rule which requires yachts, after their starting signal has been made, to sail a course consistent with the intention of crossing the line. (2) A fuller and clearer statement of the so-called "bearing away rule" under which a yacht may not, where overtaking conditions exist bear away from her proper course to the mark to prevent another yacht from passing her to leeward. (3) A change in the rule in regard to the right of a yacht on a new tack, under which change she will not acquire her rights on such new tack until she has gathered full way thereon.

It is reported that the work on the quartet of America's Cup defense yachts at the Layley yard at Neponset, Mass., and the Harreshoff yard at Bristol, R. I., is progressing satisfactorily and all four are expected to be in readiness for tuning up before the first of the scheduled trial or elimination contests. While the professional sailing masters have been selected for all four syndicates, still there remains considerable doubt as to what Corinthians will be at the wheels of the big single-stickers.

J. Christiansen will be the pro aboard the Crane, designed by Morgan-Nichols syndicate sloop *Weetamo;* Gus Olsen aboard the Paine, designed by Boston syndicate sloop *Yankee;* John Muir aboard the Herreshoff, designed by Thorne-Hammond-Paine syndicate sloop *Whirlwind* and George H. Monsell aboard the Burgess, designed by Vanderbilt syndicate sloop *Enterprise.*

This part of my work, dear people, opens up on the beautiful morning of April 1st, 1930, and after a not very pleasant winter, the birds are singing and the people all gay, looking forward with pleasure to the coming yacht racing days.

Oh, for the good old summer-time, for there is nothing in the world to be compared with it, when one may go down to the sea in boats, strip off and take a good refreshing bath, and be prepared to sail his or her boat, and her or their admirers sitting on top of the world looking on, my word!

We are awaiting the launching of both *Enterprise* and *Shamrock V*, April 14th, followed with our other three American yachts from which we hope to have chosen a suitable American defender, to sail against Sir Thomas Lipton's *Shamrock V*, for the glory of winning or losing the America's Cup.

And now, with our four beautiful yachts successfully launched we have the great pleasure of travelling to the seashore and sit and watch them in the jockeying or sailing for their tryouts, prior to the arrival of the real races of elimination.

But much is to be said and done before the racing committee so ably chosen to pick a defender, is able so to do, for we first of all have to depend on the moods of old Father Neptune, and the kind of weather that he at his pleasure wishes to hand out, we are at his **mercy.**

What a pleasure it is to see these two famous yachts; *Resolute* and her old pal *Vanitie,* sailing the ocean blue, as they did away back in the Spring of 1914, when built to be chosen America's defender against *Shamrock IV,* that Sir Thomas Lipton was so proud of, and well, he might be, for *Shamrock IV* was the first and only challenger that had won two races, or two legs on the American side, and by so doing, prolong the life of Sir Thomas and the boys of the crew and their bonus, but alas, it was in the bag to lose the famous cup, thereby starting the grand old Chief on the tobogganing slide from which he never recovered.   Don't you think so, readers?   Well, let us ask Skipper Burton, he may make a confession of fate, or maybe faith, that's all.

However, he should at least have sailed his boat, under the circumstances, for there was everything to be won and nothing to be lost on that sad and sorrowful day in July, 1920, that we, the onlookers will never forget.

We must learn more about our two famous defenders or wouldbe defenders, for our own country and her glory comes first, at all times, we hope that our glorious country will always be in the right, but my country, right or wrong, is and always will be the principle of all true blue-blooded Americans.

In the tryouts of *Resolute* and *Vanitie,* the writer like many others were of the opinion that *Vanitie* was the best yacht, and should have been chosen the defender, and while stopping on the *Erin* as the guest of Sir Thomas, I remarked to Sir Thomas at the luncheon table that to my mind *Vanitie* was the best yacht, but she was not chosen and why? Many of my readers may know, and many others might like to know, but the writer is not at liberty to tell tales out of school, and I am not going to try.

Resolute was chosen, and lost the first two races, and might have lost the third if the man or men responsible had done their duty, and that was to sail the third day of these series of five races, but three out of five to win the Cup, yes we know that it was a very stormy day, but when you sit down and think of the thousands of pretty ladies and their escorts who sailed out to see this race that was to be, and old sea dog like the skipper of *Shamrock IV,* should have sailed his sea dog, but he laid down on his boss, Sir Thomas Lipton, thereby causing him both the loss of the America's Cup, and the much worry and expense that followed.

From a cable just received, April 2, 1930, I was pleased to read that King George V is thinking seriously of taking a week's vacation, to be present at the tryouts between *Britannia* and *Shamrock V* at the end of May next, at Cowes Isle of Wight.

The King's health has so improved that it will be a pleasure to have His Majesty join the crew of the *Britannia* in his special races against *Shamrock V,* Sir Thomas Lipton and his crew.

It will be a pleasure to have King George, who is so fond of yachting and a lover of the sea, and known for many years as the "Sailor King" who has improved in health, and will enjoy these contests.

It is mighty hard to describe the building of *Shamrock V* and all of its preparations and design that Mr. Charles E. Nicholson has spent so much time to perfect and prove successful in her coming races.

The very flat sheer of only six inches induced by the rating rule gives *Shamrock V* an unusually straight deck, relieved by a foot rail, which is mighty low, and her after guard and friends must watch their step, for the yachts of today utilize every inch of space.

Speaking about King George V and his beautiful yacht *Britannia,* they made good by mixing up with *Shamrock V* in her tryouts, and for the King's kindness, darn me, if *Shamrock V* didn't run away from her beating *Britannia* badly, that first time out.

That looks very much as though *Shamrock V* was a member of Eamon DeValera's Irish Republican Party—shame on you *Shamrock,* you bit the hand of him that was looking to be your friend, you poor gossoon.

But, King George did not let *Miss Shamrock* get away with that beating very long, for the next day the *Britannia* beat *Shamrock* and all others of the five or seven racing machines contesting, and sure, who could blame His Imperial Majesty for beating them, for they would all take great delight in beating her, the King's beautiful 30 year old yacht.

But outside of the *Shamrock Metre 23,* the King and his *Britannia* can fly away from them all, and having made out mighty well, the King returned to his palace feeling mighty happy, forgetting his illness.

Over in Gosport, England, the work of making *Shamrock V* a winner by Duncan Neill and his boys are hustling to beat the band, and you can rest assured that when the whistle blows, *Shamrock V* will be ready to take her place on the firing line off Newport, September 13th, 1930, God willing.

Don't, for a moment think that all is sunshine for the men responsible for the rigging and preparation of these racing yachts, they have a lot to contend with, and one can find them studying up the weak spots of their charges while the world is sleeping. One don't know just what these good men have to do and think of doing, an idea may strike them when trying to snatch a few winks, and right away they are up at the bench and making notes of this or that idea or maybe a suggestion, this is when the racing is in the infancy and then they have to prepare for the races of elimination.

Here we are, April 6th, 1930, quite some time before any of our new yachts are launched, and we find this committee busy working on the matter of preparing our yachts for the races of elimination, so that the two that are to race together will be as near equal as possible, and no man or set of men or nation could do better. There are so many things to be attended to and often two or three of them will enter one's mind, and he has to resort to every bit of diplomacy at his command to set them right, and speaking of diplomacy, reminds me of a story told me in Perry's back room, by the late William W. McLaughlin, "Waurra Waurra" of the old "New York World" editorial staff.

This episode happened many years ago, when the "busy-bodies" first made their fight against J. Pierpont Morgan, the grand old man and finance wizard, who more than once had saved the world from bankruptcy, and the papers wanted the news, particularly an interview with Mr. Morgan, but how could they get what they wanted, had the editors all tied up.

The managing editor of the "World" called upon Bill McLaughlin, and he said, "McLaughlin, I want a story from Pierpont Morgan, and you are about the only man that I know can get it," and off went Waurra, Waurra McLaughlin.

He knew that Mr. Morgan could not be found at his beautiful home, and that he was spending his time on the beautiful yacht *Corsair,* his second home, and off went McLaughlin to locate Mr. Morgan.

Having located the *Corsair,* the next thing was to get aboard with the crew and others guarding her and ready to throw any newspaper man into the waters of the East River, and McLaughlin, to brace himself up for the fray, had dropped in the nearest saloon to have a highball or two.

While there he fell in with a sailor from the *Corsair,* and after several more drinks and a private chat with the sailor, they started for the *Corsair,* and unknown, Bill McLaughlin tumbled over the rail of the *Corsair* and down into Mr. Morgan's cabin, and this is what happened:

Mr. McLaughlin, "Good morning, Mr. Morgan" — Mr. Morgan, "Who the hell are you, and how did you get here" and it was then that Billy McLaughlin blessed himself and said a few prayers, and resorted to his grand old Irish diplomacy, and he was not long in winning Mr. Morgan over, and Mr. Morgan said, "Do you drink, or will you have a drink," and anybody that knew good natured Bill McLaughlin, knew that a drink was right into his wheelhouse and they had one, yes, two, and the Lord knows how many more, and he came much closer into the heart of that grand old man, who had done so much to save the world from the rascals that would destroy the house of Morgan, but he gave McLaughlin the interview, and as happy as a pea in a pot he bade Mr. Morgan good morning and hurried on to the office with his story.

And old boy McLaughlin wrote such a fine story which pleased Mr. Morgan so much, explaining in a general way the whole story, in a good old honest-to-goodness way of writing that his paper went over the top, for it turned out to be one of the greatest beats ever known, and Mac had no trouble in seeing Mr. Morgan after that publication.

But alas, these hungry wolves looking for the downfall of Mr. Morgan, got on his nerves, and he went to Europe and died in exile, so also did Richard Croker, and other good men, all of them good blue-blooded Americans, forced to die far, far from home and motherland, peace be with them, and I am writing this story in fond and loving memory of these good men, who had made their fortunes by the dint of hard work and good sound judgment, and would love to stay in their own homeland and spend their wealth, but the "villian" still pursued them and they have all of them, including McLaughlin, passed away, and happy in their new home, and the house of Morgan, stronger than ever before, and still open and doing a land office business, and why? Simply because J. Pierpont Morgan the first, built his castle on a rock like St. Peters at Rome, that will live forever, and being a good broadminded American banker, father and husband, he often dropped into St. Peters and on more than one occasion enjoyed a cup of tea with the Holy Father.

And when we think back thirty or more years when the hero of this work, Sir Thomas Lipton, arrived in New York, unknown and uncared for, it was this same kind-hearted banker that welcomed Tom Lipton into the circles of the New York Yacht Club, and had him elected to honorary membership, and this when everything looked black to him he having been defeated for America's Cup.

At the time Tom Lipton possessed little money and made no friends, the kindness of Mr. Morgan gave him new hopes of a brighter world, and it was then that I first met Sir Thomas, who often told me of how much he thought of Mr. Morgan, for if it was not for his help, I would never have returned to America. Going back to the question of producing a winning yacht, and the hard troublesome days and nights the owners, designers and racing committee have in store, to successfully have the racers in shape and watch for results, while the racing committee are thinking of the many handicaps they have to surmount, the weather, and troublesome waters, and the percentage allowed after each race is a real man's job alright.

But they never weakened, not for a moment, they went right along manfully to do the job that they were appointed to do, and did they do it well? Yes siree, they certainly made a proper job of their very hard and trying task to succeed and this in spite of many handicaps.

It was a mighty nice time for them, when after the races between the *Enterprise* and *Weetamoe,* they sat down to dinner, afterwards sitting in conference with every man, laying their cards open on the table from which, the winners of every race was chosen, and particularly that of the big race for the America's Cup, and everyone of them agreeing and having faithfully performed their duty, adjourned Sine Die, a tired, but happy bunch of famous sport-lovers and yachts-men with records of many victories.

We must never forget these trying times, and our conscientious workers.

Words of wisdom and to the point, coming from the lips of a humane King, namely George V of England, to wit—

It happened that one of those busybody gossipers, asked King George V, the following question: "How are you getting along with your labor party your Majesty?" "Very well was the quick reply, my grandmother would have hated it, my father would have tolerated it, but I move with the times."

Why, that old blaherskite Bernard Shaw, could not better that, no, no.

In that week's activities, King George V, won two first and one third prize and was very well satisfied, and both the King himself and his old standby and Pal, Queen Mary, both of whom were brown and healthy looking, having enjoyed the sport at Cowes, left for Buckingham Palace with a stopover at Glamis Castle to take a peep at the new Grandson, before leaving for Sandringham for the shooting season, after which they are due at Balmoral Castle, in Scotland.

King George, before leaving took the time to invest Miss Amy Johnson, the leading woman flyer of Great Britain, with her title and having said a few words of praise bade all goodbye, feeling well in health and spirits.

And now that the yachting season is through in England for another one of those drawn out years, it will be mighty gloomy along the coast, not one of the best places to live I assure you. Lovely in summer but not so lovely in winter, no, not at all.

But that will give these rich Lords and Dukes yacht owners and yachting lovers a good chance to come over to America and see how we race our boats both big and little, for we will keep racing here for nearly another month, and they can enjoy our sport to their heart's content.

Oh, if it could only be that the summer last for nine months and the dark cold winter but three, for nothing is more beautiful than the sunshine with beautiful warm days and balmy evenings. Oh Boys, who could ask more.

But some day, things may come much nearer our way, for the Gulf Stream is moving closer every day, and 100 years from now, if we old New Yorkers could but return, we might find things different with all the miserable men and women prohibitioners gone and forgotten, and their false teachings and ill gotten wealth sojourning in that place where the fires are always going, and in the company of the murderous bootleggers that they were responsible for their introduction and maintenance, bringing about the destruction of our glorious Constitution, and the shaking of the very foundations of our great and glorious country, beautiful America, the home of the brave, with no beer but high wages, very much craved, spent in the speakeasy, but none of it saved.

THE ANNOUNCEMENT PUBLISHED THAT LORD DUN-
RAVEN WAS TO BE A PARTNER WITH SIR THOMAS
LIPTON IN THE COMING RACES

Part IV—Chapter II

This little story opens up in the early spring of April, 1930, when my attention was called to a newspaper article, stating that the late Lord Dunraven had announced that he was to be a partner with Sir Thomas Lipton, on his next try to win the America's Cup, which to my mind, was a damn lie.

I lost no time with asking questions, but notified Sir Thomas of same, and the grand old man was very angry, and his friends were at the time very busy organizing a dinner in his honor, and this is what happened.

London, England, April 12th, 1930. At a dinner given to Sir Thomas by his followers on the other side, just two days before the launching of *Shamrock V*, the great hall being packed and every one present happy, Sir Thomas was called upon to say a few words, and he opened his remarks by denying the so-called pact with Lord Dunraven. "It is not my purpose to upset the peace of mind of my good friends present, for it is my desire for you all to eat, drink and be merry, for tomorrow is another day."

"I was very much put out when I opened my mail the other morning to read the following": 'The eighty-five year old Earl of Dunraven, announces that he would be associated with Sir Thomas Lipton, in his next effort to bring back the America's Cup, a dirty deliberate lie, and I will donate one thousand pounds to any man or group of men that can verify this announcement, and you can take it from me that if there is going to be any cup lifting to be done, it will be done by Sir Thomas Lipton, and no other man, or group of men while I am above ground," this brought about a tremendous outburst of enthusiasm that lasted for five minutes, and the health of Sir Thomas was proposed time after time, that beautiful evening, with all present happy.

Many of my readers will remember that Lord Dunraven made several attempts to win the cup, the first in 1893, with his Yacht *Valkyrie I* and he was defeated by our defender the *Vigilant,* in three straight races.

Again the good old Irish Earl came to our shores with his *Valkyrie II* or *III,* and he again was defeated three straight by our defender, who did not give the old Earl or his yacht a look in, the second race by a foul, and the third by a walk over, the Earl withdrawing his yacht claiming he was not getting a square deal. This was a very unfortunate incident, for it caused bad blood between the racing officials of both countries, and at times this looked very serious; this you will read about in another chapter of this work. Oh yes, Lord Dunraven was given his day in court, and lost out, and passed on a few years ago.

That unfortunate episode brought an angel of peace into the game in the person of Sir Thomas Lipton, thanks and praise be to the Lord, for he has ordained his angel of peace Tom Lipton, is here to stay.

I recall reading the remarks of Laurence Stallings, one of our many able book reviewers, then of the *Sun* and by all that is good and "Pious" if you see it in the *Sun* it's so. Mr. Stallings, was busy reading the autobiography of Sir Thomas Lipton, published by an English newspaper man and Mr. Stallings said that in his opinion, Sir Thomas Lipton, died of a broken heart, brought about by the vile treatment he received from the very men whom he had himself proposed as members of the Lipton Limited.

But while I hate like the dickens to disagree with Mr. Stallings, for several reasons, there is one good reason why I should agree with him, for his remarks bears me out that Sir Thomas did die of a broken heart, but not caused by the unfair treatment accorded him by the Directors of the Lipton, Limited, not at all man, not at all. He had been betrayed, I fear.

Mr. Stallings may be right, but there is nothing on earth can change my mind or opinion, but that Sir Thomas died as stated above, of betrayal purely and simply, and I came to that agreement, after his many conversations following that rotten turn down, by his own proteges of the Lipton, Limited.

Perhaps that when Mr. Stallings is busy reading over my book and the many letters published in same, he may change his mind as to the cause of the sudden death of Sir Thomas, alone and at the time simply forgotten, yes forsaken. No doubt Mr. Stallings will give me credit for writing the real story, and will give him more pleasure to read than did the Englishman's book, for I have the facts, and these from the warm lips, of Sir Thomas, or at least as near the facts as any person could have that goes to make up the life's story of the saintly old man, one of the whitest that ever drew the breath of life, too darned honest, to be so treated by a band of selfish employees, whom he trusted too well and this brought out this Hero's downfall, no doubt if Sir Thomas had become a New York Bobby, he might have learned the tricks of the commercialized rascals bred into this cockeyed world, to damage and destroy all.

We are also informed that Lord Inverforth, the able successor to Sir Thomas, and the other members of the Board of Trustees of the Lipton Trust among them Commodore Taylor, American representative, has returned the fine Lipton Loving Cup, subscribed for by the American people, and presented to Sir Thomas on October 9th, 1930.

For some reason or reasons unknown, this cup was ordered turned over to the members of the New York Yacht Club, but why should this be, here they hold this, the America's Cup won from England in 1851, and none but a few are permitted to look that valuable prize over, whereas, if these two cups had been given over to the Board of Trustees of the New York Museum, every man back of us interested could take our children to the Museum and having looked the cups over, tell the kiddies the life story of Sir Thomas, for by so doing, the name of this great charitable sportsman, would live in the hearts of the people forever, his life story descending from Father to Son or Grandson, thereby keeping up the good work, and the memory of this past master of the famous sport of sailing.

I don't know where to place the blame, it surely could not be placed at the door of Lord Inverforth, for he is a stranger to America, other than he visiting us often, but whoever advised this good man and his associates to my mind advised him wrongly. What should have been done with the Loving Cup was to have same turned over to the Mayor of New York, and he in turn hand it over to the Trustees of the above mentioned Museum.

What a pleasure that would have been to the common people, who dressed up in their Sunday clothes, they and their wives and kiddies, could enjoy all the Sabbath afternoon looking over the exhibits, and that happy custom no doubt would be forever their pleasure, taking their friends and visitors from other parts of the country, to look the exhibits over.

No doubt many of my readers has been blessed, or cursed, with the great big question of world travel, and they know that they are not long in a new city or town when they go hunting to see the sights and compare them to those of their own beautiful city of New York, the finest and grandest city in all the world, and I say this without fear of contradiction for I have travelled, slept, and drank in them all.

But what's the use, it is done now, but it is never too late to repent, and after the politicians have tired talking, and the busybodies go back in their holes for another few years, forever I hope, and pray, for then we, the real good Citizens of New York, might have our say, towards rectifying the mistake formerly made and have these cups put on a higher grade.

I often wonder how it is that our great Democratic men of standing in New York Society, both politicians and others, can close their eyes to matters of this character, thereby failing to have the hearts desires of their supporters looked after, and placed as they should be placed, for in this, as in all other cases, the concern of one is the concern of all.

We have for a long number of years been reading or listening to the Scotch part of the life of Tom Lipton, the many grand old Scotch stories, and his well known battles with his old chum Sir Harry Lauder, the famous vaudeville star, known the world over.

Also of his Scotch connection with the late Lord John Dewar, the world's famous London Scottish whiskey King, and his Scottish military record, he having held the position of Colonel of a Highland regiment, that you read about in another chapter of this book.

Now let us have a little of the Irish side of the late Sir Thomas Lipton, born in Glasgow, Scotland, of Irish parents, who at the time were visiting the beautiful highlands and the low lands of Bobby Burns.

And by the way, this reminds me of a passage of arms between Ireland's great poet, and Scotland's great bard, they met one night while Burns was in the act of sweeping off the sidewalk, and Tom Moore approached, and here's what happened between them. Tom Moore, "Remove your broom you Scottish Loon, and let Tom Moore pass by." Bobby Burns, "You Irish ass, there is room to pass between the wall and I." Now we will go along with the story.

The people of every country of God's footstool, have known Sir Thomas for some kind act or the other, and they looked upon him as a real Irishman, because of his charitable heart, his wonderful achievements in the sporting world particularly that of yachting, when he dared to battle for the America's Cup year after year, smiling in defeat and victory.

But you know that it was not the old worn out "Mug" that Sir Thomas wanted, not at all man, not at all, it was simply to stimulate interest in that noble sport of "Hit, stop and getaway," my yacht and your yacht racing up and down the Bay, the sport of Emperors, Kings and Queens, he wanted no more cups, he was annoyed with the 365 cups he then held. They were taking up room, and causing extra expenses. And Tom Lipton decided to not accept any prize but gold, in his winning of a 1st, 2nd or 3rd prize in which *Shamrock V* won sixteen first prizes, four second and three third prizes, all of which were paid to him in gold, and he at once sending this good money to some worthy charity and that is the Tom Lipton that we all know, then why should his heart be in this old mug, without a bottom?

But, my friends, how many of us know the family history of Sir Thomas, and that he came from a fighting race, the Lipton "One's of The Shannog Green Mills" of County Monaghan, Ireland.

It is the desire and great pleasure of the author to lay before you the Lipton history of 1767 and 1770 inclusive. This will be found in my 2nd edition, a true story of self sacrifice and patriotism that all lovers of freedom delight to read of, and of course particularly so when we know a member of that great Lipton family, in the person of Sir Thomas, whom the author has the honor and pleasure of knowing for thirty years, and is at all times the last to say goodbye when leaving our shores each year, and the first to greet that grand old Dean of the yachting world on his arrival every year, for those past thirty, long, long but happy years, for Sir Thomas is always happy and full of good cheer.

May 10th, 1930 was a beautiful day and there was a big crowd gathered at the shipyards of George Lawley & Son at Neponset, Mass., to cheer *Yankee* when sliding down gracefully off the ways and into the briny ocean, that lovely day, after a nasty miserable winter, everybody was happy.

It was Miss Isabel Lawrence, the pretty little daughter of John S. Lawrence, a member of the syndicate that built *Yankee,* that broke the bottle of health restorer champagne, on the bow of the yacht at the same time saying, "I christian you *Yankee,* go your way and make good" and *Yankee* certainly made good getting into the water fast and looking pretty.

While another but much smaller crowd were present at the second attempt to launch *Weetamoe* over in Bristol, and the reason of that was the contraryness of *Weetamoe* at her first christianing and launching, that was also well attended, and a gala day declared, in her honor, but that fluke on the first launching day, kept many of her friends and well wishers away.

It was a very fine party that stood and watched *Yankee* take the water among whom, were Mr. Frank C. Paine, her designer and the son of that grand old yachting expert, General Paine. Frank Paine is also a member of the syndicate that built *Yankee,* and with Mr. Lawrence another member of the syndicate and manager of same, with Mr. Chandler Hovey, and many others, too numerous to mention, Gov. Allen of Massachusetts was to be present, but a prior engagement prevented this, but the city of Boston was ably represented by their Mayor the Hon. James M. Curley, and his staff.

These down East yachtsmen are great for producing defenders of the America's Cup, for the writer well remembers the yacht *Puritan,* that was designed by them to race *Genesta* in 1885, and a memorable race it was.

It was in December of 1884 that J. Beaver Webb, a famous English designer forwarded a challenge for a series of races for the America's Cup, and this challenge was received by the racing committee of the New York Yacht Club and acted upon in short order.

The challenge was sent in behalf of Sir Richard Sutton, owner of the cutter *Genesta* and Lieutenant William Henn, of the Royal Navy, who owned the *Galatea,* with a request for three races all over outside courses would be granted, this challenge was received and the appeal granted by the members of the New York Yacht Club.

To retain the cup, the defender would have to defeat one of the English yachts in the series, but in separate races, while victory on the part of either *Genesta* or *Galatea*, would have won the cup.

The New York Yacht Club agreed to name the defender a week before the first race, and the yacht *Priscialla,* was designed by a Mr. A. Cary Smith, and in the form of a sloop.

But just then our down east friends woke up and entered a yacht to be known as the *Puritan,* and *Miss Puritan* was chosen, and owned by General Charles J. Paine, and J. Malcolm Forbes, of Boston.

And at that same time it was reported that the *Galatea* would not be in a position to arrive here in time to race in 1885, so that this made the second series of races in 1885 unnecessary.

Genesta arrived here in good shape, and the first race was ordered to take place on September 8, after a day's delay, due to fog.

An accident occurred even before the starting signal, as *Puritan* on the port tack attempted to bluff *Genesta* as they jockeyed before the start began.

But the skipper would not be bluffed and he kept his right-away, and the collision followed, *Puritan's* mainsail being torn, and the bowsprit of *Genesta,* snapping.

The racing committee decided that it was a flagrant foul and *Puritan* was disqualified, but Sir Richard Sutton, owner of *Genesta* refused to accept this decision. This act of the Englishman made of him a hero, for the American people were very much pleased at this action.

And after several days in dry dock the yachts were brought together again on September 14th. This race was sailed over the club's 38-mile inside course. At the start *Genesta* was set down to leeward by the tide and *Puritan* crossed the line first, and when passing Fort Wadsworth, the *Puritan* was seven minutes ahead, for again *Genesta* ran into more trouble bothered by a bark in her way.

But nothing daunted, *Genesta* braced up and cut down the *Puritan's* lead to three minutes, passing the Southwest Spit Buoy.

The next leg was to the Sandy Hook Lightship, and it was here that the excursion boats were allowed to crowd in on the two yachts, the *Puritan* was ahead, and did not feel this as much as did *Genesta,* a darned outrage, and one that should never have been allowed.

And in justice to both yachts and fair play, the race should have ended then and there with a decision of "No Race."

But they were allowed to continue, and at the Sandy Hook Lightship the *Puritan* led by 5:22 and increased this on the two reaches home.

The corrected time recorded was: *Puritan,* 6:06:05; *Genesta,* 6:22:24.

The final race of the series was called two days later over a 20-mile course to leeward and windward course in a fresh nor-wester.

Genesta got away first by 15 seconds over the line and 45 seconds ahead of the *Puritan*. And to the dismay of the American sympathizers, she held her lead and rounded the leeward mark an eight of a mile ahead.

Genesta then set a topsail, while *Puritan* seeing that the wind was freshening, stowed her topsail. And with this advantage the *Puritan* was not slow in working to the windward, while the *Genesta* was suffering from the blunder made, slowed up with her topmast flapping.

The wind had reached a velocity of thirty miles and off Long Beach the two yachts were abeam, with *Puritan* three-quarters of a mile to weather.

The wind then hauled to the northward, allowing both yachts to lay the line. The finish of the race was a very close one with *Puritan* getting across the finish line a little ahead.

The corrected time given was *Puritan,* 5:03:14; *Genesta,* 5:04:52. Remarks: This was the closest and most exciting race that had ever been held, and it gave the New York Yacht Club continued possession of the America's Cup.

This race to my mind was a disgrace to our great ballyhooing of our American fair play, Boston, trying to win on a bluff, and failed by fouling, for which she deserved the condemnation of the people, and in spite of Sir Richard Sutton's refusal to accept the decision of the racing committee who had termed it a flagrant foul, should have stood that of disqualification, for they were justifiable in doing so, in the spirit of fair play.

And again, when the excursion boats had crowded in on the two racing yachts, and without police protection, it was the proper thing for the racing committee to call this contest No Race.

This, the writer claims, should have been done in all fairness, this may not be the opinion of others, but to a fair square shooter, a real live sportsman, that is just what should have been done that day, for these mean acts are contemptible even to a piker, if there are any around, and causes a very unpleasant feeling to exist.

There, for instance, is a sample of why our good sport loving yachting experts are busy working out plans for the rule of the sea, in events of this character, for it is a disgrace for any man to take a mean advantage of another, either on sea or on land, that is one of the first lessons that we receive at our mother's knee, and should be remembered, honored and respected by all, particularly a body of men that are chosen to see fair play, and justice between men and yachts.

Would it not be better that America, or at least the members of the New York Yacht Club, to lose this cup than to lose our good name as sportsmen, and gentlemen, a proud title handed down to us by the Father of our country, the great General George Washington, and his noble followers, who fought and bled for the freedom of our great country and our people, bringing about the fact that we today stand before the civilized world, as the richest, peaceful loving God fearing nation on the face of the earth, then why stoop to little things?

The writer earnestly hopes that the good men that are drawing up what will be forever known as the rules of traffic on sea, just as are the traffic rules and regulations that are working so successfully on land today saving many lives and much property, in the shape of smashed up autos.

THE DAY WE ALL CELEBRATE, APRIL 14th, 1930

PART IV—CHAPTER III

Well, here we are folks, this is that grand and glorious day of April 14th, 1930, and word has just arrived stating that the first of the seven beautiful sailing yachts, two of whom will toe the mark of the starting line in their series of races for the America's Cup, on September 13th next. God willing, no fires or destruction.

I remarked that it was a glorious day, and who could say otherwise, when two of the prettiest swan-like sailing yachts ever designed slid off the ways into the waters of their respective rivers, *Enterprise* and *Shamrock V*, about the *Enterprise*, well she is all right, but about the *Shamrock V* we cannot say that, at this or any other time.

I mean by that, that *Enterprise* is in her home waters and is O. K. but that wee little yacht, the dear little *Shamrock* of Ireland, has a tough lot of fighting to do, firstly off the treacherous coast of England, and after she has whipped everything over there, she must face the terrible high seas of the Atlantic ocean, that even a *Leviathan* is afraid of sometimes, and who, that has ever crossed that big pond, is not afraid at times?

Heavenly Father, we that are happy enjoying our homes and firesides on land, do not imagine the sufferings of the poor men that have to leave their wives and children, perhaps for the last time, for this duty must be strictly attended to according to that old dusty deed of gift that should have been destroyed fifty years ago, or never drawn up at all.

It certainly is a happy relief to the designers of these two yachts to have them floated, and the world will never know all the sleep that has no doubt been lost by both designers, Mr. W. Starling Burgess for *Enterprise,* and Mr. Charles E. Nicholson, for *Shamrock V*.

My dear readers, we do not realize all of the worry and torment that comes to the man that accepts a contract to design a winner of a famous trophy, like the America's Cup, from the very time that her keel is laid until she is successfully slid into the ocean, at least that is the case with our American Designers, but not so with the designer of the challenger.

His worry and torments are not through until his small little yacht has safely crossed the Atlantic ocean, and is resting snugly in her berth at either the Jacob's dry dock at City Island, or some other dry dock, but that is over two months away yet, but Nicholson's worry never ceases, until she is about finishing the last race of the series, win or lose.

183

Of course as is the custom of the people of Bristol, and her owners, she was permitted to slip into the water by just breaking a bottle on her bow, with perhaps a thousand people attending the festivities, and for all that we know *Enterprise* was very well satisfied.

But not so with the *Shamrock V*, it took a Welsh band to ask permission to be a party to that greatest of all celebrations that of landing in the water, a real honest to goodness winner of the America's Cup, Providence permitting.

And it is a well known fact that when an Irishman dies, his folks has to stay up three nights, to be sure that he is really dead, for the Irish are so ably known to be a great body of fakers, they learned that from the rack renting Landlords of Ireland since time immemorial.

And when the Irish baby arrives, glory be, it takes a whole week to celebrate his or her coming, and the boys and girls from the Emerald Isle, are noted for their hospitality on the arrival of a new Shamrock. At least that is how it used to be, A. D., Before sad depression.

Shamrock V, slid gracefully into the water today, and was christened by the same person that had christened *Shamrock IV*, Lady Shaftsbury, and she smashed the bottle over her bow, in the presence of a very distinguished gathering, of England's most prominent citizens.

King George V, of England being represented by Sir Philip Hunloke.

Sir Thomas, tried hard to be merry for this would have been one of the happiest days of his life, had it not been saddened by a telegram received by his secretary, John Westwood, and handed to the poor old yachtsman, stating that his dear old friend and boyhood chum, had just passed away, in the person of Lord John Dewar.

To my mind if Mr. Westwood had any thoughts about the feelings of his employer and the many friends that came a long way to congratulate him on that auspicious occasion, he would have held the telegram back a few hours for there was nothing to be gained, and Sir Thomas would have heard of it soon enough, for he could not bring the dead back to life.

After the launching, all present sat down to lunch in the saloon of the new steam yacht used to take the place of the *Erin*, and they drank to the health of His Majesty, King George V, and *Shamrock V*, success, and a silent toast to the late Lord Dewar was drank in sorrow.

The chairman of the occasion presented all present with a bunch of real live shamrocks from Ireland and the speech-making was then in order. Sir Thomas was first called upon to make a few remarks; he did his best under the circumstances and, among others, he made the following remarks: "I believe in my heart that Mr. Nicholson has built a flyer," and he hoped that with the help of Skipper Ted Heard, Commodore Duncan Neill, and the crew, to bring the cup back to its Irish home again.

Sir Thomas declared that in his four previous occasions of trying to win the cup the American people always had treated him fairly and squarely, and were always loyal to him in making these unsuccessful attempts in the years of 1899, 1901, 1903 and 1920.

Commodore Duncan F. Neill, when called upon, remarked: "That though the *Shamrock V* had to meet the best of four American yachts, he was not unduly alarmed." It was this same Duncan Neill that superintended all of these Shamrocks in their launching tryouts and races, and will be with us again mighty soon, God willing. "This newest challenger for the cup that was taken from us in 1851, and has never been recovered," declared Neill, "has less beam than any of the four American yachts 'from which the defender is to be selected. Her greatest beam is nineteen feet seven and one-half inches. She is one hundred and nineteen feet ten and one-quarter inches in actual length and eighty-one feet one and a quarter inches long on the designed waterline and has a displacement of 134 tons and she draws fourteen feet three inches of water. She is shorter on the load waterline than three of the American defenders. She has seven thousand five hundred foot sail area. Built to the rating laid down by the New York Yacht Club's measurements rules, the *Shamrock V* has a sail area of slightly more than seven thousand five hundred square feet. *Shamrock V* is rigged with the single-masted Bermuda cut.

"Examination of *Shamrock V* indicated that her designer endeavored to build a yacht securing the best performance in light or moderate breezes such as may be expected to prevail when the yachts would be racing off Newport, R. I., in September, 1930. And she will have a height of about one hundred and fifty-two feet six inches above deck. Her center board is steam-lined and can be raised and lowered in a sort of trunkway running through the middle of the yacht. Her keel was laid five and one-half months ago."

All present were pleased to hear these figures explained and they had a very pleasant afternoon, with the Royal Welsh Band playing "The Dear Little Shamrock" and other popular airs, while those ashore were happy drinking to their heart's content, for the mayor of Gosport had declared April 14th a holiday, and they took every advantage of it, to be sure.

There were more than five thousand people present at the luncheon, and after this was over Sir Thomas had ordered that they be taken care of, and they were in good old English style, singing the praises of Sir Thomas Lipton and his beautiful *Shamrock V*, that they thought sure was a winner.

Sir Thomas, standing motionless, his shoulders squared and his body rigid, watched the launching with tears in his eyes, and the sympathy of these good people went out to him that lovely day, for they knew all that he had done for them, both past and present, but nothing could cheer that faithful old sportsman that day. When the news was broken to him, he wanted to postpone the launching, but that was impossible, for all arrangements had been made and could not be changed, and no doubt, it was well they were not.

Sir Thomas cheered up some when he received a telegram from His Majesty, the King, stating that he was going to leave a sick bed to see and give *Shamrock V* a few tryouts before she sailed for America, and the King made good, as you already are aware, for she was tried out good and plenty on Royalty's playground, the "Solent."

Let us all hope that there are going to be no mistakes, for mistakes will and have happened in many families, both rich and poor, and the family of England's Prime Minister, Ramsay MacDonald, was no exception, and why?

As the story goes, Premier Ramsey MacDonald was called upon to make an address in a town called Lossiemouth and in his address he publicly denounced and condemned gambling in all its forms, such as sweepstakes and lotteries, and while that may be all right, if the newspapers of this town named Loosiemouth, or loosemouth, as it should be named.

For even a great Parliamentarian like a Premier must eat, so it happened that a meal was ordered to be prepared for Mr. MacDonald and his party in the next town, and everyone seemed to be happy and satisfied, for we were all invited to a good meal, and when the seats were filled, one of those unlooked-for blunders happened, for at times Dame Fortune behaves very wickedly and often unjust; at least she did on this sorrowful occasion.

The country waitress that day that was to wait on the Prime Minister and his family was a beautiful "rose" from the Emerald Isle, who had just won $50,000 on the Irish sweepstakes and, of course, women like her must tell the Prime Minister all about it, and good natured enough, never thinking of the blunder he was making, Mr. MacDonald congratulated her upon her winnings, and glory be! what an explosion followed. Why?

Well, like America, England is cursed with some of those rusty-faced old scandal mongers of ministers of the cloth who, if they preached the Gospel of the Lord, would and should be the first to kill scandal, but no, that was not the case, for quickly the news was heard in Loosemouth, and Heavenly Father! what a rumpus. One minister wrote to the other minister; he told his wife and then wrote to the other minister, and soon the wires to London town were burning and all London got lit up. Why?

The Rev. F. E. Watson, secretary of the Scottish National League Against Betting and Gambling, of which Ramsey MacDonald is an honorary vice-president, laid the matter before that body and resolutions denouncing Mr. MacDonald passed, a copy of which was sent to the Prime Minister at the House of Commons, and the laugh was on that great Parliamentarian, and for what?

If those psalm singers were not so fond of publicity, and robbing the people of their rights, yes, and money, had done the right thing they would have had the foolish but good-hearted mistake covered up, but not a bit of it, for among those ministers of the Protestant church, both here and there, you have a group who, if they are not robbing the people of their liberty, they are busy robbing some poor parishoner of his wife, thereby breaking up many a good Christian home. God forgive them; I cannot.

So that the moral we learn from this is, for heaven sake avoid mistakes, both rich and poor, high or low, for mistakes have ruined many a bright Parliamentarian, for instance, the late Charles Stewart Parnell, the uncrowned king of Ireland, Sir Charles Dilke, the member of Parliament from Chelsea, and no less a personage than the former Kaiser Wilhelm, and his former teacher and very able leader, Prince Bismarck, and many others.

If these faking ministers had God in mind and had gone out and preached His teachings, the world would be far better to live in, but no, the almighty dollar and the devil himself has too tight a hold on them, and they do not have time for God. Yes. Many of them hold down their jobs under false pretense, for they do not believe in God—at least, so we are told.

I recall the late Monsignor Luke J. Evers of St. Andrew's Church, New York, of fond and loving memory, speaking from the altar, telling of another one of those scientists that did not believe in God; in fact, he made his living telling the people that there was no God.

This was in gay Paree, Paris, France, until one fine day a poor old parishoner with his hands rolls up in a shawl, approached the atheist and when in front of him dropped a brick on his foot, and the fakir that was so busy telling the people that there was no God, did not have time to wash his dirty face, and the first thing that happened when the brick landed on his foot was to shout: "Oh, my God!"

They are the fakirs that the world is up against, so keep your eye on the gun, and two eyes on these unmitigated liars and sneaking rats and scandal-mongers.

My, how Sir Thomas used to laugh when I would tell him of them, for he was one of the greatest story-tellers the world ever produced, and many a story was told over that happy table in Gosport that day, for yachtsmen, like the good old salt water sailors of old, used to tell them when on shore, that is, when they could get away from their new-found wives.

We all love to hear a good story, and we chuckle over them often, for there is no harm in a story, for while the other fellow is telling the story and we are attentively listening, we are not scandalizing our fellow man, so keep that in mind, my warriors bold.

Speaking about the miserable group of ministers, always ready to spread scandal, reminds me of a story told by a Catholic mission father, to wit:

When Napoleon was confined on the Island of St. Helena, one of his big generals asked him who was Jesus Christ, and the defeated warrior answered: "Jesus Christ is the commander-in-chief of the world, and if I had paid one-half the attention to Him, my God, as I did to my country, I would not be lingering here in durance vile."

YOU BAD MINISTERS, PLEASE COPY!

Mr. Nicholson added "America's Cup had a hole in the bottom, which was a fitting thing for a dry country."

Commodore Col. Duncan F. Neill said, "It was a good augury for her success that the *Shamrock's* launching had taken place a few hours ahead of any of her contenders."

"*Shamrock V* to Be Shown in Boston Harbor."
"*Shamrock V* to Take Part in the Tercentenary Celebration."

"Boston, April 14th (AP)—The *Shamrock V*, Sir Thomas Lipton's challenger for the America's Cup, will participate in the tercentenary celebration here this year, former Mayor of Boston, Hon. John F. Fitzgerald, an old friend of Sir Thomas, announced today.

Sir Thomas Lipton announced that he had accepted the city's invitation, Mr. Fitzgerald said, and he has offered to sail his famous yacht into the Charles River Basin for exhibition. The noted sportsman has offered trophies for a yachting regatta and a proposed fishermen's race to take place from Gloucester to Boston.

These are not the only trophies that this great Irish Baronet has given for the advancement of sport in this country and every year one hears that the Lipton Cup, given for this or that sporting event, was won by such and such a person, or club, for such and such an event.

And Sir Thomas is constantly ordering others, for he loves America and is always ready and willing to advance its sport.

There were present at the launching of *Enterprise* the following men of note and standing in America: Mr. Harold S. Vanderbilt, Winthrop W. Aldrich, Governor Norman S. Case of Rhode Island, Commodore E. Walter Clark, George Whitney, and C. Sherman Hoyt, with the designer, W. Starling Burgess, and Mr. Herreshoff, the builder of this and, in fact, most all of the defending yachts in the last thirty-five years, for two of the oldest and most prominent names in American yachting history are those of Burgess and Herreshoff, who built the famous sloop, *Vigilant,* in the spring of 1893, and we all know of her record, and of all the great yachts built way down in Bristol, at the Herreshoffs, who are still going strong.

Weather conditions were not very favorable, but while the weather marred us in America somewhat, death marred the launching of Sir Thomas Lipton's yacht, *Shamrock V*, for the death of Lord Dewar, was an exceptional hard blow to the Irish Baronet.

But, of course, the man above knows all, we have to take it or leave it, for the weather is sure one thing that money cannot buy, and it is mighty fortunate that it cannot, or God only knows how the weather would be commercialized like everything else of importance by the grafters of America, yes, and of England also, and for that matter, most all nations since 1914.

They all seem to be much quicker picking up the evil side of the things of life, than they do their prayers and the love of God. Why?

However, here we are on April 16th and we find everything O.K. both up at City Island where the *Enterprise* is riding on the water and about to have her big mast stepped in a day or two, and boy! she looks mighty fine to the writer, and while I would love to see the *Shamrock V* win this year for many reasons, among them to satisfy the heart's desire of my good friend, and for the good of the shipbuilders of both countries, for it would mean the spending of much money and great competition next year, but nevertheless, I wish all of the seven yachts that are mentioned good luck.

And the *Shamrock V* floating on her own waters waiting to be dressed for the fray; they will soon be harnessed up and then we will be happy to hear of their doings, so let us look forward to the launchings of the other three yachts in this country and pray that their launchings will also be successful, and again I say, good luck to you all.

All arrangements are pretty well completed among the sail-makers who are working night and day, with the house-boats for the crews in pretty fair shape, and most of the crews picked for each yacht. We may take a bit of a rest, for heaven knows, some of us need it badly, particularly the good men that did the designing of each yacht, staying up nights to see all things, yes, everything, in first-class shape to measure up with all other parts of its design, with neither a screw nor a bolt out of place.

The *Valkyrie* was then in drydock and we were all interested in looking her over, for she was a pretty looking craft, and like a swan skimming through the waters off Sandy Hook, with her English steel spar that seemed to appeal to all lovers of yachting at the moment.

However, we are living in the modern age and the wise men of today do not have to go back to the year of our Lord, 1895 or 1898, so we will confine ourselves to the class of yachts that our present-day designers and builders are turning out.

Let us see how the four American yachts measure up, and then we can compare them to the measurements of the *Shamrock V*, and then be in a better position to judge them all, something that is impossible just now.

The *Whirlwind* of the Thorne-Hammand syndicate has a length overall of 127 feet; length on water-line, 84 feet; beam 21 feet; weight, 158 tons.

The *Yankee*, the John Lawrence of Boston syndicate, length overall is 125 feet; length on waterline, 84 feet; beam 20 feet; weight, 145 tons.

The *Enterprise*, the Vanderbilt-Aldrich syndicate, length overall is 120 feet 9 inches; length on water-line, 80 feet; beam, 21 feet 2 inches; weight, 148½ tons.

The *Weetamoe*, the Morgan-Nichols syndicate, length over all 125 feet 11 inches; length on waterline, 83 feet; beam, 20 feet 8 inches; weight, 143 tons. The ballast on the keels will consist of from 55 to 60 per cent of the total weight of each yacht and about 80 tons of Tobin bronze plates will enter the construction of the three metal yachts, while some 50,000 rivets is the average used on each yacht.

My, but how I do long to live in the past, when all was happiness and sunshine on every side with a happy home and loved ones, among them your parents, wife and children, to greet you, that are no more.

An episode of 1920 is worth the telling relating to the *Shamrock IV*, and her troubles preparing for the series of races that were to take place in 1914, but postponed on account of the World's War and finished in 1920 when Sir Thomas and his *Shamrock IV* won two races out of five, and may have won the third if the captain attended to his duties. The smiling Irish Baronet came closer to winning the cup than did any other challenger.

My attention was called to this episode after reading of Mr. Vanderbilt taking the *Enterprise* for a sail on Easter Sunday, 1930, having an enjoyable and a very successful sail, all on board smiling at the beautiful stand before the wind of pretty *Miss Enterprise*.

Sir Thomas was bitterly opposed to sailing his yacht on a Sunday, but we were blessed with so much rain off Sandy Hook that he was forced to give his consent, but he never forgave himself and he did not meet with the same success as did his rival, and he made up his mind never to sail his yacht on the Sabbath, and he often spoke of that tryout.

Sir Thomas was a pretty clean-living man, and he respected the Sabbath so much that he would prevent any unnecessary work aboard his yachts, and his Heavely Father, no doubt, is paying him double for his many good deeds on earth, happy in his heavenly home.

I have often wondered if my readers ever stopped to think of the enormous weight the masts and rigging of our America's Cup defenders and the challenger have to carry while racing.

It is surprising just how these frail little yachts can stand up to the heavy burden of, in most every case, some fourteen hundred pounds of the best sail material to be produced, and the tremendous pressure of the wind; it is truly remarkable,

Imagine all of this weight and pressure must be tied from a height of about one hundred and sixty-five feet, or in some cases one hundred and seventy feet, and on down to a space of perhaps twenty feet, so that to keep all of this vast amount of rigging in place is a very serious problem, when the wind is blowing good and hard or, in fact, any little blow at all.

The designers of these racing yachts have spent hours, yes, days and nights, studying every conceivable method that the brain of man could suggest to strengthen this rigging and its supports, for nothing in the world looks more untidy than a flabby sail, and the slightest mistake would bring this about, with the designer's reputation at stake all the time.

It takes more than a ton of the best canvas to be had to make up the sails of these yachts as we like to see them plunging through the ocean, with the mainsail alone weighing 1,400 pounds, and then added to this is a jibsail, a jibtopsail, forestaysail and a spinnaker.

Several of our yachts will be supplied with two sets of sails in the case of an accident, and that costs a lot of money not only the providing of the canvas, the sewing and other particulars, such as the handling and storing of these necessary appliances, both before and after the races. But, if our millionaires must have kingly sport, then they must pay or quit the game, but look at all the happiness that this big outlay brings to others and their homes and families connected with that profession, and also the hours of pleasure and happiness that it brings to us all, we fellows who are lovers of the white sails that never grow weary, but carry you cheerly over the sea.

It is always very pleasing to hear nice things spoken or written of or about a friend, and I delight in writing them in this work, for this whole-souled sportsmanship has brought about many changes, and the one that stands out more than any other was that it was thought that he would never again go hunting for the old "Mug."

But to one that has known him and has studied his mind and thoughts as has the writer for more than a quarter of a century, for in that time Sir Thomas has confided in me, and has told me more than he would the press or public. He made few confidants; he never wanted to be tricked, but he was, all right, and in the end of his days at that.

But when it was published on June 10th, 1929, that the New York Yacht Club had just received another challenge from Sir Thomas, they woke up, and many for the first time commenced to sing the praises of the London grocer and the newspapers run headlines, the snobs saying, "I told you so."

One London daily commences its story as follows:

"A Veteran's Defi Within the Rules Governing the Race."
"Sir Thomas Lipton's sportsmanship has won high regard from the followers of yachting both here in London and elsewhere,"

"London, May 19th, 1929. British yachtsmen believe that Sir Thomas Lipton's challenge will be accepted. They cannot see how it can be rejected under the deed of gift, and they are wholeheartedly wishing the Irish Baronet every good luck, which they feel he deserves."

"Sir Thomas Lipton deserves to win the America's Cup for two reasons," writes Major B. Heckstall, in the *Daily Telegraph*.

"On no fewer than four occasions in the last thirty years he has raced for it and has been fairly beaten by a better yacht or perhaps better yachtsmanship, as the case may be.

"Each time he has built a Shamrock specially for the purpose of the race and has done his best. There is another reason that did not exist when Sir Thomas built *Shamrocks I, II, III* in the years of 1899, 1901 and 1903.

"In those years he was widely known to the world as a great businessman and industrial magnate, but he had no special claim to be regarded as a representative British yachtsman. Times have changed.

"In 1908, after he had challenged for the cup three times, Sir Thomas Lipton built another yacht, the 23-meter *Shamrock*, but she must not be confused with *Shamrocks I, II, III, IV,* which were specially built for the winning of the America's Cup. She is the present Shamrock meter 23, which is at the moment lying off Hythe in Southampton, England. And has been racing for 20 years and winning most of her races at every British port where a yacht racing regatta flag flies. This yacht has been the mainstay of our regattas and she is second in popularity only to the King's cutter *Britannia.*

"Everywhere and in all weathers, Sir Thomas has raced in the *Shamrock* himself. In the hottest of clashes last year against the big schooners, namely, the *Westwood Oh,* and the *Elena,* and against the cutters *Britannia, Asrea, Cambria,* the *White Heather* and the *Lulworth, Shamrock* won the title of champion British racer of them all.

"Wherever Sir Thomas has sailed in England, Scotland or Ireland, he has endeared himself to the yachting public by his manly sportsmanship.

"No racing yacht has been consistently better handled, as well as our *Shamrock,* and although when Sir Thomas forwarded his first challenge, and even after that for the America's Cup in the bygone days, he was little known to British yachtsmen, today there is no man who has done more for our sport and none more popular than is Sir Thomas Lipton. As the senior supporter of our premier international class, none is more deserving of victory; none a more suitable yachtsman, to challenge for the America's Cup."

My word, but that was a wonderful statement of facts, and having been issued by an Englishman, it comes sweeter and better, for they are never of that kind of mettle to throw bouquets.

Heavenly Father! how happy Sir Thomas was to read that publication, for to use a common phrase they never gave Tom Lipton a tumble, and when he wrote me enclosing this grand statement, he was the happiest man in all creation, and when he next visited New York, we spent many hours gossiping about that and others that followed, for the grand old sportsman knew that he had lived down the aristocrats' hue and cry about the poor London grocer.

How pleasing to the writer and, in fact, to all that these very kind remarks were published while the grand old sportsman was in the flesh, for to quote the words of his old friend, the late President Teddy Roosevelt, to quote that grand old Colonel of the world's famous regiment of Rough Riders when they were much needed, "It would please me much better if you were to place a flower in my hand while living, than a bouquet on my grave."

It was very pleasing news to us all to learn that in spite of that terrific storm raging on the Devonshire coast, that troubled the Lipton fleet for a few days, had calmed down and the boys are on their way to the dear old U. S. A. and with the help of God and the assistance of Father Neptune, they will arrive here on time.

We will be kept informed by radio, from day to day, of how the fleet is making out, and we will look for glorious news, morning, noon and night, and by the way, Sir Thomas is highly elated at the wonderful royal reception that was accorded him and his fleet on their return to the Royal Dock in Portsmouth, there to be made ready for the swim across.

Sir Thomas was not slow in sending his ambassador with portfolio, to J. J. Hickey, a full account of this reception and parting to the Tom Lipton Irish armada, when bidding farewell to the briny shiny hills and rocks of Albion, and the chalk hills of Southampton.

The quays and rivers for miles around were filled with the yachts and motor boats of many of the foremost men in all the British Isles, and they kept up this happy vigil until long after the *Erin* and *Shamrock V* had disappeared from view, and that, too, was most pleasing to our grand old man of the yachting world, and no longer the poor London tea merchant.

I fear that our yacht racing committee, or whoever is responsible, made a big mistake in transferring the championship racing course from Sandy Hook to Newport, for the challenger is going to have much better sailing in Newport than she ever got off the Jersey coast, what with old mud scows and snooty little motor boats dodging around like bums in a low down fantangled speakeasy, but it is all over now.

Of course, like all good soldiers, Sir Thomas takes his orders and is always ready to obey them, for he was never known to object to leaving everything in the hands of our American officials, that is all, and that is why our great yachtsmen hold out the right hand of good fellowship and respect to this famous Irish sportsman, and Sir Thomas is ever keen to appreciate that.

Sir Thomas would much rather pack up and go back home than have any misunderstanding with the men whose friendship he admired.

BIDDING SIR THOMAS AND HIS *SHAMROCK V* GOODBYE AND GOOD LUCK

Part IV—Chapter IV

London, England, July 8th, 1930. At a luncheon given to Sir Thomas Lipton, owner of the *Shamrock V,* the 1930 challenger for the America's Cup, by the yachtsmen of England today, presided over by His Royal Highness, the Prince of good fellowship, known to the world as the Prince of Wales, and held in that famous old historical building known as Fishmongers' Hall.

The luncheon was given by the Honorable Company of Master Mariners of England and composed of the leading yachtsmen and others that go down to the sea in boats, as a farewell to Sir Thomas on his departure for America with his *Shamrock V* to lift the old "Mug" lying unused and uncared for since 1851. Everyone present, at the request of the toastmaster, the Prince of Wales, stood and drank to the health of Sir Thomas, and sang the well known song. "He's a Jolly Good Fellow," followed by remarks and speeches of the toastmaster and our great Ambassador to the Court of St. James, the Hon. "Hellfire" Charles G. Dawes, a soldier of few words, but thinks and works quickly. This was a very noticeable gathering and it cheered the grand old Irish Baronet very much, particularly when the gallant young Prince of Wales, the future King of England, arose to say, among other things:

"All we ask is a turn of luck," and turning to America's great Ambassador, Charles G. Dawes, His Royal Highness said: "I venture to say that it would be as popular in America as in this country if Sir Thomas at 80 should bring back the cup which was taken from England when he, Sir Thomas, was but one year old, he having been born in 1851." Loud applause followed with more drinking and toasting and the Ambassador took the center of the dais, and stated in a few brief remarks the following:

"Now that Britain has shown that she has the fastest airplane and the fastest automobile," Ambassador Dawes said, "America will be slightly disappointed if she shows also that she has the fastest yacht, but that disappointment will hardly equal the disappointment which will be felt if this great sportsman does not win," and fighting Charley Dawes sat down amidst the applause of all present.

The toastmaster, the Prince of Wales, then called upon Sir Thomas to address the distinguished gathering, and when Sir Thomas arose to speak he was so much cheered that it was several minutes before he got his breath back to commence his remarks, which were as follows:

194

"Your Royal Highness, the Prince of Wales, Hon. Ambassador Dawes and distinguished friends, it is true, I am going to lift the blooming old 'Mug' and bring it back home with me, for I have a feeling deep down in my heart that I must, and am going to win, that 'elusive mug,' although I love the American people, for there is no country today that fights more fairly and squarely than do American sportsmen, whom I have learned to know and respect, for we have for many years met in contest and fought our battles fairly and squarely and parted, as good friends, with a friendship that will forever live live and endure. I love good friends, but still give me the dear, dear friends of old."

The Royal Launch was in waiting at the foot of the stairs leading from Fishmongers' Hall to the River Thames, at which spot I, the writer, saw the grandfather and grandmother of the young Prince, alight from the Royal Launch, Albert Edward, Prince of Wales, in after years King Edward VII, and his beautiful Queen, Alexandria of Denmark, in the year of our Lord, 1863.

Many such luncheons and dinners are being given in honor of Sir Thomas Lipton on his departure for America to lift the cup, for at last the people of England are commencing to feel and recognize the fact that Sir Thomas Lipton has done much for them and their country, and that the poor London grocer, the wee little Irish and Scotch orphan boy, proved himself to be a world-beater, known, loved and respected by the rich and poor the world over, and this great peace arbiter does not have to sing the old song anymore, to wit—"Though poverty daily looks in at my door, I am hungry, footsore and ill, I can look the whole world in the face and can say: 'Though I am poor, I am a gentleman still.' "

And in conclusion we are all going to be singing very shortly the following old ballad, "When Tommy comes marching home again, hurrah, hurrah, when Tommy comes marching home again, hurrah, hurrah, the village bells will ring with joy to welcome home our Irish boy and his blessed old Queen's Cup, when Tommy comes marching home."

My, but what a wonderful day that will be when Sir Thomas returns the cup and has it placed in the drawing room of the Royal Ulster Yacht Club of Ireland, that so many good men and true have tried but failed to do and their last words being, "Sir Thomas, it is up to you."

Yes, and Sir Thomas is going to make good, for as those good people did say, we are looking for Sir Thomas most every day.

Portsmouth, England, July 9th, 1930. *Shamrock V* with Sir Thomas, her owner, on board, sailed into Gosport today flying sixteen winning flags at her masthead. Oh boys! what a wonderful reception they both received, for the large number of townsfolk that took a holiday the day the *Shamrock* was launched on April 14th of that year, the very day that the *Enterprise* was launched, took another holiday the day she left Portsmouth to defeat the best of yachts and yachtsmen in the British Isles, and my word, how they did whoop it up, for the whole of the Isle of Wight was just one big pageant of glory, and so well it might be.

The *Shamrock V* is now being put in shape to leave England for America in about a week, and may God protect her and her noble crew and land her safe in New York harbor, there to be put in shape again to face America's best, or to be right, pardon me, the New York Yacht Club's best.

And won't we of America be proud when we see the *Shamrock V* sailing up the bay with these same sixteen flags flying at her masthead. Oh boy! but after all, it's all in the game.

How happy the crew and her commanders will be when they take up their quarters on the new boat that Sir Thomas bought and is having put in shape for them, they sure will enjoy a good night's sleep in the busy harbor of protection, before preparing to get ready for the firing gun or signal to stand ready to cross the line in her first race for the America's Cup on Saturday, September 13th, 1930.

Dear readers, for your information and guidance, I am about to write what the writer deems a wonderful address, that given by that famous man among men, and one that the whole world is proud of, who at the age of nineteen took his father's place and visited the bloody fields of Flanders in the great World's War of 1914 to 1918, cheering up the men, both of his own country and their allies, who were very busy fighting with their backs to the wall, who by the cheers and comfort given them by His Royal Highness, the Prince of Wales, the heir to the Crown of England.

It is a well known fact that King George himself also visited the battlefields, and so, too, would his honorable father, the late King Edward VII, had he lived, and again if King Edward VII had lived, there would not have been any war at all; this I am confident of.

The writer has written this story before in my book of history entitled "OUR POLICE GUARDIANS," a second edition of which was published and sold.

The address in question was delivered by His Royal Highness, the Prince of Wales, at the luncheon given by the Honorable Company of Master Mariners of England in honor of Sir Thomas Lipton, the dean of the yachting and sporting world, in London July 8th, 1930, previous to his departure for Newport, Rhode Island, America, to try again to win back the world's greatest trophy, the America's Cup. Speech of His Royal Highness, the Prince of Wales, who was the Royal Toastmaster at the luncheon. To wit:

"The yacht *America* won the cup in a race around the Isle of Wight in 1851 and American yachtsmen have held it ever since.

"Sir Thomas Lipton's first *Shamrock* was built in 1899. The selected defender of America was the yacht *Columbia,* which won three straight races somewhat easily. *Shamrock II* was his second challenger, and raced in 1901 against the same defending yacht, the *Columbia.*

"This series of races was remarkable for the close finishes—the difference in the times being a matter of seconds—and in the final race the *Shamrock* finished ahead of the *Columbia,* but lost the race through having to allow some thirty-odd seconds time allowance, the *Columbia* winning the series.

"A notable incident associated with the *Shamrock II* was that of her being dismasted when engaged in a trial race on the Solent, on which occasion King Edward VII was on board. Fortunately no one was injured.

"The *Shamrock III* was built to race in 1903, and was opposed by the *Reliance,* which was regarded somewhat as a freak, being of the scow type with the immense sail area of 16,000 square feet. The *Shamrock III,* though a fast and very beautiful yacht, could not keep pace with her huge rival, and was defeated in three straight races.

"The *Shamrock IV* was built to race for the America's Cup in 1914 and left this country, convoyed by Sir Thomas Lipton's Steam Yacht *Erin,* about the middle of July of that year. She passed through the great fleet, then assembled at Spithead, on her way across the Atlantic and when war was declared on August 4th, she was well over her long, tiresome voyage to America.

"The *Erin's* wireless operator learned the news of the declaration of war by intercepting a message to a German cruiser in the neighborhood, and later got in touch with a British cruiser, on whose instructions the *Erin* towed the *Shamrock IV* to Bermuda and later to New York, where the *Shamrock IV* remained until 1920, when the contest was held, with the result that although the *Shamrock IV* won the first two races, she was finally defeated by the *Resolute* winning the remaining three.

"The *Shamrock V* is built to the American's own universal rule under their J class. All interested in yachting know that she has shown remarkable pace and racing qualities.

"In all this great effort Sir Thomas has upheld the great tradition of British yachting and British sportsmanship, and while we congratulate him on his great efforts in the past and proudly acknowledge the stimulus and encouragement he has given to all those who are engaged upon, and interested in, this sport of the sea, I think it is his pluck that calls for more admiration. We wish him the very best of luck, and no body of men in the world will watch and hope for his triumph more than the Honorable Company of Master Mariners. All we ask is a turn of luck, and, in the presence of the American Ambassador, I say and I believe it will be as popular in America as it will be in this country if, at 80 years of age, Sir Thomas brings back to this country the cup which was won for America, when he was one year old." And the Prince of Wales sat down amidst the applause of all present, and so well they might applaud, for this was one of the noblest addresses ever given by the son of a reigning monarch, and that by a dutiful son whom God willing, will be called upon to succeed his democratic father in spite of the overthrow of kings and high potentates has succeeded to rule with a kindly hand, thereby winning the love and respect of his people the world over, and when the day comes that day that we hope is yet far distant that King George V is called upon to join his great father, King Edward VII, we will all say in one big voice, "Long Live the King, the King Is Dead, Long Live the King."

And when the Prince of Wales called upon our great Ambassador, "Hellfire" Charles G. Dawes, to say a few words, the young Prince knew well what he was doing for all England as well as America knew that "Hellfire" Charley Dawes, was a fighter, and not a talker, and when Ambassador Dawes arose to speak, he was received with round after round of applause, for they like that whole-souled democratic American, and glory in the fact that they are blessed with a fighting American Ambassador at the Court of St. James.

I will quote for your pleasure the remarks of Ambassador Dawes at that great representative luncheon on July 8th, 1930:

"Now that Britain has shown that she has the fastest airplanes and the fast automobile," Ambassador Dawes said, "America will be slightly disappointed if she shows also that she has the fastest yacht, but that disappointment will hardly equal the disappointment which will be felt if this great sportsman does not win." And Fighting Ambassador Charles G. Dawes sat down amidst applause that might have been heard in the Parliamentary Halls of St. Stephens at Westminster. And since that memorable luncheon Sir Thomas Lipton, aged and worn, is being besieged with invitations to the farewell parties of all prominent men and organizations throughout England.

Sir Thomas Lipton, that grand old Irish Baronet, and dean of yachtsmen, in his 80th year is receiving so many invitations to dinner and luncheons just before taking his departure from Ireland to win the America's Cup that he is forced to take a rest, for he does not want to upset his stomach before leaving, for he thinks more of winning the blooming "mug," than he does of all the dinners and suppers and luncheons tendered to him.

And rightly so, for human nature is but human nature after all, and must at all times be considered, and while Sir Thomas does not seek postponements or offer excuses, nevertheless, he was in duty bound to call off several of these kind invitations, for the time being.

Sir Thomas hopes to have the *Shamrock V* ready to start bucking the wild Atlantic Ocean next Thursday, but if not ready, under no circumstances will he ask his skipper and crew to start out on Friday, the 18th, but will see to it that all being well she will sail on Saturday July 19th.

And again Sir Thomas is perfectly justified in standing by his decision, because before that world-destroying war of 1914 to 1918, no English skipper and many American skippers would sail on Friday, but since that time the world has gone money-mad and they care not Friday, Sunday, or any other day; they want the trade, and being mad after the almighty dollar, they throw all caution to the winds and sail anyhow, and any time.

From the latest dispatches received from over there is one stating that the *Shamrock V* has been visited by a "Talisman" to insure winning the cup.

Portsmouth, England, July 11th, 1930.—Sir Thomas Lipton received today from a famous old lady a talisman packed and sealed in a large case, which is intended to insure the *Shamrock V* winning the America's Cup.

It was handed to Captain Ned Heard, the skipper of the *Shamrock V*, with the blessings and the good wishes of the lady in question, wishing the *Shamrock V* every good luck, asking heaven to protect her and her crew every step of the way over and success follow them until the cup is won, and ever after.

Captain Heard said: "Without doubt, the *Shamrock V* is the fastest challenger that ever undertook to bring back the cup. I feel so confident of the *Shamrock's* success that if she doesn't win it will be the biggest surprise and disappointment of my life."

Now we hear that the British Sportsman's Club wants Sir Thomas to be their guest at a dinner to be tendered him on Monday night next, at which dinner Lord Birkenhead is to propose the health of Sir Thomas, and our great warrior Ambassador is to be present also, and no doubt the Prince of Wales.

But it is alright for them to be mailing invitations to Sir Thomas, but Sir Thomas is his own doctor, and is using good judgment in asking a postponement to all of those rich and kindly invitations so that he will be able to conserve his strength and after he has won the America's Cup, his thousands of friends and fellow club members may whoop it up to their heart's content, but until then, please refrain from undermining the present good health of Sir Thomas, and a good purpose will be better served by all.

For after Sir Thomas adds a few more flags to the sixteen that he now flies from the mast head of *Shamrock V* and the good American flag that fought and won just as hard was these sixteen. Sir Thomas is taking things easy, but after that, well, all the world will rejoice. The falling of the *Shamrock's* mast, I am pleased to say, was not so sorrowful an accident, for there was no one injured when the mast of *Shamrock II* fell while the late King Edward VII, father of the present King George V, at the time a guest of Sir Thomas Lipton, was on board and had just left that part of the deck, but the good game old sport, prepared to jump overboard when the crash came, and when the excitement had passed, good old King Eddie and his hospitable host, sat in the saloon of *Erin* and filled up on champagne instead of water, that they sure would have filled up on if they were forced to jump to save their lives, peace be to that good King Edward VII and success follow his host of that time, the great Irish Baronet and father of the yachting game today the world over, Sir Thomas Johnstone Lipton, Bart, K.C.V.O. which in English means, Knight Commander of the Victorian Order, and many other titles of note, but Sir Thomas don't want titles, all he wants is the America's Cup, and this he is going to get before God calls him, his one heart's desire, that he would be willing to give his all to obtain, and the wish of this grand old Knight of the sea is going to be fulfilled, believe me.

Sir Thomas hopes that the weather will be favorable as it was during the southerly crossing in 1914, for the races that took place in 1920.

In the crossing, it was remarkable to learn that the crew of *Shamrock IV* were able to transfer in a dinghy to the escorting steamer frequently to obtain new provisions, or if they were not able to do that, then they of course would be in hard luck, eating hard tack.

One month's rations for a crew of twenty-two men and fresh water to be used for the whole trip over, that is by taking on new water at the Azores.

Shamrock V expects to arrive in America in time to spend a month tuning up. Sir Thomas wishes it known that he will cancel several of the races on the Clyde, so that he can send *Shamrock V* away as early as he possibly can, giving the boys a good chance to rest up, and be in the pink of condition when they arrive off Newport. This the writer hopes will be about August 10th, Providence permitting.

In June, 1920, Sir Thomas Lipton, in an interview, made the following statement. "I think I have the key this time."

"Haven't you a home of your own?" How well I do remember being amused by these words under a cartoon from the pen of the famous McCutheon, which depicted a party of my American friends busily engaged in nailing down the America's Cup, while your humble servant, Tom Lipton, was shown making valiant efforts to break down the door in order to wrest the much coveted prize from their custody.

"Well, here I am again at the door—this time with a magic key in the shape of *Shamrock IV*, which I hope will prove effective, achieving the ambition of my life by winning the blue ribbon of the sea and solving the problem which has puzzled British yachtsmen for seventy years.

"Whether I have the right key can only be proven in the coming races off Sandy Hook. Whichever way the victory goes, however, my admiration and respect for the great American people will remain unaltered, and my recollections of their unbounded kindness and hospitality continues undimmed and unimpaired." Sir Thomas came near making good, winning two races.

"SHAMROCK V" LOST ON THE HIGH SEAS, LOSING SIGHT OF HER CONVOY ON HER WAY TO NEW YORK

PART IV—CHAPTER V

The crew of *Shamrock V* worked mighty hard to get her in ship-shape to tackle old frosty faced Father Neptune and his roaring seas before sailing for America, on their way to win the America's Cup.

It appears that *Shamrock V,* by the orders of someone unknown, sailed alone, having lost sight of the *Erin,* before calling at the Azores to take aboard the provisions for this long nasty trip.

The famous little greenbird, the *Shamrock V,* running into another storm was forced to return to port, and run into the Azores also, and how happy the gang was to see the *Shamrock* in her good old form, sailing right into port, none the worse for her lonely sea roving. My, but what a mad, desperate chance they took of disaster, but the boys only laughed it off and jumped in to help their buddies in provisioning the *Erin,* No. 2, for they were all crazy to get under way and get the anxiety off their minds.

So that's the pretty little Queen *Shamrock V,* that Sir Thomas has chosen to meet our yachts, neither of whom has yet shown their ability to stand a moderate breeze of from 17 to 20 miles, and that looks bad for our yachts, unless something unforeseen shows up before the races of September, 1930.

But all is well that ends well, and *Shamrock V,* being tough, she took all that Father Neptune could give her, and that was nothing good, for the horny faced old rascal has raised hell with our own yachts of late.

Imagine the feelings of those poor boys getting knocked around, and none but our Supreme being a witness in these awful storms, that one runs into at sea, it takes a stout heart to face it, but these poor fellows were counting on the bonus, and how happy they would be returning to their homes.

But wait until you see those same boys, after a good night's drinking of alf and alf, throwing off their coats and going to work, you would never believe that they are the very same heroes of the deep, that stole *Shamrock* and brought her over here, to beat all before them. It won't be long now and we will know all about it, and then we can settle down in a chair to rest.

We also hear good news from London, July 31, and that is that our dear old friend Sir Thomas Lipton, has booked passage for New York, to sail with his good old friend of long years, Commodore Cunningham of the *S. S. Leviathan,* leaving Southampton, August 10th next, and the grand old Baronet is in the best of spirits, feeling fit and well again, and ready to tackle whatever might come along for he knows that he has the winning yacht.

On the high seas, July 24th, 1930. In spite of the report published in London yesterday, stating that *Shamrock V* and all hands had gone down, the latest reports from the wireless of the *Erin,* her escort, today, July 23rd, 1930, time, 7 o'clock P.M., to Sir Thomas, at his beautiful residence, Osidge, London, was that all is well, we are now three hundred miles west of the Lizard, and everything and everybody doing well. And again next day.

Aboard Sir Thomas Lipton's *S. Y. Erin,* convoying the *Shamrock V,* July 24th, 1930. "All is well, and we are now at the half-way point between Britain and the Azores, so far so good."

These stories that have been circulated about the Lipton boats being in serious trouble are a pack of lies, that have originated in the brains of some darned fool reporter, who ought to be cast into jail, for having in his own selfish way written for publication such a damnable story.

But it just goes to show dear readers how far some of that profession will go, how low down they will stoop, hell be to their dirty souls, they do not care what sorrow and torment they carry into the homes of the wives and children of these good men that are bringing the *Erin* and *Shamrock V* over to this country. Nor do they care for the sorrow and lament that a lying story of that nature brings to Sir Thomas, and his staff, whose only desire is the safety of his men, the protection of life first, property may come after. But let us all thank God and be happy, and pray for the best, kind Providence permitting, August 15th will soon be here and so too will *Shamrock V* and her heroes and the escorts on the *S. Y. Erin.*

We may rest assured that the skippers and crews of *Shamrock V* and the *Erin* is not going to lose any time in getting away from the miseries of this long miserable ocean travel facing gales and strong headwinds continually for they are looking forward to a much deserved and a much wanted decent night's rest, and they may surprise us by slipping in ahead of time.

However, all that we can do is to watch and pray for their comfort and safe landing in America, God willing. They arrived O.K. on August 13th, after a nasty, stormy passage, and was met by Police Commissioner, Grover A. Whalen and Staff, Police Glee Club and Band, followed by the Newport reception under the supervision of Mayor Mortimer Sullivan, and a Jim dandy it was.

SAILING FOR THE PROMISED LAND

True to form, Sir Thomas Lipton's *Shamrock V* sailed for America today, just as promised, for Sir Thomas never goes back on his word.

And in sending his pretty little yacht out here to give our yachtsmen a few lessons, as it were, it is at a mighty risk, for *Shamrock V* was met with one of those terrible English coast storms, the like of which finished Lord Kitchner in 1916, and would have finished Lloyd George, had he too have gone with that great soldier on his mission to Russia.   And that canny little man, the hero of Wales, owes his life to fighting Ireland.

Ireland's troubles in the British House of Commons is all that saved him for the Carson Amendments to the Home Rule Bill had then passed the House, and that canny little Welshman, Heaven had no room for him then.

But to treat that poor frail little chicken *Shamrock V* that way was a terrible act of indecency, and that too with the thousands, both on land and on sea waving goodbye, she sailed forth, but had to return, too much storm.

That is why I have been saying that it is an inhuman act to ask your fellowmen, in fact order them to sail over on their own bottom, for such things as brutal storms is a constant menace on the Atlantic ocean.

It is Tom Lipton's fleet today, it might have been an all American fleet tomorrow, and Tom Lipton was always known as a good soldier. did not stop to reason why, it was for him to do or die.

Sir Thomas, who was not able to attend, met the newspaper men at Osidge cheerfully and he told them that he was sure going to win the "Mug" this time, for he had today the best yacht that he ever had, and when you take into consideration that *Shamrock V* has won sixteen first and four second prizes out of twenty-two starts, and racing against much larger yachts, it is easily seen that *Shamrock V* is a world beater.

"I have never before felt so confident about a yacht as on this trip, it of course is not so pleasant when one has to send his yacht alone over the stormy Atlantic ocean, but these are the rules as promulgated, and we must of course, obey them, but I am in hopes it will be my last, for I am sure going to win, and take the cup back with me," and all present gave a loud cheer.

Aboard the *Shamrock V* were Captain Henry Paul, her ocean pilot, and a crew of twenty-two good stouthearted fellows, and all longing to get to America.

Commodore Duncan F. Neill, Captain Ross and Albert Bardour of the Royal Ulster Yacht Club.

We read with pleasure, the joyful news, that Sir Thomas Lipton has now fully recovered from the disposition that he was suffering from, and today he is in good health, but very busy preparing to bid goodbye to dear old London town, on his way to New York to lift the cup, all London is happy and in a blaze of gaiety, for never before did they think so well of Sir Thomas when leaving on this same errand to lift the cup.

And on Saturday last, August 9th, 1930, Sir Thomas was kept mighty busy bidding his friends goodbye, and good luck, on his mission of mercy, that is to, if possible, restore a wondering child to her home and loved ones, a Cup that strayed away from home, away back in 1851, and forgot to return.

His was a wonderful send-off this time, with parades and bands of music marching down through Hyde Park, to the Green Park, past Buckingham Palace and the Royal Family at the open windows wishing him God's speed, and the big men of Parliament waiting to bid him goodbye and good luck.

Along they marched, down through Rotten Row, over Westminster Bridge, arriving at the Waterloo station to entrain for Southampton, there to board that beautiful ocean greyhound the *S. S. Leviathan,* under the command of his old friend and crony, Commodore Harold Cunningham.

And there he was given another wonderful reception, the good people turning out to say goodbye Sir Thomas, good luck, and prosperity follow you so that when the grand old sportsman got aboard, he was mighty tired, but so happy at his send-off, particularly that of the poorer folks, whom he loved so well, and after a few hours rest he was on deck with his old friend, the Commodore, seeing which of them could tell the greatest and best story.

It was reported that the reception given in London to the parting of Sir Thomas and his staff, was the greatest ovation ever before given a man. With the men of the Irish Guards from the Wellington Barracks and the old and tried members of the Scots Guard and their Kiltie Band, lined the curb along both sides of Rotten Row, down to Parliament Street.

Was there any reason why Sir Thomas was so happy, well I'll say there was, for next to the opening of the Parliament by the King, there was no other pageant to equal this one accorded, our grand old friend, for we were all happy.

And after a very fine voyage over, he was again welcomed by the Police Band and Glee Club, under the able management of Police Commissioner Grover A. Whalen and his Staff of Deputy Commissioners, representing Mayor James J. Walker, the good people of the great municipality, New York.

And he was given the time of his life by all, and of course, that cheered the good old sportsman more than anything else in life, for his love for America and her people was ever foremost in his heart, and remained so until his dying day.

And again the good people of Newport, Rhode Island, under the supervision of Mayor Sullivan, received Sir Thomas with open arms. Some reception, one grand and glorious day it was, O.K.

I often sigh for my good old Broadway friends of the past, among them Jim Churchill, Paddy Roche, the former owner of the good old "Rossmore" Hotel and the Brighton Beach Hotel and others. But today I ran into that noted Broadway character actor, George W. Callahan, noted for the big hit he made in that world's famous actor and play writer, George M. Cohan's play of "The Meanest Man in the World", George Callahan in the part of the (Cobbler) and I was mighty glad to meet my old friend, just as funny as ever, and O.K.

THE CITY WELCOMES SIR THOMAS LIPTON

I recall vividly the grand reception accorded Sir Thomas, on his, what rightly might be termed a home coming, for New York, more or less, was his home, for he had more friends here than in any other part of the world.

Yes, Sir Thomas loved the good old name of New York, and the thousands of dear old friends that he had made and was continually making, and when Sir Thomas made a friend, then this friendship existed on through life.

Saturday, August 16th, 1930, time, 7 o'clock A.M., the good ship *Leviathan* was to enter the harbor about this time and the Mayor's Committee of welcome went down the Bay on the steamer *Macon* to greet the old sportsman, and after his medical examination, he was taken off the *Leviathan* to the *Macon,* and a jolly old time was had by all on the way to old New York.

Police Commissioner Grover A. Whalen, always a very busy man, had not yet arrived and Sir Thomas felt somewhat lonesome, for they were old friends of long standing, yes from 1919, for Mr. Whalen was then secretary to our Mayor, John F. Hylan, also Chairman of the Mayor's Committee for the reception of distinguished visitors to our city, and Oh, Boy, how he did receive.

It was far from being a morning that one would wish, for it rained so, we all had to take to the saloon, and we will again soon, now that the President Franklin D. Roosevelt is going to give us our beer back again, God bless his heart, he is a Godsend, if ever there was one.

Sir Thomas looking hale and hearty, had a handshake and a happy smile for all, and when called upon to address them all, or tell some funny stories, for which he was noted, the grand old fellow peeled them off and kept them in fits of laughter with his stories after he had made the following remarks, that was very pleasing to all present, to wit:—

Of course, the Radio was much in evidence, and the Police Band

and her Bon Ton Singers of the Police Glee Club made all present, happy when Sir Thomas started his remarks, by first of all asking where is Mr. Whalen?

Like a boy on his way to meet his girl, Sir Thomas was happy when he stepped up to the transmitter and made the Radio do the rest, and he said, "I am pleased to be with you again, and to think of it, sailing into good old Castle Garden, near where I landed a wee poor boy of 17, in the year of our Lord 1867, and I assure you gentlemen the reception is very much different, and no doubt many of your grand old fathers and mothers arrived here in the steerage and had been through the mill, and was well acquainted with its miseries, yes, almost tortures.

"The life of a steerage passenger in the past was far from sunshine, and that is why you have in America today such a strong, healthy nation of fighters, men and women alike, they are all able to fight and do their bit, God bless them all, they were never found wanting.

"When one landed at Castle Garden, often without a copper in his clothes, believe me, one had to fight or go hungry, and I have had to do both, and here I am today by dint of hard work, and my love for your country and my friends, I am being received in a style that would do credit to my dear good friend of the past, the late King Edward VII, of England.

"There is nothing like work, and no doubt most of you good men know the same, for money don't grow on tree tops and you are all in the millionaire class with myself, so what's the use of trying to tell you folks something that you already know, but did I ever tell you how I became an Irish Scotch boarding house runner over there at the battery," and he told this and many other stories that morning, and between the remarks of Sir Thomas and the men of the Police Commissioner's Staff, the famous Police Department of this great city of ours, composed of one hundred singers were through the Police Band, composed of another one hundred of the finest boys in blue, entertained Sir Thomas and guests until we arrived at the Atlantic Boat Club House, West 86th Street and the Police Club House on Riverside Drive, yes, that was a wonderful reception, one the likes was never before seen.

By that time Commissioner Grover Whalen, who had been detained on some very important business in New York, had arrived and grasping the hand of Sir Thomas, they moved over to the radio transmitter, and this is what followed. "You are no stranger to New York, Sir Thomas," said Mr. Whalen, "As an old friend of mine, Mayor Walker has asked me to convey to you his heartiest greetings with the hopes that Sir Thomas would call upon him at the City Hall later on.

"With the greetings of Mayor Walker comes the wish that you

will win the America's Cup this year so that our yachtsmen here can sail over and bring it back, Mayor Walker thinks, Sir Thomas, that you are the greatest and happiest yachtsman of all time."

Commissioner Whalen, the one-hundred per cent American that opened the eyes of our Government in Washington to the dirty work of the Russian Communists right here in America, then welcomed Sir Thomas on behalf of the Reception Committee. Sir Thomas replied as follows:

"Mr. Chairman and gentlemen of this big Reception Committee, I am very thankful to you for your kindness to me, and I am delighted to be here, and in reply to your great Mayor, Mr. James J. Walker, and his greetings, I am most thankful, and it will not be long before I visit the Mayor at the City Hall there to thank him personally for each time in other years that I had had the happiness to meet Mayor Walker, why I go away happy for I never met an abler speaker or a finer amuser, witty and sociable to the last point, again I thank you all."

Sir Thomas speaking into the microphone, had this to say, "I have been very fortunate in all of my races so far with *Shamrock V*, she is a new yacht and I hold out great hopes of her winning the cup, this year for sure."

WELCOME TO OUR CITY, SIR THOMAS

COMMENTS OF THE PRESS

Notes of greeting to a welcome visitor, who today is no more.

Just as though kind providence had ordained that this would be the last welcome to this great sportsman, Sir Thomas Lipton, and had sent out a quiet tip, he received one of the grandest welcomes ever before given to such distinguished persons, and this made him very happy.

The aristocrats of Newport, the yachtsmen of America, the newspaper men of the country, the expert newsmongers and in fact from the bootblack up, they all did their bit to make that grand old man happy, and cheerful.

Among the many kind things the newspapers had to say about Sir Thomas are the following: "We Toast You Never Say Die Sportsman" because your Shamrocks suffered defeat on four occasions in their attempt to lift the America's Cup, here you are again visiting us ready and willing to, if it must be, take another licking, and keep right on smiling.

A noble old sportsman past eighty, and still in the swim of life's activities, when younger men have long since retired, here you are a credit to the great nation and her people whom you represent, her greatest representative of all time, with no man or party of men to take your place.

Born of humble Irish parentage, you advanced yourself from a penniless, honest and energetic youngster to that of a peer among the British, and others, who by the dint of hard work, established one of the largest tea and coffee enterprises the world over. Through your own personal achievements you merited Knighthood and a Baronetcy from the British Crown.

In all of your dealings with your fellow man, or men, you have proven yourself true blue and four square, and a man among men, that we are all of us proud of, and wish you every good luck.

Another writer has this to say, about Sir Thomas Lipton:

"Persons who can neither name one end of a yacht from the other, nor the difference between spinaker and mainsail, are beginning to get more than mildly excited over the coming races for the America's Cup between Sir Thomas Lipton's *Shamrock V,* and the defender, which ever one of our 6 yachts is chosen and men who never read about or see a yacht race are prepared to go to Newport this year, elated at the opportunity."

Speaking of 6 to 1, reminds me of a remark made by Duncan Neill, at a dinner party given Sir Thomas in London, to wit—"Although they have six yachts to our one, we have no fear." Although they kick at England having six votes in the "League of Nations," Why. Now you ask one, if you can?

Sir Thomas, was very proud of his many winnings, of cups, plaques and prizes of every conceivable color and make, and one day he ordered that a photographer should be called in to take a photograph of them all, and he having autographed each copy, he mailed a copy to each of his many friends among them his old friend, J. J. Hickey, and I am proud to be the possessor of such a historical souvenir, and will always keep it in sight.

Now is the time Sir Thomas, take to yourself a wife, but be sure, pick a good one.

Oh yes, there was one cup that Sir Thomas threw out from among his set and that was the cup donated by old Kaiser Bill, or the former Emperor of Germany, known as the Gold Cup and won by *Shamrock IV* in the "Kiel" Regatta, for after scratching this cup it turned out to be just a pewter cup. This was not the only case of chiseling, there were others I could write of, My word!

The fourth and last race of the series of 1930, for the America's Cup has been won and lost, *Miss Enterprise* the winner, and *Shamrock V,* the loser, and once more history repeats, we won you in 1851, and we are not going to lose you any more, at least while the noble spirit of yachting exists.

It seemed to me that *Shamrock V* was having a little fun to herself, for the last race of these series were fought out better than the first *Shamrock*, leading *Enterprise* over the starting line and gaining a little advantage, but not for long, for when Skipper Harold Vanderbilt, woke up he said nay, nay, *Miss Shamrock*, get back in your place, "Thou Shall Not Pass."

No. *Shamrock V*, did not pass, but little did we know that it was Lipton and *Shamrock's* last, for the hand of death was so shortly after to be placed on the shoulder of that famous international yachtsman and sport king.   May the Heavens be his bed, on this beautiful "All Saints" morning of 1933.

This the last race, was sailed over a triangular course, and noted as the best race of the four, and if *Shamrock V*, could have kept her gain and improved upon it, it might have been a more interesting show, and Sir Thomas made happy after witnessing the race, but alas, that was not to be.

Skipper Vanderbilt has a mortal detest in being held a prisoner, for he was forced to experience that before, and it stuck in his gizzard ever after, oh, yes, he knows what it is to be forced into the leeward and kept there, as he was in the races of elimination by *Yankee* and *Weetamoe*, and he will never forgive them, although they just got Harold napping.

But they had laid their plans in fine style, when making ready to tie Mr. Vanderbilt and his beautiful yacht up in the rear of both yachts, this to my mind hurt the souls of the Vanderbilts more than did the beating accorded him by the two old pirates of Buzzards Bay, *Vanitie* and *Resolute*.

But let me tell you racing experts, that there is not a man living today that can beat Harold Vanderbilt, and keep him under their lee.

Sir Thomas Lipton has met with many setbacks, and his ups and downs were increasing since he first entered the yachting world, but no one can ever say he quit, for he never knew what the word quit meant, and woe be to him who would dare mention such a thing.

Of course troubles will come and troubles will go, and no man can find fault with a man that worries when everything is not going right, and Sir Thomas was sure that all was not right off Newport, September 13th, 1930, that is what caused him to cave in, and pass on to the great beyond, both loved and respected by all the world.

My word, how that grand old sportsman's heart did raise, before the race and how quickly it did fall after the yachts were across the starting point, and that was enough for him, he then and there gave vent to his feelings that brought sadness to the old man's heart, that carried him away from us all, oh yes, he managed to keep up, for his never say die policy never left him and he gloried in seeing *Shamrock V* winning most of the races from the cream of the British Isles, and while writing this story and about to close this brief statement, I received a dispatch from Bangor, Ireland, dated June 21st, 1930, stating that Sir Thomas Lipton's *Shamrock V* had won a very hard fought race beating the *"White Heather"* by six minutes, and this over one of the rockiest old yachting courses to be found the world over, off the rugged Irish coast and against a fleet of much larger yachts, than his wee little *Shamrock* of Ireland. That and other such victories gave him hopes that his Bonnie Prince *"Charley"*, of a yacht, would be fit to race against any yacht either in America or the British Isles, and who could blame him? I know that I could not after seeing *Shamrock V* win one of the grandest races, and over a forty mile course, and this against all the big yachts, the King's *Britannia,* one of the best in British waters was a mile behind *Shamrock* at the finish line.

When Sir Thomas had arrived here with his beautiful *Shamrock V,* our own yachts were all doing badly, and the remarks were passed that if they did not do better, then *Shamrock V* would walk away with the America's Cup, it was acknowledged by our experts that *Shamrock V* was in fine shape, and prepared to make the fight of her life. But what happened to *Shamrock V* right after that fast sail yesterday, August 15th, 1930, who can, or who will, tell us the grave news?

The following incident of note took place while Sir Thomas was sailing homeward with his good friend, Commodore Cunningham, on the *S. S. Leviathan.*

Just as the *Leviathan* reached the spot of a bloody encounter in war time, ending up with the sinking of the U. S. S. *"Ticonderoga"* by an enemy Submarine taking 240 officers and men to a watery grave.

What thoughts must have been running through the mind of Sir Thomas, at this sad time, thinking back to 1915 and the loss of his beautiful steam yacht *Erin* by the dastardly act of the enemy, taking with her many of the Irish Baronet's favorite employees, and within an inch of taking his Commodore, Duncan F. Neill, who had just joined up with his colors and was in a number of sea battles, arriving home after the Armistice with the D.S.O.

It so happened that Sir Thomas was ashore dining with the King and Queen of Serbia, or he too may have been aboard the ill-fated yacht *Erin,* and with the other poor souls taken from us when we needed him most.

Among the passengers on this trip was a member of the crew of the lost ship *Ticonderoga,* who had helped fight the battle of freedom for all, a glorious act, taking from us our sons and daughters, who had given up the comforts of both home and motherland to fight for Freedom and the Democracy of us all, and never returned, but after all "Sherman" was right, "War is hell."

John Michael, was the name of the survivor, who at the services for the dead held that day, told about the actions of the U-boat 153, of the German Navy, and he dropped overboard on the very spot a small bag of dirt taken off the grave of Captain J. J. Madison, commander of the *Ticonderoga,* at the time of the battle, and sank with his officers and crew.

Commodore Cunningham, and Sir Thomas each made a few remarks, among the passengers were Inspector Griffin and Sergeant Coy, on their way to bring back a desperate prisoner, to answer in court for his many crimes.

Who knows but that these two heroes of the Police Department of New York were thinking back to 1909, when Detective Sergeant Joe Petrosini, was murdered in Palermo, Italy, on a like errand. I quote that great American steel magnate, Mr. Charles Schwab, to wit— "Something may soon come along to give us new impetus—something now unseen, may answer my inquiries above."

The records state that after the battle, and the ships were sinking, Captain Madison was swimming to save his life, and became unconscious, and one of his men dived after him, pulling him into a small boat and transferred to a passing steamer with 21 members of his crew, were taken to the Naval Hospital in Brooklyn, where he passed away.

It was recorded that this was the first time that a U-boat of the enemy, had ever had the courage to fight her rival above water, fighting to a finish, which to say the least, was a creditable act of its commander, his officers and crew, but Heavenly Father, keep us out of such world destroying wars forever and forever, if such can be done, for Thy will be done.

The reading of the many episodes of that same character, in war time, is in a sense pleasing, for it is mighty hard to get your son or sons to speak about their own activities on the battle front, in the great war, or of their own personal transactions, and I love to hear these things, and to know that they were able to "take it."

As stated in another page of this work, my orphan or motherless sons, when their mother died in 1912, were minors, and I paid their way in a good Catholic school of learning, fitted out for boys of that character, while I would travel to forget the past.

My oldest son, Thomas, I put to work in a sporting goods house, and my son, Robert, came to me in 1916, asking me to sign his papers, he wanted to join the U. S. Navy, and I said is that the best that you want to do, well you asked for this and I am not going to stand in your way, give me the papers, I signed them and away he went, becoming a member of the crew of the U. S. line of battleship the *New York,* under the command of Admiral Sim's.

I had no knowledge of what he had done after leaving me, for several years, he would not write me, hence not knowing where he was, I could not write him, and so it went on until after the entrance of our government into the world's war, April 6th, 1917, and my son Thomas, left his desk in Police Headquarters and joined up with the colors, and sailed on the *Kilpatrick* to the Lord knows where, and I was near broken hearted, no word from either son.

Until it came to pass that Mayor John P. Mitchel had given orders to call upon my son Thomas, to resign his position in the Police Department, he not asking his, the Mayor's permission to join the colors, then I got to work through my good old friend Congressman Henry Goldfogle, and located my son Thomas as a Sergeant of the 3rd Engineers, and son Bob, at the request of Admiral Sim's for volunteers, to man submarine chasers, was the first to volunteer, and I located him on a converted cruiser, namely, the *U. S. Alema,* owned by Mr.——— Well it makes no difference, he was a good American, who at the call of his country, gave both, his yacht and his fortune, to win the war.

And it goes without saying that Thomas did not resign his job, and is sitting pretty in his same old position after an absence of two or more years, and son Bob, came back safe, and he too is a member of the same department, in the position of Traffic Cop on the Bowery, and Teddy, at 16, wanted to join the fighting Irish 69th Regiment, but I stood in his way unfortunately, for it serves no good purpose in looking for promotion, for he too is a member of the Police Department of this great municipality, thank God, all three sons married and raising families, maybe to fight for their country if ever called upon. That is why I am so interested in battles at sea.

London, England, October 4th, 1930. Sir Thomas Lipton arrived home today feeling sorry that he did not win the America's Cup, but he will try again, for this Lipton man has more lives than the cat, and like the pussy, if you threw him out of a 10-story window he would land on his feet, but can't win that infernal trophy, America's Cup.

Of course, all the newspaper men for miles around were waiting to button-hole the grand old Irish Baron at Waterloo station, and he was feeling prime to answer all questions, and they were many, but there was one answer that Sir Thomas made and I was very much surprised, for Tom Lipton is always so guarded when answering questions.

But this time, I was afraid that the old sportsman was going to spill the beans, as they say in America, and here is why: One reporter asked how he liked America and Sir Thomas answered, "America, why, I love it, always did and always will, but, there is one thing that I can't understand, but remember that this is not for publication," and he called them all closer to him and whispered in the ear of one or two, "I can't understand, and I don't think it right that America should have a faster yacht than mine," followed by a jolly good laugh among those present.

On another occasion Sir Thomas said, "Why, of course I am going to challenge with my *Shamrock VI,* and she will be provided with all the modern fads and fancies and mechanical gadgets that the law will allow, and one of old Ireland's heroes among the croppy boys, to watch over them all."

"They gave me a wonderful time," said Sir Thomas, "I wish that Vanderbilt would come over here and race under our rules." I asked him, but I hardly think he will. I have been through Vanderbilt's yacht and so has Mr. Nicholson, my designer, so look forward to seeing a much better yacht when I return with *Shamrock VI.* On his way home, Sir Thomas was kept busy signing up the autographs as requested by all the pretty girls on board.

"SOUTHGATE, LONDON,
"October 9th, 1930.

"Dear Mr. Hickey:

"The photographs of *Shamrock V* and *Enterprise* are being returned to us, also the photograph of Sir Thomas alongside of his vast pile of cups and other winning laurels, and trophies, all under separate cover at this mail. Hoping that this will find you in the best of health and with the kindest of remembrances and best wishes.

"Yours faithfully,

"JOHN WESTWOOD.

"Mr. John J. Hickey, Hotel Elton,
"New York City."

MY SURPRISE MEETING WITH THE FORMER GOVERNOR, AL SMITH

PART V—CHAPTER I

Having worked all day, busy putting on the finishing touches to this book after seven long years of compiling, and having to celebrate my introduction of track and field athletics into the Police Department of New York some forty years ago, and my winning of the championship long distance run of one mile, October 5th, 1893, holding same and retiring undefeated for thirteen years, feeling mighty happy in my lonesomeness.

I closed my book, only to reopen same, to have my readers know of one of the greatest surprises that I ever received, in the following incident to wit—Leaving my room at the Hotel the Grand Union, at Park Avenue and 32nd Street, I walked over to 5th Avenue, and at 33rd Street, I ran into my old friend the former Governor, the Hon. Alfred Emanuel Smith, conversing with friends, and before I knew it, our hands were clasped, the Governor of this great Empire State for four terms, said, "Hello Jack, how are you" and in reply, I said, Governor how are you, and passed on.

Be it known that when I won the Police championship, I was a member of the 4th Precinct, No. 9 Oak Street, near where the former Governor was born, he first seeing the light of day December 30th, 1871.

Young Al Smith grew up to be a very likeable boy, always willing to do a good favor, run errands, and if he saw one of us old Policemen in trouble he would run to the station house and report same, and on many occasions Al would go to the Fulton Market to get a can of coffee and a sandwich for the man on post for it was a noticeable fact that we old Cops could always get a ball of whiskey, when we could not get a can of coffee, until young Al Smith would be on his way to work at 3 a.m. My post was Peck Slip, through which most of the Fulton Market employees passed through coming from the Elevated R. R. at Franklin Square at Cherry Hill.

The fact of my winning the championship made me somewhat of a hero among the boys of the old 4th Ward, and young Al Smith was their leader known as the Mascot of the Cops of the 4th Ward, and the Fire Buffs of old Hook and Ladder 32 on John Street, at our ball games and outings, young Al was the hero, and much could be said of America's pride in after years, for Governor, and near President, Alfred E. Smith did wonders. F. D. Roosevelt then named Al

Smith the "Happy Warrior," I hope never to be called the "Forgotten Man."

Dear readers, what makes this meeting with the former Governor, more memorable and historical was the fact that he had just got off the Albany train, after doing one of the grandest things in his life, that was the nominating of the Hon. Herbert H. Lehman, Lieutenant Governor of New York for the last two terms, and Al Smith nominating him to succeed the Hon. Franklin D. Roosevelt, who is about to step out of the Governor's chair in Albany that he so gracefully filled for the past two terms, taking over this great position when the former Governor ran for President in 1928, but was defeated for his faith and love of church, by a pack of un-American scallawaggers.

It was a glorious sight to see standing on the platform of the nominating Convention in Albany last evening, these three great men, namely the present Governor, the Hon. Franklin D. Roosevelt and our next President, clasping the hand of the former Governor, the Hon. Al. E. Smith, the (Happy Warrior) and the Hon. Herbert H. Lehman, whom the former Governor was nominating for our future Governor, more power to them all.

I assure you folks, that I was very much surprised and amazed, for it was the first time that I had been face to face with the former Governor since the memorable year of 1928, one of the darkest days in American history, and while we may forgive, we will never forget. But alas, such matters are too easily forgotten, and by the principals at that, more's the pity.

All of those good men were close personal friends of the late Sir Thomas J. Lipton, and if with us today, he too would glory in the fact that these three old friends are again united, for united they stand, but divided they fall, and the election of President Roosevelt, and Governor Lehman, is all over but the shouting, for the voice of Al Smith sounding over the whole of these great United States, elected both, thanks and praise be to God, our redeemer and maker.

And so that you my friends will not be misled, I have not yet heard from my former good friend, John Westwood, of a letter a week, since February 11th last, 1932, Why? this, his last letter to me, was answered forthwith.

Our lives are short in this hardened world, then why not be honest in your dealings with your fellow man, as was the late Tom Lipton, may the Heavens be your bed tonight, Goodbye dear friend. Ah, but Tom Lipton only wanted the America's Cup, but others want the whole world, something that they will never get or should not. There are others, worthy too, oh, yes.

Here are several episodes that must not be passed over, just to show to the world the stupidity of some learned men, and the villainy of the scandal mongers that we are cursed with; hell be to their dirty souls, they are never happy only while writing up or telling the poor, foolish reader lies.

Remember, I hold no brief for the honesty and the bravery of King George V of England, or his son, the young Prince of Wales, for they have on many occasions proven themselves gentlemen and heroes, by playing the game fair and square, and by visiting the heroes of both America and England on the bloody fields of Flanders. I do not have to tell you good people, for you know that just as well as does the writer. So why not be decent to them.

I was amazed to read in one of our first-class dailies of August 8th, 1930, an editorial emanating from the pen of a man connected with a paper that has always been noted for its knowledge of our brothers over the sea and their advanced honesty in all things, particularly sport, for one does not hear of their squawks or protests; the game is played fair.

This kind of writing may be all right in some suburban paper, but in a noted high-class paper like the one I am speaking about, it does not fit in, or should it have ever been permitted to see the light of day, for it leaves a lot of room for argument, and that must and should be avoided, and it is to these same writers of newspapers to whom we look to avoid, and not foster scandal; enough said. Here is the editorial, read for yourselves:

"THE ROYAL YACHT

"On the day of the fatal accident at Cowes' Isle of Wight, the King's yacht *Britannia* won the race. Moreover, it developed that the King's yacht *Britannia* almost always wins the race. It has won more than two hundred races to date and still going strong. Well, it seems to us that that ought to be looked into. Our point of view of such matters may be somewhat corrupted as a result of the following, too many prize fights that are said to be in the bag; yet we must confess that too long a string of victories in any sport does have a way of arousing our suspicions."

Waurra! Waurra! What a head to be sure, for in all of my long life meeting and knowing the grand old newspaper writers along Park Row, this is the worst that I ever heard; but "none is blinder than he that does not want to see." But this is a sorry state of affairs, to say the least, and I will leave this gentleman to his and my betters. Go see a doctor, old top.

I have, on more than one occasion, seen the King's yacht beaten. This I speak of in this book, so it is no use repeating, and the race that this able writer spoke about, took place on August 6th, 1930, with King George V at her wheel, *Britannia* won, marking her two hundred races won and every race on its merits with *Lulworth* close on her heels, until an unfortunate accident, owing to the rank stupidness of the skipper of a small yacht, the *Lucille,* dashing past *Lulworth,* robbing her of her water, causing the drowning of two and almost that of its owner and family; a damn sorry mess.

That sent King George back to his sick bed again, for the King was so happy at the finish of this race, beating a large field of big yachts, and the fact of this being his two hundredth race won, helped to forget his illness, but for the moment only, for when *Britannia* got back to her base and King George was told of the terrible accident, he fell to the deck.

On recovery, the first thing the King did was to send a letter of sympathy and congratulation on the owner's family escape, and he ordered every vessel in the harbor to half-mast their flags and ordered that the skipper of the *Lulworth* be brought to his cabin and he thanked him highly for his noble work in quitting the race to save many lives, for without his aid and assistance we would have a much sorrower tale to tell today.

And now, for the enlightenment of my able friend, the writer above, let me tell him that *Miss Britannia* is often beaten and beaten badly with or without the King at her wheel, and that to my mind his remarks were very unparliamentary to say the least and he ought to offer an apology to the many thousands of good, sober-minded readers in America. No, I mention no names or editor, or paper; that is free advertising and leads on to much jealousy.

The idea, this placing of King George V of England in the same category as that scoundrel that caused all the bloodshed and the starvation that is following it, Kaiser Wilhelm of Germany, who was noted for winning every army "maneuver" or the other generals would be found on the retired list.

Having being disgusted, I did not finish the editorial, but here I ask in all fairness, was it not out of place to dare insinuate, that is, "Has the King really got a fast yacht?" Gee! If I were only free to be able to answer, it would be in a good old New Yorker's strain of voice, believe me, mixed up with a little of the Steve Brodie, Chuck Connors, Bowery slang, you bet.

And more he says, "There are things that Americans should know, and would very much like to be told about." That's damn rot, no free broad-minded American, man or woman, would be so stupid as to ask such questions. That is none of their darned business. Read the papers, they will keep you informed or if you must know, then give me a ring that you are coming and I will let you take a peep at my records of fifty years back to date. Good night!

Why, no later than May 31st, 1930, *Shamrock V*, with Sir Thomas at the wheel, played rings around the King's *Britannia* and other big yachts. Do you wish more information? If you do, turn over to another page, every word of which is real honest-to-goodness facts, and then go and teach your rotten commercializing, faking gamblers, right here in New York, that will keep you for the time, no doubt, for I have another sorrowful tale to tell.

But, thank God, this is not American. My story emanated from the brain of some rat on the Prince of Wales' staff, or one of his body-guards, but whoever dug up such damn rot ought to be left off the staff of a fine young man as is H.R.H. Albert Edward, Prince of Wales, and heir to the throne.

When I undertook to write the 800 pages of the autobiography, and now the biography of that grand old man of the sea, who so dearly loved to visit the land of the free, and finding myself doing a wrong, I came to the conclusion to sing myself a little song and story of the man that wrote much and in all his vast amount of writing said nothing at all. I re-wrote my story and will endeavor to tell this sad story to you as Sir Thomas told it to me.

"PUTTING ONE OVER ON THE WORLD'S PRINCE CHARMING"

That, to my mind, is how this should be headed, and the rascal that wrote it sent to the "Tower," there to be beheaded, for he is a failure and not fit to hold his job. My story goes back to the year of our Lord, 1919, when you folks knew what a happy time H.R.H., Prince of Wales, spent in this, the Empire city of the world, and like his grand-father, enjoyed every minute of it.

In my letter, I requested that His Royal Highness would please let me have his autograph to be printed in a book that I was then compiling, namely, "OUR POLICE GUARDIANS," published in 1925.

I received an answer when the *Renown* was at lands' end, which read:

"Dear Mr. Hickey: The Prince of Wales has requested me to write you to say that he has made it a practice not to give his signature, but to those people to whom he has been introduced."

I hold that letter, also that of the letter from his father, the King, with a copy of my book, that I sent to Buckingham Palace in 1928, stating "That His Majesty does not receive presents from any but his own British subjects," but thanking me for my kindness.

So you see wonders will never cease, here I am leaving a book with all that I am writing about the King and Prince, compiled, and for two long weeks it was at the Palace of King George V and no doubt read or looked over, by those present, for they love anything American.

And when I received the King's letter from his private Secretary, the late Lord Sandringham, who passed away in 1930, R.I.P., I was delighted, and often take great pleasure in looking over these letters and book, that I am sure was looked over by the King and his household.

And in conclusion, let me say that I think that that rotten lieing story should never have been given to the public, for it serves no good purpose, no, not at all, and I am fully sure that it will not be the means of breaking up the friendships that exists today between these two great English speaking nations, and when America follows President Wilson's advice and becomes a member of the great body of peace lovers ever before noted, I speak of the "League of Nations," then we two governments may dictate and rule the world, and allow no wild man to bring about another war.

I cannot bring myself to believe that any fellow-countryman of mine would dare or attempt to destroy or injure this wonderful Democratic young Prince of Wales, for why should they, with Ireland never so happy as now, and I don't believe they would.

Yes, it is true, that Mr. De Valera, was at the time visiting America, but was seeing beautiful California at that time, and while I am not a follower of Mr. De Valera's or do I believe in his teachings, still I don't think that he would be base enough to do, or allow it to be done, that is to do this fine young fellow grievious bodily harm. And I am quite sure that Mr. Boomer, or his trusty detective from Scotland Yard, John Smith, would stand for it.

Why should the Royalty of today, suffer for the miseries and persecutions inflicted on the people by the murderous Kings, Queens, and soldiery of past centuries, God forbid.

Why this damned question should be introduced at a time when all the people of the sad, sad world was looking for peace, I cannot fathom, and it would be hard to ask an explanation from the fools that introduced it, but maybe the Government will call upon these trouble-makers for an explanation, and I hope they do, and punish such humbugs.

I, from personal experience know right well that such treacherous business as a plot against a Host, could not exist, and when the time came for him to leave, he did not want to go from us to grieve, on his leaving the good line of battleship the *Renown* and looked back long enough to say, "Dear old New York, I am sorry to be forced to leave you, and would like very much to mix up with your people much longer to stay." So far, so good, I was a member of the Sir Thomas Lipton party, escorting the young Prince, then paying his respects to our Mayor, and on his leaving, I shook his hand mighty hard, for the moment forgetting myself, no doubt, thinking that I was in the ring with our present champion, Primo Carnera, the Italian man mountain, who spent his time the other night down in Florida, jumping on the feet of little Tommy Loughran.

The delicate young Prince raised his leg, as if suffering pain, for which I was heartily sorry, and I wrote to the Prince on board the *Renown,* saying how sorry I was for my blunder, but I thought so much of this young chap who so bravely entered the trenches to cheer along the heroes fighting for the whole world's liberty, that is why I forgot myself, an act that I shall never forget, that took place in the grand old City Hall, built in 1812.

In my letter, I asked the Prince if he would kindly send me his autograph, for at the time I was collecting photographs, letters and autographs of all famous heroes of the present day, among them our own great General and world beater, John Pershing, and I wanted the Prince to share a page with General John Pershing, who did so much to help win the war of 1914 to 1918.

And in another part of this work you may read the answer sent me from His Royal Highness, sailing out of New York bay, and for my blunder, I have nothing to say, for I deserved his rebuke, there is no question about that.

Sir Thomas, one night in his room at the Biltmore Hotel said, "Mr. Hickey, we are to be graced with the presence of His Royal Highness, the bonnie Prince of Wales and a right royal party at the coming races in September next of 1930, for the Prince is mighty interested in these coming races, and he will be here in a battleship, maybe the *Renown,* as in 1919."

But you will recall the Prince and his party did not come, why? Well, I asked my dear old friend, Sir Thomas, and his answer was, "I cannot tell you now Mr. Hickey, it's a long sad story, I will tell you all when I come back to America in a few weeks again, for urgent business if the work calls on me at the works."

Sure enough on his return to New York, Sir Thomas asked me to call and be sure to see him alone, Westwood having gone to a show, I spent a long evening with the grand old gentleman, and we were both delighted, no foreign interference or eavesdropping by John Westwood, that evening.

I was amazed at the long sad story that Sir Thomas told me that night for at his earnest request we sat knee to knee, and this is what my grand old friend told me, and I jotted down his every word, so that you, my readers may profit by my good fortune, to wit:—

"You recall Mr. Hickey, that I told you that the Prince of Wales was to be here for the coming races, up to that time everything was made ready for the Prince to sail, but unfortunately the propagandists got to work, and one of the Prince's staff heard a sad story and when related to the Royal Family, the trip was countermanded. I learned that the story was given out that the Prince was to be attacked, in 1919, while sleeping at the Waldorf Astoria Hotel, by several members of an Irish society, who had engaged the room above and the room below the Prince's suite, and to prevent trouble it was decided to call the visit off."

And so ends that sad and rotten story, which to my knowledge could not be, for Mr. Boomer, and his faithful old Scotland Yard house detective, would never for a moment allow such a dirty trick to be pulled off there, for they at all times looked for the comfort and safety of their guests, and that I am ever willing to swear to, for I spent much time at the hotel myself, and am in a position to know just what I am talking about.

The dirty work of these rascals of propagandists brought both sorrow and unhappiness to both countries, more is the pity, for such propaganda helped to keep us farther apart, until these two great Irish heroes, Mike Collins and Arthur Griffiths, instituted the Irish Free State only to be cut down in their manhood, the one poisoned and the other shot and by a fellow countryman, Waurra, Waurra!

And on the taking over of the Dublin Castle and reestablishing the Irish House of Parliament, on College Green, the people of both Ireland and England became happy and contented, and prosperity again loomed in the distance and President William T. Cosgrove and his Irish Free State Cabinet were doing wonders, until by threats of violence he was defeated for President.

A sorrowful blow for the Emerald Isle, and one they are going to rue, I fear, but God is good, and with the aid and assistance of Blessed Saint Patrick, Cosgrove will return and Ireland again return to prosperity.

"With the wolf dog lying down, and the harp without the crown, and the sunburst of Ireland between."

The following sad, villainous lying story was told the writer, to wit :—

Of course, in all such cases of Royalty, or other parties, they hire a suite of rooms, even though they may have a warship laying off shore, for when these good people that visit our shores gets a wift of our glorious sunshine and beautiful old "Bushmills," they are too tired to go aboard.

And it so happened that the Prince of Wales and his staff hired that world's famous house of welcome to all nations, the old Waldorf Astoria, a meeting house for the crowned heads of Europe, Princes, and the diplomats and parliamentarians of the world, whose doors were closed by the Methodists under the command of that noted fakir, Bishop Canon, Jr., and his group.

That is the kind of news our newspapers are turning out each day, and all that is left for us poor simps, is to read the press for the benefit of our coming prosperity, and —the N.R.A.

Who instead of preaching the Gospel of the Lord, they robbed the citizens of this great and glorious country, making it a land of boot-leggers and grafters, who thought no more of violating our great and glorious Constitution, than they did of taking a wet English steamer to Europe, Why?

A story emanating from some imaginative brain, no doubt, when bleary eyed, to have the young Prince of Wales think that they were good, careful protectors, not caring for the sorrow that they were bringing on the world these miserable propagandists, which to my mind was a damnable lie.

That was at the Waldorf Astoria Hotel in 1919, but not made public until the coming yachting season of 1930, for such cussedness would never for a moment be tolerated by the owners of that former famous hotel, and I know of what I speak, for I used to spend my evenings there with friends.

That was the reason that the bonnie young Prince did not visit New York for the yacht races of 1930, much to the sorrow of Sir Thomas Lipton, and his party composed of the foremost men of both England, Ireland, and Scotland, causing Sir Thomas many hours of worry, who never believed the darned story.

King George always had great faith in Sir Thomas Lipton, and knew full well that his son would be well taken care of in 1930, as he was in 1919, who like his grandfather, loved New York, for the late King Edward spent many happy hours here in 1860, who like thousands of others when they arrive here, they hate to leave it. But, that was of another day when we had no mad dogs of war and their propagandist spies and sharks, and no such men as the fellow that we call Bishop Canon, the hypocrite, who helped to bring depression.

This was an explanation that I wanted badly, for I could not see why the Free State of Ireland, would give this contract to Germany and the people of Ireland needing money very badly.

But an explanation coming from a diplomat like Mr. Cosgrove must be taken in good spirit, but from anyone else, well we would have to ask for further explanations, and at times that is mighty hard to do.

Mr. Cosgrove after handling every question of note wound up his remarks as follows. "I have tried to draw you a picture of our economic position as I see it. I do not claim that the future is all plain sailing.

"But I do assert that we have laid our foundations firmly and securely.

"We are doing our best to educate our rising generation in a spirit free from party hatred and to make them realize their duty towards the State which is now theirs.

"I am under no illusion about the magnitude of our task, but I am convinced that our people appreciate the responsibilities they have shouldered and that they feel confident of success."

In conclusion let me ask my readers to join with me, in wishing this wonderful leader every success, and good luck in his every undertaking, and let us all appoint ourselves a committee of one to assist Mr. Cosgrove, by advising our friends at home to vote, and work for this good man, until Erin's Green Isle will again come back to their own, and peace and prosperity will once again be ringing from the mountain side, just as it did in 1914—before that cursed war was forced upon us to destroy the world.

I am happy to learn that good old Rebel Cork, stood by Mr. Cosgrove to a man.

"Here's to the land of the Shamrock so green. Here's to the boys and their darling Colleen. Here's to the one I love dearest and most, may God speed old Ireland, is an Irishman's toast."

Great preparations are being made in Dublin today for they are expecting 200,000 people to attend the Field Mass, a colorful ceremony will mark the one hundred years passed since Daniel O'Connell, M.P., wrung from the English Government Catholic Emancipation.

Dublin, June 22nd, 1929.—Religious demonstrations, the like of which, it is said, have never been equalled by any single nation, will be conducted in Dublin tomorrow, when the week's celebration of Catholic Emancipation in Ireland reaches its climax. Olde Ireland, you're my jewel sure, my heart's delight and glory, but the happenings of today makes my heart bleed for thee.

More than 200,000 people to say the least will be gathered in Phoenix Park to take part in the field mass, and the trains will be running night and day so as to accommodate the great mass of people attending.

They are taking every precaution for there will be a body of 50,000 attendants at this mass, for God willing, there must be no accidents at this notable service in commemoration of the passing of the emancipation bill.

Police Booths and Red Cross stations are being set up, and a staff of doctors and nurses, and many members of the Civic Guard, to care for those overcome, or taken ill, for William T. Cosgrove, President of the Irish Free State is doing everything possible to avoid accidents or trouble of any nature, and we of America today, wish Mr. Cosgrove and his people every success, and again I must repeat, that God is good to the Irish, so with God at our side or in our houses, we have nothing to fear.

Immense altars have been erected for this mass and all the streets are decorated with the Papal flags. A network of loudspeakers will broadcast the services to the outlying crowds while the talkie cameras will preserve the day for the rest of the world.

All of the past week the people of Ireland have been celebrating this wonderful event, concerts, lectures and musicals have kept the people going night after night to commemorate the one hundredth anniversary of the passing of this act by which most of the disabilities under which the Catholics had long since suffered, were removed by the passing of this bill. Irish political differences have been forgotten. President Cosgrove and Eamon de Valera will be found in this great line of march, side by side, peace and happiness will be the watchword in that great procession, for every section of the country will be represented, even the North, has united in the spirit of rejoicing.

The writer well recalls the great masses of people that attended the Eucharistic Congress held in Chicago, June, 1926, for both night and day that wonderful assemblage could be seen for a whole week, marching from one church to another and attending that notable field mass, I shall never forget that wonderful sight, one that will go down into American history.

Lord Dunraven was a loyal Irishman, and supported the Cosgrove party, showing that he was not so bad as painted, we all have our faults, but like many others of us, he was not rightly understood, but I hold no briefs for the dead.

And now Earl Dunraven is with Sir James Bell, the owner of the *Thistle* that was beaten by *Volunteer* two races to none in 1887, and other good men who were owners of America's Cup yacht racing yachts of both countries, may they rest in peace. Sir James Bell, died December, 1924.

Another item of interest dating back to June 19th, 1920, off Sandy Hook, New Jersey. We recall reading in large type as follows.

Sir Thomas Lipton's challenger, *Shamrock IV*, showed what she could do today, when in competition with her trial horse, the 23-meter *Shamrock III*, she outsailed her completely in windward work, reaching and running, and over a course of slightly more than twenty-eight miles, won by a margin of 13 minutes and 15 seconds.

The course was a triangular one with a handle and the challenger showed that her best work was to windward, in which she severely trounced her friendly rival. The breeze at the start was very light, but freshened considerably later on and was typical of what may be expected ordinarily off Sandy Hook during the summer months. There was no fluke about it.

The course originally selected for the first trial race between the challenger and the *Fife* designed yacht, meter 23, was from black buoy at the turn of the Hook, thence down South Channel, southeast one-quarter south to the Scotland lightship, a distance of three and three-quarter miles; and then down along the New Jersey coast for a distance of six and one-tenth miles in a southwest one, quarterwest, direction to, and around, the Shrewsbury Rocks light buoy off Sea-bright; thence east north east eight and one-quarter miles to, and around, the buoy off the lightships; thence west northwest, one-quarter west for six and three-quarter miles to, and around the Scotland light-ship and thence up the channel northwest one-quarter miles north for three and three-quarter miles to the starting buoy off the Hook.

Or a total distance of 28:60 nautical miles. At the last minute the triangular part of the course was reversed.

The course originally selected for the first trial spin, or race, between *Shamrock IV* or any challenger and the *Fife* designed champion of the British Isles.

SIR THOMAS AND HIS ACTIVITIES WHILE STOPPING IN LITTLE OLD NEW YORK BEFORE LEAVING FOR THE GOLDEN WEST

PART V—CHAPTER II

On his arrival we find Sir Thomas today in his eightieth year of age just as nimble and as spry and as willing to do things as ever, with that same old get up and do it spirit constantly on the go, never thinking of a rest while there is still something to be done, and if not done he will do it himself, just as though it was his second time on earth, reincarnated.

Speaking of Sir Thomas and his activities, while visiting his business here in America, New York in particular, he trots over to his factory over in far off New Jersey, hears all reports and then settles back in his easy chair with a boiler of tea always ready for any old friend that may pass his way, at five he is ready to return to the Biltmore Hotel, his New York home, and after dinner prepare to visit some of his old friends.

It might be the Hon. Morgan J. O'Brien, former Supreme Court Justice or it may be Commodore Taylor and his family, who by the way was and is Sir Thomas's legal representative here in New York, or it may be R. A. C. Smith and his family, former Deputy Police Commissioner under the administration of Richard E. Enright, when Police Commissioner, 1918 to 1926.

Or it may be a call on Mr. and Mrs. Enright, for he always did like their company, and then back to the hotel, read his mail and have orders given for the next day and to bed, some game old man, and he could stand a long number of years at this, for like Jimmy Walker whiskey, he was noted for improvement with age.

Barring accidents, I'll bet a new hat that with no more troubles and tricky manipulations, by those whom he has been a father to, he will live to serve out his one hundredth birthday, and Glory be, if he wins the Cup, he won't want to leave mother earth at all.

Sir Thomas delights in visiting the coast of the Golden West, if there are no yacht races to prevent him, he goes there to visit his friends at Hollywood, and they are many, among them the celebrities, Jack Dempsey, Tom Mix and others. Sir Thomas gave me while stopping at Osidge, 1928, the picture post card which was taken in the fall of 1927, to be correct.

NOW A WORD ABOUT OUR OWN CHAMPION, HAROLD S. VANDERBILT

Of course you will agree with me, that it is pleasing to be recognized as a member of the press, looking for information, and by chance listen in on all that is being said, for our racing men have off moments, and it makes no difference if he is a rich batchelor or a poor married man.

They are just as human as is you or I, and just as full of hell as any other old New Yorker, and we are noted for how far we will go, yes, we will go the limit, and that may be the sky, if it's worth going after, so don't be shocked at what you hear quoted to you, for none of us have got wings.

In one of those off moments, one fine day, after Mr. Vanderbilt and his pretty *Enterprise* had defeated the field, and he was feeling mighty fine after dinner, the boys of his staff gathered around, and each having his little say, and of course the question of beautiful women arose.

Here I will quote one of our experts present that day, "Mr. Vanderbilt limbered up some and got himself into a speaking humor, and this is what he told all present, and he was perfectly within his rights while so doing, and truthful to the point and pleasing to any man or set of men that loves to stand face to face with the common truth, and I deny the right of any man to question the remarks of Harold Vanderbilt, or any other man acting within the law."

And to prove my assertions, that Mr. Vanderbilt was not a woman hater, but the reverse, he took to himself a fond and beautiful wife, since and he having tucked the America's Cup under his belt, we wish them joy.

The question of women yachtsmen came up, and this is what Mr. Vanderbilt had to offer, all of which was received with open ears, "Women may learn to wear trousers, and to drink their whiskey straight in this age of emancipation, but they will never know the thrills of sailing a yacht in one of our coming America's Cup races."

"Women have made great strides in their ability to master small sloops in recent years," said Mr. Vanderbilt. "Yes, they have entered races and won the prizes from the men folk by defeating them and carrying off the victory, and there is no reason why they should not compete with the best yachtsmen of the day. But this mind you, is in the field of small yachts sailing 14-footers and other craft of less formidable classes."

"But when you are talking about sailing in an American Cup race, you are dealing with something very different, and it is unlikely that women will ever enter that majestic event."

The question was asked of Mr. Vanderbilt, and this is his ready answer:

Question—Do women lack the strength to sail so large a yacht?

"It is not so much a matter of strength," answered Mr. Vanderbilt. "Strength is only required in emergencies, it's the ability to handle a crew."

"I doubt that a woman, even of the most aggressive type, could make a crew respect her orders at times. And someone must be in supreme power during the progress of a race."

"There is also the vital question of money," said Mr. Vanderbilt.

He believes it improbable that a woman could induce owners of the big yachts to put her in control of one of the fabulously expensive toys.

This season the syndicate that has built the *Enterprise* has spent around a quarter of a million dollars for canvas alone, and the international races are more than two months away.

So expensive are the yachts that even Commodore Vanderbilt, who it is estimated owns the third largest fortune in the country, owns but a part of the shares of *Enterprise,* the yacht that he is so successfully handling, and he don't hold any portfolio in Washington either.

That my friends, is a highly privileged conversation, and you will of course, use it accordingly, for I, the writer wants no trouble with our good friends in America, or elsewhere as far as that goes, I am simply writing to amuse you all, and not to abuse, no, not at all.

From a cable just received from London, we learn that the members of the Royal Yacht Squadron were not in favor of Mr. Sopwith challenging for the America's Cup this year, on account of the depression and unemployment a noble idea indeed, and they left the matter in the hands of His Majesty, King George V, their Commodore.

I also learn that King George summoned Mr. T. O. M. Sopwith to court, and they talked over the matter, for a long time, each giving his reasons for and against the proposition, and when Mr. Sopwith stated that like the late Sir Thomas Lipton, he too wanted to fill the dinner pail of the hundreds of unemployed ship and yacht builders, of both countries, his point was well taken, and Commodore King George V gave his consent, forthwith.

This folks is just another reminder of the broadmindedness of England's ruler today, for King George V is noted for his words of wisdom, just as that other famous yachtsman, our great American President, Franklin Delano Roosevelt, in his flying send the N.R.A. racing to victory, day after day.

There is no getting away from the fact that Harold Vanderbilt is one of our born yachtsmen, like President Franklin D. Roosevelt, and young Patsy Raskob, the daughter of John Raskob, former Chairman of the Democratic National Committee, who at the age of twelve is winning championships.

Mr. Vanderbilt, must have been born on a yacht, for his main hobby in life and since early childhood, is that of yachting, in fact he has gone so far as to forget everything else but finance and yachting, more power to him, his next hobby in life may be, to take a wife, and settle down and be happy for the rest of his life, a long and a happy one I hope.

He first started to sail a 14-foot sloop, that he bravely sailed out into the harbor of Newport, a very courageous act for a kid of twelve, and he always thinks back, and loves to speak of his first yachting adventure.

My word, how a courageous millionaire with a pleasing smile and a charming personality could have escaped the women, I don't understand, but he is still young and handsome, and their being no more call for a defender of America's Cup honor and glory, he may get hooked up to some pretty girl.

But when he becomes that way inclined, I pray that he will side-step the gold hunters, and stolen highball fiends, for once they get their hooks on you, your life is one of worry and trouble, so watch your step.

And since the disgracing of that grand and glorious document, the Constitution of these United States, by adding the 18th Amendment, it has made for us a very hard road to travel, but after President Franklin D. Roosevelt gets through with them, we will again be free and independent, so there is still a chance for all old bachelors to become happy.

But there is no use talking, but the gold digging, rum seeking, frosty face dictators of women of the past has done much to destroy the happiness and pleasure of many homes, and the lives of our young heroes, to date.

They first looked for the 16th Amendment and they got it, and then, many of our clever women, helped a group of crooks to put over the 18th Amendment, a curse to our nation, for this introduced the bootlegger, the gunman, and the racketeers in most every profession, even to resorting to murder, to put over their dirty rackets of every conceivable character.

And that in the Empire City of the known world, it's a damn shame that we, the citizens of this great city have to grin and bear it, instead of our organizing a Vigilant Committee as they did in California, years ago and hang the rascals to the lamp posts on the street corners. Hanging such men as Corri the gambler, and sending his pal Yankee Sullivan to jail to die.

Until something of that kind is done, we will be a nation of suckers, giving up to every Tom, Dick and Harry, surely we have not lost our manhood.

While travelling through the different countries of the old world, in my rambles, I made myself busy attending the games and meeting places of the athletes of every country to obtain all the information that I could as to their condition, and times in every event, and mailing my information on to New York.

I had been asked by one of the oldest officials of the A.A.U one of the few living today that played in the same old school with the late James E. Sullivan and good old Bill Curtis, the real fathers of American Athletics and founders of the A.A.U. of today.

Fred Rubien, and the writer did much hard work to help place the A.A.U. on the high pinnacle that it stands on today.

Good old Colonel Charley Deiges, Johnny McHugh, Dan Ferris, Bob Kennedy, John O'Brien, and the late Johnny Welsh, and others who have passed away. Joe Conlon and Dick Enright did their bit always. Both living, T. G.

It was indeed a pleasure to me to be able to serve my old friends, and keep them in touch with information that they were unable to obtain otherwise, and even at the ripe age of 70, I did not let the grass grow under my feet for the Olympics were soon to take place and our officials wanted all the information they could get, and get it from your humble servant of the old Police A. A. of New York.

Yes, from Lille Bridge in London to Athens, and from there to Bombay, searching for information with very little to say, "for he that does not profit by his past experience, turns his best schoolmaster out of doors."

One not dumb, learns a whole lot travelling under such circumstances and I lost nothing of note, believe me, interviewing this one and that one, all members of the same club, the sporting fraternity of the world.

It was alright in the Far East and Bombay, with the mercury as high as the Empire State Building, but when I got to Moritz, oh, boy, how cold, and believe it or not, my stay there was brief, for it would freeze the nose off a brass monkey.

I had all that I wanted of the cold bitter nights on post around the monument of Ben Franklin, at Nassau and Park Row, doing police duty, when New York was New York, until the bloody hand of war, destroyed the whole world.

It is often asked, "What is the meaning of the word "Corinthian" that one reads about so often in sporting pages, when referring to yachtsmen who are termed "Corinthians."

Much could be said or written on this question, but suffice it to say for the information and guidance of my readers that a Corinthian, is one who takes part in sailing his boat purely for the love of sport, and with no intention or desire to profit financially from his or her ability in that line.

In other words, he or she, is an amateur as contrasted to the professional sailor.

This and other such questions of such character that will crop up now and again are well to know, for one never knows when such questions will be asked of you, by some person or persons, that may love the game, but never has the opportunity of seeing a race unless in the case of a championship race like that of Sir Thomas Lipton looking to lift the Cup.

I recall while the races for the Cup were being run off Sandy Hook, July, 1920, I like many other guests of Sir Thomas on the steam yacht *Victoria* was dressed in my best suit of yachting clothes, Johnny off the cattle ship, as it were, knowing less about yachting than did Bishop Canon knows about the bucket shops of New York.

On a number of occasions I was addressed as "Captain" and asked this question and that question, about the tacking and jibing of the racing machines and numerous other questions such as the one above, all new to me, but my good old New York Police learning stuck to me, and I found an answer for every question fired at me, for it would not be good policy to say I did not know.

But believe me, when I saw these fine old inquisitors coming my way, say for instance they were forward, I would have some particular reason to go aft, for I did not want to be assuming a position that I knew nothing about telling these fine old people a lot of fibs, for one fib after another soon counts 99, and 100 makes a lie, so with all the diplomacy at my command, I would bow myself from their presence, when I had counted 99.

I often felt that I would be far better off pounding my beat on the Bowery, back in beautiful little old New York, back in the old days when men were men, and no one running foul of a gold digger.

So be advised by your humble servant, and don't ever be caught as I was, prepare yourself for all such emergencies, by writing to the Government Maritime or Survey Department in Washington and ask them to send you a copy of their valuable book, for your future information and guidance.

I well remember, after the races, the evenings sitting down talking to Sir Thomas, we would enjoy many a good laugh over my story, of my trials and tribulations of the day, for Tom Lipton himself has been often cornered in much the same way, but he like the old Bowery Cop, always had an answer.

Yes, Sir Thomas was always ready for a good laugh, and I often have seen him advising the folks asking questions to go ask Captain Hickey, for he is more familiar than I am on these questions, and my, how he would laugh, and I would sweat blood, Heavenly Father.

So take my advice and don't be a walking encyclopedia of facts not worth mentioning, for you can try anything once, if the Cops don't get you.

Here are a few secrets of yachting, that may help you out should you ever be caught napping as was the author of this work, on the memorable July week of 1920, when Sir Thomas and his *Shamrock IV*, broke records.

And to further assure my questioners of the nationality of Sir Thomas, I will write for their information and guidance the records as copied by the writer of this little story, while visiting in London, the summer of 1928, to wit:—

Sir Thomas Johnstone Lipton, was born of Irish parentage in the city of Glasgow, Scotland, first seeing the light of day on the morning of May 10th, 1850; and today he is fighting his way through this world without a living relative, for the records state that he has no heir.

Sir Thomas loved his dear old mother dearly, but kind fortune did not smile upon them so that young Tom Lipton at 17, bade goodbye to his home and loved ones and struck out into this cold hard world to make his fortune, and the world knows how wonderful young Tom Lipton succeeded.

Arriving in New York, he first went to work for Patrick McQuellan, at 17½ Washington Street, as a boarding house runner, taking this job, just so he could get his bearings, and when he was good and ready he again took the trail, his itinerary taking him first through Silver Street, then along into Gold Street, never stopping until he had landed himself in the house of good fortune, that he so richly deserved, but he carried on in spite of his riches, until today he stands out in the front ranks of the millionaire, known the world over for his charity and wholeheartedness, and his manly honest bearing and charming Irish personality.

But remember, in all this time Tom Lipton never once forgot his dear old mother, for she was then, and is today his guiding star, and if this good International world's sportsman lived to be a hundred, his mother will always be his first thought and his guiding star, his "Star of Bethlehem."

To write at this time the progress made by this Irish immigrant boy would take up much space, yes, his life's work will fill any good sized book, but some day, God willing, the writer of this story is going to write the life of this wonderful Irish character, from the cradle to the present time, with my own personal experience for the past 25 years of friendship of this hardworking Irish immigrant boy.

Often when alone with Sir Thomas our conversation would cease when Mr. Westwood beckoned to me to go, stating in his, Westwood's Room 614 that Sir Thomas was up too late at that, he having some important business for the morrow, with several important appointments to be met, oh yes, the same old story of Sir Thomas meeting his old friends not at all suitable to this gentleman, John Westwood.

But, I did not spend twenty years knocking around the slums of New York and have to stand for a jealous gentleman to tell me what I should do and when I should do it, not at all man.

I would manage to get the tip that Westwood was going out, and that was all I wanted, went up to Room 618, show my passport and walk into Room 222, with Sir Thomas all alone, we were free to talk, and he always had something important on his mind to tell me about, and my presence was a happy relief to the game old scout, and of course I would sail home happy.

But before he would let me go the night when Westwood stepped in, he asked me why I did not return with him and stay at "Osidge", and I answered, Sir Thomas, I hope to visit you some time later, but under no circumstances will I stay in Osidge, for they darned near killed me the last time I called on you, and I must beware, I had reference to my visit June, 1928.

You will find this story in another part of this work, and then you no doubt will understand it far better than I am able to explain, right now. What with Westwood's strange actions in Osidge, June 1928, and Mr. Fields locking me in his office, he going home and leaving me there, no doubt to be shot down by his night watchman as a burglar, and the fact of Westwood, not mailing me my invitation to the City Hall at the presentation, that brought about a run in with a fresh Policeman in the halls of the City Hall, I to my mind had my troubles, with these fellows, yes, the invisible committee or invisible government, if you wish.

But when I think back to this man Westwood, going under the knife, and pulling through, a man who would resort to anything to further his ends, and make life harder for his employer, and maybe drop a pill into his coffee as well as in mine.

The life of such a man is spared, while his employer, a man of charity and benevolence is taken from us, as for me, no doubt that it was ordained that I should outlive them all, so as to expose their dirty work.

Glasgow, Scotland must be a very lucky city, to be sure, for besides they having produced a number of millionaires, not one of them more worthier than is our own famous Irish yachtsman, Sir Thomas Lipton, who went out into the wide, wide world without a shoestring, and finished up a millionaire and the most advertised and best loved man living today, in either business or sport, and that from a poor unknown kid.

But what I most want to call your attention to is the statement in the papers today relating to the remarks of Sir James Barrie when addressing a meeting in Glasgow the other evening, he stated among other things that from his own experience Glasgow was a safe place to live in, for if you invested your money there, you would sure get in return two hundred per cent profit, one of Sir James Barrie's pipe dreams, no doubt, and to further make those present happy when speaking so proudly of their dear old city, he stated that he once lost a penny and he went back and found it and two others, making three pennies all told, some find!

Then let me ask, who of you will dare call a Scotchman stingy, for we have been hearing for many years that the Scotch are mean and stingy, but the remarks of Sir James, proves to the world that the Scotchman is not stingy if you wish to listen to those loud mouthed rascals who are constantly knocking everything under the sun, but the fact that Sir James lost one and picked up three pennies, proves those vagabonds liars.

But to quote the words of Sir Thomas Lipton, that when Sir Harry Lauder lost a threepenny piece in the coals on an cean liner when speeding for God's own city, New York, and when I say New York, I mean that part of it we now call Manhattan, for outside of Manhattan, one will run into meaner men and women, than any Scotchman, and to recover his threepence, he paid the coal passers a quid, that means five big handsome looking Bucks, dollars in beautiful America. Moral, please be careful and don't let a Scotchman ever hear you say again that the Scotch are stingy.

Yes, it might be all right to say that Sir Harry Lauder is a good fellow, to pay a pound to recover a threepenny piece, I will bet that this fun-maker Harry, had the laugh on all the other fellows with a big bet, winning 10 Quid.

And we surely must not forget the great work and expense that Harold Vanderbilt and his associates of *Enterprise* have sacrificed to make this coming contest a success, and we of New York are indeed proud of these good men, that did so much to get the turning up of their boats under way.

Of all four boats to the writer's way of thinking, *Enterprise* is most of all worthy of being chosen our defender, and if *Enterprise* can but make the same successful progress on deep water as she did, off Glen Cove and old Oyster Bay, I think that she will be entitled to the honor of being chosen defender. Imagine what Mr. Vanderbilt has done to make this a success, why he has spared no expense whatever, for the sails alone of *Enterprise* will cost over two hundred and fifty thousands of dollars, and that is only one of the small items that is to be considered, there are many more.

And *Whirlwind,* that has not proved herself in the past, but that there is a possibility will do much better in the future, her owner, Langdon K. Thorne, has spared neither time or expense to make her our defender, but if fate is against him and his boat, then no blame can be placed at his door, or at the door of his associates, or designer, it's just hard luck, that's all.

Weetamoe, another fine speciment of American designing, has had her own troubles, and yet no one is to blame, for Mr. Morgan, Mr. Crane and Mr. George Nichols have done all that could be done to make her the fastest and best boat, so what is the use complaining, *Weetamoe,* might yet beat the field.

And last but not least, *Yankee,* she has been cunningly spending her time tuning up in the kind of waters that they will race on next week, and she may have something up her sleeve that will surprise all, who knows?

We all know how hard Mr. John S. Lawrence, and his associates have worked, and at this writing they are still working, and with the valuable assistance that Mr. Paine, is rendering, it would not surprise the writer the least to see *Yankee* out in front, after July 7th, so let us hope for the best, we wish the four boats and their owners and designers every success.

And when we take into consideration that Sir Thomas Lipton, overseas, is spending his health, his time and his millions playing a lone hand, and up against this combination of American millionaires, we must remove our hats.

I just received a telegram from Sir Thomas J. Lipton, stating that he and his party were about to sail on the U. S. Line Steamship *Leviathan,* with his dear old friend of long standing, Commodore Harold Cunningham, and to be at the pier to meet him next Monday, November 3rd, 1930.

It has been my honor and pleasure to be the first to greet Sir Thomas, on his many arrivals, and the last man to say goodbye on his leaving, and both Sir Thomas and the writer appreciated that very much, and that has been so for more than thirty years, long before there were any invisible governments running the Lipton, Inc., for there were very few of that time in the Lipton employ of today.

Many of the employees of Sir Thomas and the Lipton Tea incorporation would tell you that Sir Thomas was a hard man to get along with, and why?, it was them, and their actions that made Sir Thomas a hard man, for if he was not stern and hard enough the tremendous business that he established may have been a thing of the past, but unfortunately he did not get wise to these many ingratitudes until too late, and it took J. J. Hickey, the old N. Y. Cop to have him get wise to himself, but alas, too late.

Why, I have seen and heard of many things that did not have to be, for there was not a move Sir Thomas would make but what the invisible gang would set the wires burning all of course unknown to that grand old sport, that thought that everybody like himself was honest.

Heavenly Father, is there any wonder that J. J. Hickey was not wanted either at the factory or hotel to have a wee cup of tea, at the request of my good old friend, no, they thought that I could spill the beans, and have my good old friend find out what he was up against.

Yes, when I think of the many humiliations that I was forced to suffer at the hands of the leader of that invisible government. I often imagine that I was a damn fool to stand it so long, but I wanted to be with my dear old friend to the last, and I was the last to say goodbye Sir Thomas when leaving here on his return from that trip, his last.

And here we are today, Sir Thomas dead, Commodore Cunningham retired and our grand old Queens of the seas the *S. S. Leviathan* making a port of call in Hamburg, or Berlin in the German trade, a bum finish.

For a grand old steamer, captured from the enemy, and did great service carrying our soldiers to France.

Among the many stories told by our grand old friend Sir Thomas, this story to my mind is the best and sweetest, for it shows the human side of our beloved Chief, who loved to repeat, when the opportunity presented itself, and I am sure that my readers will delight in reading same.

The story opens at the pier in Southampton, England, just as our grand old friend was about to visit us on one of his yearly visits.

We will let Sir Thomas tell the story, for I know that you, my friends will enjoy it much better, and may imagine Sir Thomas sitting telling his many dear old American friends, that he loved so well.

"Just as we were waiting for the steamer to blow off and hoist anchor, take in her gangplank and sail away, we, the first class passengers lined along the rail on the portside, heard quite a commotion and looking down the gangplank, we saw a poor woman struggling hard to carry her children aboard, and seeing no one willing to help the poor woman, I jumped out of the lineup, and taking one of the children from her, I carried her aboard.

"The Chief Steward seeing what I had done also grabbed one of the many children, and got them on board for the steamer was three hours late then, and the Captain was very much put out that day.

"The poor unfortunate woman, after resting some, thanked the many kind hands that so gallantly ran to her assistance, and when asked why she was so late, she said, 'I could not help it Sir, I had no money to ride, so I had to walk a long distance to the ship? I then asked her how did the other children get here on time? 'They came with the wagon, Sir, with my luggage.' Then you have no money I asked? 'Very little Sir, was the woman's reply.'

"I asked to see the Stewardess, who hailed from the same home town, as did the woman and children, Yorkshire. Then I said, you do all you can for the poor woman and present a bill to me for expenses, before we leave the steamer in New York, and I retired to my quarters.

"I lost no time in spreading the sad news among the first class passengers, among whom was a Catholic Priest, and he suggested taking up a collection, and soon a Protestant Minister happened along, and when he heard of my sad story, he too got into line to help us pick up a little money to aid and assist the poor creature, and soon we had collected the fine big sum of one hundred and twenty-five pounds, and this was turned over to me. I gave the woman one hundred pounds, and placed the other in a bank in her name, and the poor creature was delighted and personally thanked the donors with tears in her eyes and a light heart to help her over the jumps.

"I asked the Stewardess to attend to the banking of this money, and to keep me informed from time to time, and to reimburse her, I placed her on the Tom Lipton pay roll, and she, too, was delighted to be chosen for same.

"I had previously asked the woman 'where is your husband', she answered, 'dead, Sir, he was killed in a railroad accident, and seeing nothing but starvation before me, I decided to sell off my home and leave for America, and I wrote some friends in America, and they said yes, come right out, we will be looking for you.' Sir Thomas having the promise from the Stewardess that she would keep in touch with the poor woman through her friends, Sir Thomas handing her a good fat tip before leaving the ship, happy and contented knowing full well that he at least saved one life, for. it was so mighty hard on the poor soul, that she came very near dropping out of the picture.

"The woman had asked the Stewardess, who was that fine man, who so kindly helped her, and when told it was Sir Thomas Lipton, she was amazed, saying, why I thought that he was the Captain of the ship.

"And after recovering from her surprise, she said, 'God bless Sir Thomas, I often heard my mother speak about him home and his many charitable acts reciting to us children the story of the poor Lipton boy, who by dint of hard work, became a millionaire. God bless and protect him forever and forever, for he has saved my life, as well as to make myself and my children happy until we get settled down, and my children at work.'

"Some time later a letter was handed me from that same woman stating that she had been delivered of a young son, whom she had christened Thomas Parker Leviathan, and Sir Thomas being delighted at the good news mailed her a very fine check to both Mother and Son, and forever after Sir Thomas kept an eye on Mother and children, on until death."

This dear readers is simply another one of Tom Lipton's charitable acts, and to support my assertion of the human side of this grand old man.

SIR THOMAS WAS VERY MUCH PLEASED WHEN I
SHOWED HIM THE REMARKS OF THAT FAMOUS NEW
YORK BANKER, THE HON. THOMAS W. LAMONT, SPEAK-
ING OF THE LATE J. PIERPONT MORGAN

PART V—CHAPTER III

As an old friend of Sir Thomas Lipton, I was very much pleased
to read a statement issued by the famous New York banker Mr.
Thomas W. Lamont, deploring the loss of the biography of that great
American banker, who was persecuted in his old days, and driven to
die in exile, far from the good old city of New York that he often
had helped out of a hole.

I know of no biography that can surpass the kindly actions of any
man, more than the kindly action of this grand old man, the late
J. Pierpont Morgan, father of the house of Morgan, the backbone of
American Finance, who was so charitably disposed as to take Tom
Lipton to his heart after losing his first race here in America, at a
time when Tom Lipton wanted friends and sympathizers more than
he ever wanted them.

And in spite of the fact that Tom Lipton, came here to try to take
away from us a Cup, that was deemed a great pleasure and happiness
to us Americans, this grand old man, J. P. Morgan, Sr., laid his warm
hand on the shoulders of this famous international yachtsman, just
starting out in life, saying, Lipton, I like you, for you are honest and
a mighty good loser.

What better cheer can one man offer to another? Is there anything
on earth could equal this manly act? No, I guess not, for if there
is then I never heard of it, but this I do know all about, for one of the
very first stories told me was the story of how Mr. Morgan was the
one man above all others that kept him in the yachting fields, for if it
was not for his kindness to me then, "I might have never returned to
seek that darned old Cup but this noble act of Mr. Morgan gave me
courage and inspiration that I was badly in need of, and I shall never
forget his kindness".

Not only did Mr. Morgan give his comfort and cheer to Sir Thomas,
but he did not stop until he had seen to it that Sir Thomas was elected
to the proud position of honorary member of the New York Yacht
Club, a title he honored until his dying day, for Tom Lipton never
forgot a kindness, and I, the author, hope and pray that Mr. Morgan,
and Sir Thomas are resting in peace and happiness in their Heavenly

home, where there are no enemies, and hungry busybodies, that brought about this good man's downfall, not at all.

Sir Thomas often used to tell this story in our little chats years ago, long before he got so busy in "Foreign entanglements'" long before there was a Mayor's reception committee of distinguished visitors, or a Police Commissioner named Richard Enright, and he had less friends.

My evenings with Sir Thomas 25 years ago were of more pleasure to me then, than an evening at "Roxy's" for he told me many things about these two pigs, and how his business increased with their advertising, around the town, before which he could not hire a boy, but sweep the store out himself and sleep under the counter nights, but after the coming of my pigs, well I lived more happily, making all kinds of money.

"After the court proceedings that day, the judge letting me go when I had told my story, said Sir Thomas, a big crowd followed me and my piggies back to the store and I had to hire two boys to help me, and so that these pigs would not lose their popularity, I built a sty, fed the pigs well, keeping the cloth coats on them with the signs, 'The Lipton Orphans.'

"And when business got slow, I would give the boys some pennies and have them take the pigs for a walk through the town, and then my business would jump aplenty, often the Piggies reneging, I would swat them on the hass, and the divil himself could not keep up with them, or my bank roll."

Sir Thomas was a very humorous story teller which many of you know, but the stories he tells today, are not as rorty, as they were in the long ago, and I delighted to hear them, one and all, every evening when I'd call.

Again Sir Thomas visited New Orleans, on a business trip, and again he met his foster mother taking tea and talking of the past, but he had to be on his way, leaving an order that this woman be taken care of, he departed promising to return some fine day later.

Sir Thomas had about at this time bought up his tea plants in Ceylon, and he loved his beautiful Ceylon home, and one day a few years after leaving New Orleans, he received a letter stating that his foster mother had died, and her last words to her son was "Write and tell Sir Thomas that my last words were 'May God and his blessed mother spare and protect my dear good friend and foster son, Sir Thomas Lipton,' and in a few minutes she was dead."

Sir Thomas, after reading the letter, was very much affected and with tears in his eyes he ordered his secretary to forward forthwith a check to pay the expenses of her funeral, but he never forgot her, after, and often he would speak of this kind old lady, and his boyhood days in the sunny South.

Surely a man of that sterling character ought to have better treatment in his last moments than he was given. Why?

Young Tom Lipton was mighty nervy and willing to try anything once and while he did not succeed in winning America's Cup, nevertheless everyone of his endeavors proved successful, thanks to the unruly "Two Orphans."

What could be more pleasing to the friends of our dear old Chief than to see the photograph and a long story of the Chief and his generosity on the front page of the "New York American," thanks to his very able successor and the Lipton Trust, two years after his passing, brought Sir Thomas once more before the people and the limelight that he was fond of, with a check for $500.00 to buy baskets for the unemployed. Peace be to you, Chief. December, 1933.

When one thinks of the fact that young Tom Lipton arrived in America flat broke and all through those years finds time to write out his check to help the poor and distressed to the amount of $500.00, not only in this country but in England and Scotland. Oh, yes, and in dear old Ireland.

My thoughts are carried back to 1903, when at 1 A. M. on a summer's morning we met for the first time, just around the corner at 17½ Washington Street, and where he started in to make his fortune. Shades of Jenny Lind, who sang in old Castle Garden in 1850, and the two little Irish "piggies" that started him onward and upward.

Now that the tide of battle is over in the matter of our four yachts, namely, *Enterprise, Weetamoe, Whirlwind* and *Yankee,* racing for the honor of being America's Cup defender, against *Shamrock V,* everybody is happy that the races of elimination have passed and the best yacht and the best skipper picked by our experts in the person of Mr. Harold Vanderbilt and *Enterprise,* we are all happy and contented, for it is the consensus of opinion that the racing committee of the New York Yacht Club made the best of a bad bargain and picked the best yacht and the best skipper for that honor.

That is, the honor of being chosen defender, but, can they win? That is the question now being asked by all, and just one week before the sailing of the first race of the America's Cup series September 13th, this question is answered by none, for as things stand today it is a matter of the utmost impossibility to pick the winner.

Both yachts have a vast assemblage of followers, and the owners and skippers have their friends and followers by the thousands, but if per chance Skipper Vanderbilt and his pretty sloop, the *Enterprise,* are defeated, then the highbrows of the N. Y. Y. C. will get no sympathy, nor can they expect any from the good people of New York and New Jersey, lovers of yachting, because of their not being satisfied with Sandy Hook, for after 79 years they find Sandy Hook too troublesome and the people of New York and New Jersey too darned common, and the highbrows of Newport had to be taken care of.

But that move was a sorry one for all concerned for many reasons and those responsible are going to sup sorrow, for it has already played havoc with our yachts in their trials of elimination and has the racing committee half looney, so far gone that they were satisfied to pick the winner with ten or twelve races uncontested, that is, of the three series of races of elimination, but they judged rightly and picked the best.

And now but a few days of grace the two principals are unable to get a fair tune up, what with fog and rain, it is simply impossible, and the men behind the guns are frantic, for what can they do but loaf, and you know it comes pretty hard on a successful, hard-working business man, men like Thomas L. Lipton (Tom Lipton) or Harold S. Vanderbilt (Mike), to lay, after the races of elimination, on and around the Sound. The boys were given a rest of a week or ten days before opening up off Newport, and that gay young American champion of ours was like a fish out of water, laying around day after day, all dressed up and no place to go, for they cannot be traveling back and forth to New York, using up their valuable time and hard-earned money, for Heaven knows that they are heavily taxed now, and it is going to be so until long after the cup has been lost and won.

And while the writer hates to be constantly harping about the highbrows of the N. Y. Y. C., nevertheless when one has to listen to the tales of woe of the poor unfortunate working man and working woman, friends and rooters for both Sir Thomas and Mr. Vanderbilt, telling you that they are borrowing the money to go see one or two races, as they cannot afford to borrow, or see more than one, or perhaps two, races, the expense is too great.

Never before in the past fifty years has the challenger for the cup been so highly applauded and so many wishing that Sir Thomas win the cup, and with *Shamrock V* he is going to try hard.

And you ask, why rooting for Sir Thomas and *Shamrock V?* and the answer you get is, well, he is a grand old man of the people and with the people and his noble spirit and charming personality; that is why.

And, remember, that in all of his business and other contacts in this country or elsewhere, he has always played the game fair, with his cards on top of the table every time, not under the table, not at all, that is why we love him and respect him and pray for him to win the cup.

But, that is not all, it is to aim a blow at the highbrows of the N. Y. Y. C. who took it upon themselves to steal the races from the old course, and to amuse and please their friends, the highbrows of Newport, at the expense of the common people, we want to see those guys get a good trimming.

But what about Harold Vanderbilt? He is not highbrowed, not at all man, he has always proved himself a chip of the old block and always on the up and up, a second edition of his grandfather, good old Commodore Vanderbilt, a man of sterling character, that never weakened to a man in his life until he was confronted with a summons handed to him by another grand American High Constable of New York, Jacob Hays, in the good old days of the forties and fifties, when men were men—all true blue Americans.

And so that you will know this grand old man, former Commodore Vanderbilt better, I will let you in on an inside story, and that is that this grand old man of the long ago, like his nephews and grand-nephews, had no use for the American aristocrats or highbrows, that are destroying this country today, for the Commodore was a real he-man, and proud of it.

Commodore Vanderbilt of the early fifties feared neither man nor beast and he carried on a thriving business along the coast, and could be seen strolling along Broadway at night on his way to visit the gambling parlor of the greatest fighter of all time, John Morrissey, from sweet Templemore on Hibernia shore, that stood at 816, and bye the way, the old building still stands with its old brownstone front, and in pretty good condition at that.

The only man that ever made Commodore Vanderbilt take water was good old High Constable Jacob Hays, in the late forties, and it was when the Commodore had violated a corporation and Hays was serving him with a summons down along the old North River, and he refused to be served, no, not even from the High Constable, but he took this summons all right.

After a hard day's work, he was often seen trudging up Broadway, making for 816, to meet his old pals and cronies of that time, and was often found with his cards above, and not under, the table in the wee small hours, often paying his bill of ninety dollars for ninety cigars, costing a dollar a piece.

This grand old gentleman thought a whole lot of that wee little green-horn boy, that fought and licked Bill Poole, the Washington Market butcher, and drove his know-nothing party to hell and damnation, and winning the big title of John Morrissey, champion heavyweight of the world, by his defeat of Yankee Sullivan, and John was nominated for the legislature at Albany, and the House of Representatives in Washington by his followers of that grand old bed of democracy, the Seventh Ward of little old New York.

The great men of the past, like many of today, loved and loves a real fighter, just as we love Jack Dempsey, our dethroned champion of today, and the grand old real Americans of the past, alas, very few of them living today, were all silk, and yards wide, and would go to hell to see a good fight, and if living today, would be very proud of the forebears, just as we are very proud today of our champion yachts-man, Harold Vanderbilt and his *Enterprise.*

But here is a proposition that I would offer for the benefit of our bachelor friends, a very simple measure that is sure to bring happiness and comfort to many American homes, and that is, if pleasing to the powers that be, have Harold Vanderbilt and his *Enterprise* declared our defenders.

Then call on Sir Thomas Lipton and Mr. Vanderbilt to what we may call a bachelors' dinner, and with a big bunch of friends, have articles of agreement drawn up, to read that the winner of the American Derby, America's Cup, shall take himself a wife and forever after live in real happiness.

So that when old age and the infirmities that follow, comes your way, you will always have a protector, one that you are sure will take care of your interests, and not be forced to leave your business in the hands of a self-seeking secretary, as we read of in every-day life.

Is that not a fair bargain? It seems to me that it is, and one that will set a good example to others who are unfortunately obliged to take comfort in some one of those many infernal night clubs, spending their evenings among murderers and grafters, waking up in the morning with a big head and an empty pocketbook, singing, "I Will Never Go There Anymore," or some other following reminder, with no beautiful wife to sympathize with you and speak lovingly to you to cheer you on, that I am sure would be comfortable.

A faint heart never won a fair lady, so take a chance, for none of us knows what is before us, and when adversity comes your way, as it has to many of us, then you will be fully prepared to meet it, young or old, for the older man in particular, to avoid the sharks of crooked employees.

If you follow out this plan, the gold-diggers and rum hounds would have to go to work, and then life would be well worth the living, and crime of all kinds would be banished from the fair name of our grand old city for all time, and we would not have to rob the one to give to the other to keep the city from bankruptcy, and that thought alone would make us all happy.

Think this over men, before it is too late, for it is never too late to repent, and there is yet a chance to save both your lives and your money, your homes and your business, with a good watchdog of a wife who would be forever at your side to cheer you through the world, and with a son or daughter around the house, what could be better?

Here we are folks, off Brenton's Reef Light, ten miles outside New-port, Rhode Island, July 7th, 1930, and we have gathered here to celebrate a long awaited commencement of the first series of three races that is to be known as the elimination contests, same to be supervised by the racing committee of the New York Yacht Club, and with a fair field and no favor, may the best yacht win, if not, then why.   The racing committee are hard pushed, trying to bring about an even contest, by seeing that all entries must be guarded and kept free from collision, with her rival or rivals, for that above anything else must not happen, that is final.

And to help the committee we should all, yes, every mother's son of us, peel off our coats, and aid and assist the committee in their good work.   While I know that our committee on racing are a staunch and true blue body of men that are able to master any such situation, nevertheless, they cannot be in two places at one time, nor can they see all behind the scenes, while us freer fellows can see much that should not be, and if we were given the power of a Police M.P., that we could stop this nonsense if compelled to throw the offending rascal far into the sea.

Yes, I know that this is strong language, but what else can be done, if those boobs so far forget themselves and ignore the experts of the racing committee, the very men that we all should help, for they are appointed to a very disagreeable job, and while willing to serve and do their bit, they must be both respected and obeyed at all times and if not, then we must find out why not, for these good men must be obeyed, no matter the cost.

Here is an instance you will recall that on the first day of the big races, the pilots of some of our steamboats just lost their heads and came darn near causing serious trouble and loss of life, and this in the face of the fact that there were two government vessels present for the purpose of regulating the traffic to prevent disasters, and in spite of that, these damn fools with thousands of lives in their keeping, want to crowd the track, yes, even to cross the racing course if allowed, one of them, the *Lowell,* coming very close to having one of our destroyers open fire on her.   Heavenly Father!   How long is this thing going to be tolerated?

Our champion, *Enterprise,* made a lovely showing with her hull and that white mast towering 169 feet above her deck.   She often resembles a white-sheeted apparition—particularly in the filmy mists that frequent this coast.

"MUST BEAT VANDERBILT

"If *Shamrock* is to win the cup, she will first have to conquer the combination of wind, water and weather and after that she will have the tall and lithe figure of Harold S. Vanderbilt to work on.

"And Mr. Vanderbilt in the role of an opposing skipper is no bargain.

"Get yourself under his lee as we have remarked before, you may just as well be in jail.   If captain Ned Heard, Skipper of *Shamrock V,* gets away to a bad start and finds *Enterprise* to weather of him, he will need a flock of outboard motors to get him out of the predicament.

"When you are under Mr. Vanderbilt's lee there is nothing to say except that 'It's just too bad.'   No one can tell what sort of weather will prevail here during the week in September when the cup races are to be sailed.

"September is regarded by seafaring men here, which is to say, coast guards-men and rum-runners, as the most fickle and unreliable month of any one of the twelve. There may be days of dead flat calm and there may be days when if you were out there off Brenton's Reef—you might wish you had never been born.

"The best feature about the defending *Enterprise* is that she can take it on the chin from old man ocean and make an appearance of liking it.

"Despite the fact that *Shamrock V* sailed here from England under canvas, it is doubtful whether she will stand up under the racing and show speed under a blow.

"She has proved conclusively that she is good in light airs, but what she will do in heavy weather is something else again."

These comments are very fine and interesting and do not give *Shamrock V* the worst of the argument. But in all that is good and pious, what happened to *Shamrock V* between this day in question when she made such a notable showing under the watchful eye of Jack Lawrence? is what gets me. Were her people too damn confident in not giving her more practice and keeping that grand old boat in trim, or what really did happen to bring about the breaking of this grand old man's heart, bowed down in one defeat after another. He became full of grief that ultimately brought about his death, and Sir Thomas is no more.

"*SHAMROCK* IS A PUZZLE

"The Lipton Irish Yacht Astounds Critics by Sailing in Calm

"Newport, R. I., August 27th, 1930."

Under the above bold caption or head lines, we read a dispatch pub-lished in one of our evening papers of the above date, and this by one of our ablest newspaper experts, and one that I enjoy his writings very much.

The two writers just quoted are darned good experts and both mem-bers of the same club and when you see their names attached to an article you may be sure it has merit, for in all of my experience of more than fifty years along Park Row, meeting and knowing the most of these good fellows personally, and I take off my hat to them always.

WHAT HAPPENED TO SHAMROCK?

OUR AMERICAN CHAMPION

YACHTS BEFORE NEWPORT, R. I., LED BY COMMODORE VANDERBILT AND *RAINBOW*

Part V—Chapter IV

And here we are before Newport, R. I., September 7th, with Skipper Harold Vanderbilt who, in that same old true sportsmanlike spirit that he has shown all summer in sailing *Enterprise,* the sloop selected to defend the cup against the challenger, Sir Thomas Lipton's *Shamrock V.*

Yes, you can believe it or not, but Mr. Vanderbilt requested the men of the *Shamrock V's* afterguard to take a spin with him on the *Enterprise,* for the men on the *Shamrock* were busy getting things in shape to dock *Shamrock V* on Monday, and she was tied up at her moorings all Saturday.

Unfortunately, this prevented Colonel Neill and Mr. Nicholson from being able to go along, but several of Sir Thomas Lipton's friends accepted the very welcome invitation, and we find Colonel, the Right Hon. Sherman Crawford, and Major Brock Heckstall Smith enjoying the invitation and very much pleased to be present. Colonel Crawford is Vice-Commodore of the Royal Ulster Yacht Club of Belfast, Ireland, of which the Prince of Wales is the Commodore, and Sir Thomas Lipton is Rear Commodore.

Enterprise tried out her No. 3 mainsail and found everything O.K.

The following is the official measurements and record of races of both *Shamrock* and *Enterprise.* To wit:

MEASUREMENTS

Shamrock V		*Enterprise*
119.98	Overall length ....(ft.)	120.40
81.43	Waterline length ....(ft.)	80
19.66	Beam ....(ft.)	21.80
14.78	Draft ....(ft.)	14.49
20.72	Forward overhang ....(ft.)	20.40
17.83	After overhang ....(ft.)	20.00
7,524.10	Sail area ....(ft.)	7,540.00
2,956.70	Fore triangle ....(ft.)	2,679.00
4,567.40	Mainsail ....(sq. ft.)	4,861.00
4,779.00	Displacement ....(cub. sq. ft.)	4,494.00
546	Free board ....(ft.)	5.47
74.50	Quarter beam length.........(ft.)	73.32
76.00	Rating ....(ft.)	

RACE RECORD

Won 16	Won 11
Second 5	Second 12
Third 1	Third 0

I am sorry for the commitee of experts whose duty it is to pick a winner to carry the flag of defense. They have not been given a chance, not at all, for first one yacht would win, and then the other, and so it has been going on and to use a biblical expression, "The first shall be last, and the last shall be first," for *Enterprise* has swopped places with the *Weetamoe,* and this last race should decide the winner, for *Enterprise* defeated *Weetamoe* in her (*Weetamoe's*) own weather, in spite of the assistance given her at every point by *Yankee.* So, tonight the committee is all up a tree, for it was a known fact that *Weetamoe* was in the minds of many to be chosen defender; yes, right up until the finishing up of today's race *Weetamoe* was a great favorite and the betting on her was a one-to-five shot, but we all make mistakes, and they are in duty bound to make *Enterprise* the one-to-five bet if they know where they are at, but that is their business. I wish them luck.

On this run back to Newport the crews surely earned their salaries, for it was one continuous change of sail from the commencement of the race to the finish. *Weetamoe* watching *Enterprise* and *Enterprise* watching *Weetamoe,* for just as fast as the one would change the other would follow suit.

And the crew of the *Enterprise* had it on the crew of the other yachts. Why? Well, because Commodore Harold S. Vanderbilt gave up his time and pleasure to forward the launching of *Enterprise,* and by so doing giving the world a good chance to read of her activities, on the one hand, and also giving his crew four or five weeks' advantage over the crews of the other three yachts and that was a great assistance to Mr. Vanderbilt and *Enterprise* in all his contests of elimination, and he deserves great praise for his good, wise and efficient judgment.

What other man, let him be a rich bachelor or a rich married man, would take it upon himself to give up his time and money to forward an ideal? Mr. Vanderbilt did, and when he ordered sail to the value of $250,000 and a mast that cost $150,000 more, he showed the world that he was willing to spend his last dollar to win the glory of being the owner of the yacht to be chosen the defender against the wonderful yacht built by Sir Thomas Lipton, *Shamrock V,* and the writer expects to see *Enterprise* chosen.

You will recall that on more than one occasion Mr. Nicholson, designer of *Shamrock V,* had stated that *Enterprise* was the best yacht, even though several of our experts and many good Americans thought that *Shamrock V* was the best of the two yachts.

Then, why did Mr. Nicholson take things so easy before the races that were about to commence on September 13th? Was it not his business to see just what *Shamrock V* was lacking and make all necessary changes, so his much bragged of yacht, *Shamrock V*, would not have to suffer too much of a handicap when the appointed time arrived?

In my estimation, the men that were getting well paid by Sir Thomas loafed a hell of a lot when they should be at the master's work, and not be fooling the grand old man and his many friends, having them believe that there was nothing to the races but *Shamrock V*.

Someone of them has a lot to answer for the bringing about of that Lipton broken heart, and not a solitary man Jack of them able to explain; four richly paid doctors, two or three well paid secretaries, designer, and several captains. Sure, someone of them ought to be able to say what happened to Sir Thomas in his last moments.

And all this at the time that we were led to believe that he was then about to sail for New York, to leave London on October 2nd, and I to meet Sir Thomas and his party in New York on October 9th, 1931, by request of his secretary, John Westwood. I am sorry for having to repeat this gruesome story, but I cannot forget my grand old friend and what appears to me to be the base treatment that he received from those whom his hand had fed for many, many years.

But when I read over many of the very fine letters that have been written and printed about our old friend, I feel somewhat cheered, and I will quote a few of them to cheer you as they have cheered me. To wit:

"SIR THOMAS LIPTON TRUE SPORTSMAN

"We are proud of Will Rogers for having suggested that the American people present a loving cup to Sir Thomas Lipton as a farewell present in appreciation of his wonderful sportsmanship.

"Nothing finer could be done for this good man, with such a charming and happy-go-lucky personality, as was Sir Thomas Lipton, the Dean of the yachting world, and all around good fellow.

"There is no doubt that for the first time in sport's history, many good blue blooded Americans, maybe a majority of them, would prefer to have Sir Thomas and his beautiful *Shamrock V* lift the Cup, temporarily at least. We have admired his sportsmanship so much that we want to see it rewarded.

"And there is something else that most Americans would like to see, and that is that instead of the rules for the races specifying only a like construction of the racing hulls that they also require all rigging above decks be similar. This would make the races absolutely even, and would resolve it down to the seamanship of the skipper of the contestants, making all future races a test of skill.

"Americans have shown their sportsmanship by suggesting these changes, by their desire to see Sir Thomas win, and by the friendship expressed for him."

A word about Sir Thomas Lipton's expert commissioner at Newport.

But with all due respect to the gentleman in question, I often think that Sir Thomas might have been better served if this expert had stayed at home, for then Tom Lipton would have paid more attention to his yacht.

But, to hell with him that starts the next war, particularly at this one grand time of our lives, the good old summer time, for the last cursed war turned the world upside down, with their modernism, the rats are forgetting that they ever had a mother or a father, while they are going mad, spending the earnings of their damn fool fathers, now cold in their graves.

That cursed outburst of the Germans has left the whole world cock-eyed, high-hatted and bandy-legged, with a lot of four-flushers digging for fame among the former good people of our aristocracy in Newport, but hell from their souls, they will never be recognized, after stealing the yacht racing of our champions away from good old Sandy Hook.

But, that is the way all the time, put a beggar on horseback and he will ride to h—l, and there is no question about that, for they are going there every day, with others following them fast.

However, we must be satisfied, and live our lives over again, among a lot of featherbed soldiers, going to the last flare up unknown and un-cared for, returning with the Kaiser's Iron Cross tattooed on their —, well, it does not make any difference, they are called majors and colonels today. We take off our hats to the real soldier, but to hell with the fake soldiers.

But after all it might be well if we did have another war, to knock some of those wise guys off their high perch, and further enrich old man Bishop Cannon, Jr., and other dogs of that character, "touching on, and appertaining to" the question before the house, are you guilty, or not guilty?

Well, here we are folks, just starting in to make another week of history in the yachting world, for today starts the first of the great racing between the four new yachts that wish to be chosen our defender, and the two old-timers will be out, of course, you could not keep them in.

The past racing off Glen Cove and Oyster Bay does not give much to go by, a poor chance to get a real line on the yachts, but this week, well, you can rest assured of a good week's sailing and out on deep water, so that we will be in a better position to judge them fairly.

Well, folks, it is all over but the shouting, for *Enterprise* won her fourth race of the series of 1930, for seven races was the number to be raced and four winnings out of this seven won the series. Congratulations are due our champion, Harold Vanderbilt, and his pretty yacht, *Enterprise.*

And while it is but fair and proper to lionize Mr. Vanderbilt, we must not forget the feelings of that poor old man of yachtdom, Sir Thomas Lipton, the good old soul, and tender to him the nation's sympathy.

That poor old broken hearted Irishman took this beating to heart and sure who could blame him, defeated four out of seven trys, and he told that his yacht was a wonder from which he expected better results.

The outside public knew these things, but they did not know of the sad private life that he was leading. The very men that he was paying well, had none, or very little respect for him of late years, the Invisible Government.

The fourth and last race of this series was won by *Enterprise* defeating *Shamrock V* by nearly six minutes. Pretty hard on old Uncle Tom, but he tried to cheer up and forget it, but he could not, had he but won one race or made a decent attempt to win a race, but alas, no.

And now that these races are won and lost, let us get together and make the concern of one the concern of all, in spite of the hard feelings that unfortunately broke into these picayune races of elimination, for much had been said and done that never ought to be, but that's all past now.

Sir Thomas may try again, but I doubt it, not that he wouldn't enjoy the sport, not at all, man, but when you are paying others to do your work and do it properly, and you find them laying down on you, that is enough to break any man's heart, no matter how strong it may be. The sin of ingratitude is the worst sin of all, and some rascal, or rascals, at present unknown, are guilty of them all. So let us do the best we can to help our fellowman, and take over a wife and enjoy a beautiful home, for this darned bachelor life is hell. Confide your business matters and secrets to your charming wife and family, if blessed with same, and throw these dumb head-sniping secretaries overboard, unless an occasional one who has proved himself or herself. They are hard to find, but a good, fond, loving wife, a real American, housekeeper, can always be found, and your happiness complete, and some day you will be writing old man Hickey, whom experience has been proven to, congratulating him on his wonderful forethought. You have proven yourselves to be good honest gamblers, so take this chance before it is too late, for a faint heart will never win a fair lady. Goodbye and good luck.

Newport, R. I., September 18th, 1930.

The winning of these races this time by *Enterprise* defeating *Shamrock V* means that the New York Yacht Club scored their sixteenth victory in eighteen races against the Lipton *Shamrocks*, the five challenging yachts since 1899. Oh, boys! That is mighty hard on the Irish, but all is fair in love and war.

AND THIS IS HOW IT HAPPENED

Year	Defender	Won	The Challenger	Won
1899	*Columbia*	3	*Shamrock I*	0
1901	*Columbia*	3	*Shamrock II*	0
1903	*Reliance*	3	*Shamrock III*	0
1920	*Resolute*	3	*Shamrock IV*	2
1930	*Enterprise*	4	*Shamrock V*	0
Total		16		2

This is great history for we Americans, dear readers, but, we must give a mighty good cheer for Tom Lipton, of the lion heart, for he went forward to give battle to his friendly foes, with defeat staring him in the face, like his ancestors away back in 1767, when they went forward to fight the fight of the much abused and persecuted tenantry of Cloynes County, Monahan, Ireland, winning battle after battle against the thieving baliffs and the hireling Red Coats of Dublin Castle.

After which the Lipton "Ones," William, Robert, John and Thomas, were arrested, charged with high treason and found not guilty by a friendly and also persecuted Irish jury of Enniskillen, in the Emerald Isle.

So we live in hopes to see Sir Thomas proudly sailing with *Shamrock V* or *VI* across the mighty Atlantic ocean, perhaps next year, that of 1931, while attending the great World's Fair in Chicago, and may the good Lord guard, protect and watch over him, and land him again safely on our happy, prosperous and welcoming shores.

And with a few additions to *Shamrock V,* who knows but Sir Thomas may yet win the America's Cup, for the Will Rogers' loving cup he has already won, with the hearts and the love of the American people. Good luck, Sir Thomas.   Come again.

Many are asking today why Sir Thomas Lipton did not win the cup, with *Shamrock V* noted to be a very fast yacht, and she proved this while racing all of the biggest and fastest yachts in the British Isles, and as Teddy Roosevelt would say, "Beating them to a frizzle."

One cannot be blamed for asking such questions, for there is a deep and unsolved mystery connected, attached to this whole story, that must be cleared up before we will be able to answer that question.

But I have this to offer as an excuse, and after reading this statement over, you, too, may agree with me that something very strange happened and it was settled that *Shamrock V* was in the bag to lose, and at the appointed time it came to the surface, and like a meteor from a clear sky, all the world was dark and gloomy, at least so it appeared to Sir Thomas.

Here is a little inside news that may help us fathom this mystery that we are at present surrounded with.   Yes, it is not widely known that one of our greatest financiers, a yachtsman of the first water, and one known to have handled an sailed his own yacht to victory more than once and one who certainly understands and knows what he is talking about.

This gentleman of whom I write offered to buy from Sir Thomas *Shamrock V* after her defeat by *Enterprise,* September 13th, 1930.

And here are his reasons, to wit: If this man's offer is accepted, he will bring *Shamrock V* back to our shores and have her re-rigged and race her in Class J.   But God help Sir Thomas, he was sorely tried and unable to overcome his feelings, for he was sure that all was not well, alas, betrayed?

This great yachtsman in question is sure that when re-rigged and handled rightly, could beat *Enterprise* or any other big yacht on our coast at the time, and he surely must know something of what he is talking about for men of his character don't often put up a big wad of money on a losing yacht. It is said to think that such a beautiful sloop as was *Shamrock V* would sail a race so shockingly disappointing to her owner and his friends, that never once deserted him, and like myself, still has the same old faith in *Shamrock V* and none moreso than the very man we are reading and talking about, whose name for the present, must remain out of the story.

This good man also feels sure that something fearful was happening to *Shamrock V* the week before the start of the races for the cup, September 13th, 1930, and I quote this man as saying that "He was convinced that in the hunt for the America's Cup yast year, *Shamrock V* possessed more potential speed than any one of the four American yachts involved."

"I am absolutely certain," said this American yachtsman today, "that the *Shamrock V* was the best of cup yachts of 1930. She had the finest hull of them all. Yes, I think it was the finest racing hull I ever saw.

"It was a crying shame that such a perfect racing machine should have been ruined by the stupidity of those who were responsible for her rigging. It is probably a fact that her needlessly heavy mast was alone enough to ruin her chances. But to make a bad job worse, they attached a mainsail to that mast which, in my opinion, was even a still greater handicap. With competent rigging and proper handling, which she never had, I think she would have taken the measure of Mr. Vanderbilt's *Enterprise,* or that of any other yachts of 1930." What better evidence could we look for than the evidence of a sound, practical American yachtsman, who might have changed the whole complexion of this case had Sir Thomas and he come together, but such was not to be. The invisible government, that I have reasons to believe, was born after the bungling races of 1920, did not welcome any foreign interference. God forbid that I would judge any man, or party of men, wrongfully, but as you know many things have happened since the failure of Captain Burton to sail and win that third race July, 1920.

But murder will out, and we may yet receive some evidence as to why Sir Thomas should be made to suffer, eventually dying of a broken heart, sad to relate, after the many happy days and years prior to the cursed World's War of 1914 to 1918, bringing with it desolation that, thank Heaven, President Franklin D. Roosevelt, another yachting hero, is trying hard to abolish.

But alas, if prosperity returned tomorrow, we will never have the pleasure of greeting our dear old friend, Sir Thomas Lipton, among us again.

Peace be to you, Sir Thomas, for though gone to your happy home, your memory shall never be forgotten, either by friend or foe, but he never made an enemy. Like all good men, he had them among the high-hatted British snobs who despised a poor man; nursed and petted by the royalty.

THE SAFE ARRIVAL OF *SHAMROCK* V AND CREW AT PORTSMOUTH, ISLE OF WIGHT

PART V—CHAPTER V

"I am sure that you will all be glad to learn that the *Shamrock V*, owned by Sir Thomas Lipton, and beaten in the races for America's Cup in 1930, arrived safely in Southampton, England, today, October 22nd, after a hard, stormy passage of twenty days, and without an escort, Sir Thomas being detained here.

"Under Captain Paul, who sailed the *Shamrock V* to America, and Captain William Paul, of Greenock, that sailed the *Shamrock V* back home, and the crew were well received by the people of Portsmouth, for the bad news had traveled ahead of them of the bad storms that started in just as they were pulling out of American waters and lasting all the way.

"Captain Paul said it was far from being a pleasure cruise, for we were bothered the day after leaving Newport, R. I., losing our wheel, that is, our steering wheel was blown overboard and we were forced to rig up boards to protect the man at the wheel and keep a sharp eye on them so they, too, may not be blown after the wheel.

"You understand I believe that many of the crew of the *Enterprise* sailed as members of the *Shamrock*, and while they did not have a day to themselves going over, they are leaving for Norway and Sweden, their former homes, there to spend and enjoy their earnings and the bonus given them by Sir Thomas Lipton, and will return next spring.

"*Shamrock V* will be rushed to drydock, looked over and laid up until next spring, for I am pleased to say that we might see *Shamrock V* again under sail in both British and American waters, for she is far from being satisfied, and asks for another chance, and that she is entitled to.

"For under the new rules adopted by the two racing committees, that is, the New York Yacht Club, and the Royal Belfast Yacht Club, there must be no more mechanical yachts, for they must build a mast that will weigh not less than five thousand five hundred pounds, and all machinery for raising or lowering sails must be kept above deck and accommodation for the crews must be provided for on all yachts that will be built from now on, to be in a position to sail for the America's Cup, or to defend the same."

That is all good news and should be pleasing to most anyone connected with sport, for these boys had an awful voyage over. My word!

With your indulgence I will quote an editorial taken from one of New York's famous dailies, to wit—October 19th, 1933.

"SOPWITH CHALLENGES

"At last there is to be an international yacht race with the yachtsmen the pilots, assuming that Mr. Harold Vanderbilt or some other amateur is at the helm of the American contender for the famed America's Cup.

"Sir Thomas Lipton was an admirable, in fact, lovable figure, and dauntless. But now England's yacht is to be piloted by her owner, a man who won his first laurels as an aviator and taking up yachting only a few years ago, immediately showed a great natural gift for it.

"It is he, Thomas O. M. Sopwith, who will pilot his pretty yacht, the *Endeavour*, now being built for him, against the best that America can offer next September, 1934.

"Sopwith, a man of solid achievement as a foremost English airplane designer and manufacturer, is a natural born sportsman and no armchair commodore, hiring a skilled professional skipper.

"The projected new contest for the ancient America's Cup will be insured of mechanical equality through the barring of the trick masts, winches and other deck equipment which gave America's *Enterprise* the edge over Sir Thomas Lipton's *Shamrock V.*

"With the sloops held to basic equality by advance agreements and understandings and with amateur helmsmen skippering them, the races next year, lacking the glamor which the great name of Lipton gave past races, will yet be more thoroughly representative."

There you are, my heroes, I have paid great attention to the copying and wording of this editorial. It is for you to judge, for my opinion may vastly differ from yours, and I have never been charged with being an expert critic, but in this, I am speaking for myself only.

But I must say that the ballyhoo that always followed the late great Irish Baronet and lover of the noble sport, was more or less the outcome of his honesty and charming personality, and we are not all worthy of this great honor, but Sir Thomas Lipton was never selfish, and he died so others could and would take his place. Peace be to him.

So that we will not forget, let me say to my good friends that we have with us still the Houses of the Morgans and Vanderbilts, and if England has a fast yacht to send over, before Starling Burgess and Boyd Donaldson get through we, too, may have a very fast yacht that will be able to go Charley Nicholson and his *Endeavour* one better.

We have defeated Nicholson and his yachts before, and it would not surprise me for a moment that history may, or will repeat, for as long as they did not let their old friend and standby, Tom Lipton, win the cup, they are not going to let Tom Sopwith walk away with it, not by a darn sight. But fate is often very contrary, for often we find that after a fellow builds a house others enjoy it. It is between them it is, may the best yacht and designer win.

THE PASSING AWAY OF COL. ARTHUR LYNCH, IN NORTH LONDON TODAY MAKES THESE EPISODES MORE INTERESTING THAN EVER. SUNDAY, MARCH 25th, 1934. R.I.P.

Episode Number Three

I am sure, dear readers, that this, my third episode, relating to the Lipton "Ones," namely, Sir Thomas, who is with us today, will please you all, for it speaks of our own times, and the hero of this story we all know so well, and is today stopping in his suite, in the Biltmore Hotel of this city, and will be, it goes without saying, delighted to read this story when published in the biography of Sir Thomas, and his doings in the yacht races of the past, particularly those of 1914, postponed to the year 1920 because of the great World's War, and the races for the America's Cup of 1930, the greatest trophy the world ever knew of.

My story opens in the City of London in 1902, an aftermath of the late Boer war that cost England so much in the loss of men and finances in the year 1899, she (England) winning the war by good judgment and long, careful waiting.

It so happened that a native son of Ireland, born in Australia, who had seen much service fighting under the flags of other countries, namely, Colonel Arthur Lynch, of the famous Irish Brigade, whose glorious flag, the grand old green flag of the Emerald Isle, has seen service on the battlefields of almost every country since time immemorial, always ready to take up arms against England, who at that time held their own country, Ireland, by the throat, and whose fighting ability was known and respected since the days when Patrick Sarsfield, the Earl of Lucan, led them into battle in the service of France in the year of our Lord, 1689.

Colonel Arthur Lynch, the possessor of a stout Irish heart, thought that now was the time to strike against their own bitter and common enemy, and he mustered his men, and being commissioned by "Oum Paul," the President of the Transvaal government, with his Brigade sailed for Capetown.

And on arrival there was met by President Oum Paul, who in a short address welcomed the men of Ireland, whose services would be deeply appreciated by their brothers in arms fighting for liberty, plans of action being drawn up and orders given to Colonel Lynch, they quickly made for camp and prepared to take the field in short order. They fought hard and often, in a spirit of revenge, only to be tried, found guilty and ordered to be shot.

HISTORICAL LETTERS OF IMPORTANCE

I quote from the letter mailed to the editor of the New York "Herald-Tribune" of November 30th, 1927, by Colonel Arthur Lynch and published on that same day, to wit:

"FROM COLONEL ARTHUR LYNCH

"Story of His Liberation; His Ideal of English Speaking Concord.

"To the *New York 'Herald-Tribune'*:

"In your issue of October 25th last you published a cable from London concerning my trial and the intervention in my favor of President Roosevelt. I wish to thank you for the correction thus given to the false version in Sir Sidney Lee's 'Life of King Edward VII.'

"That book is so smeared over with sycophancy and cant, that it is of no value, but my object in writing is to remind you of two names, both held in honor in the United States. Sir Thomas Lipton and the late Michael Davitt, for without these, the story would be incomplete.

"Mr. Davitt wrote a letter to Sir Thomas urging my release, and that letter was shown to King Edward. The King discussed it with Sir Thomas, who in that genial but effective style of his, won him over and induced him to move for my liberation. The King was so pleased with his own part in the matter that he begged to keep Michael Davitt's letter.

"I write as a great admirer of America and Americans, among whom I have many dear friends. One last point may interest you in this regard. The cable message says that I am writing a book in which will be 'set forth the idea that the English-speaking countries are all individual republics.' This is not quite accurate. The book—'The Rosy Fingers,' a title taken from Homer's image of the dawn—will advocate, not that the Dominions are republics, but that they ought to be and soon will be. The ideal which stands before my eyes is a ring, federation, or, as I prefer to call it, a concord of free republics, including, of course, Ireland, united for defense alone; that then this concord should form a working cooperation with your own great republic for the maintenance of the peace of the world. This is one of the practical conclusions of my book, which is founded on my previous philosophical work, particularly the psychology and the ethics, of which its represents various practical corollaries.

"ARTHUR LYNCH,
"London, England, November 17, 1927."

By special permission of Sir Thomas Lipton, I quote the following communication in the matter of the liberation of Colonel Arthur Lynch, and by whom same was brought about.

"NEW YORK 'HERALD-TRIBUNE' LONDON OFFICE
"Harold E. Scarborough, London Correspondent
"Bush House, Aldwych, London, W. C.
"23rd January, 1928.

"Sir Thomas Lipton,
"Waldorf-Astoria Hotel, N. Y. C.
"Dear Sir Thomas:

"I am informed by Colonel Arthur Lynch that you had some difficulty when you attempted to secure from the 'Herald-Tribune' office in New York a letter written to the editor by Colonel Lynch, and published on November 30th, 1927.

"I am sorry that the hitch arose in New York, but I am enclosing herewith from my own files a copy of this letter.

"Yours faithfully,

"H. E. SCARBOROUGH."

Copy of letter mailed to Sir Thomas Lipton by Colonel Arthur Lynch:

"80 Antrim Mansions,
"Haverstock Hill, London, N. W.
"August 22nd, 1929.

"Dear Sir Thomas:

"Herewith I return the letter you gave me last night, with the article from the New York 'Herald-Tribune.'

"It was very interesting reading, bringing back as it did memory of the old days when your intervention with King Edward was of such great benefit to myself; you may be sure that I shall never forget that kindness, although I know it was a part and parcel of your invariable goodness of heart. Needless to say (Nan), Mrs. Lynch, feels just the same about it.

"The name of Lipton is honored before all others in this house.

"Wishing you a happy time in America and hoping to see you next time able to dance an Irish jig, instead of having to go slow on an injured knee.

"Yours for ever,

"ARTHUR LYNCH, *also* ANNIE LYNCH."

Col. Lynch passed away in a London, England, hospital.

I vividly recall an editorial published by the late John Devoy, "I Am Guilty," my Lord (Johnny Devoy) in the ("Gaelic American") of March 7th, 1914, in which he called Col. Lynch a traitor, and lots of other bad things, but if this was coming from the pen of any other writer but Devoy, it would be more readable, but now it is the forgotten man.

Here we have another one of those very fine letters of approval, coming from the pen of one of Sir Thomas Lipton's dearest and closest friends, of more than thirty years, of which I am proud, to wit:

"New York, March 2nd, 1934.
"Captain J. J. Hickey, Grand Union Hotel,
"34 East 32nd Street, City.
"Dear Captain Hickey:
"I have yours of February 28th. In the first place, as you tell me, you are writing these letters personally. I am sorry I put you to so much trouble, and at the same time I wish to congratulate you on your efficiency as a typist, as well as of your literary ability in setting forth the facts you mention so clearly and logically.
"I will be very pleased to see you, as you suggest, whenever you may be in this neighborhood.
"Thanking you for your good wishes, which I certainly reciprocate, and with my kindest regards, I am,
"Very truly yours,
"John Doe."

That, my friends, is a letter that any man may well be proud of, and it coming from the mind of one of New York's greatest lawyers, whose name, for the present. I will keep in abeyance, for reasons best known to me.

P. S.—I am very much pleased that your name has been entered on the books of the Irish Historical Society for membership, proposed by that very eminent attorney at law and former Justice of the Supreme Court, the Hon. Justice Daniel F. Cohalan.

"OSIDGE, SOUTHGATE, LONDON, ENGLAND.
"15th June, 1931.
"Mr. J. J. Hickey,
"Hotel Elton, N. Y. C.
"Dear Mr. Hickey:
"Sir Thomas, who at the moment is very busy cleaning up in the yachting races over here, beating all before him, advises me to write you and to thank you in his name for the many fine cuttings that you are compiling and mailing to him. Many of them are very interesting and from which he gets many a good kick out of, reminding him of the happy past in little old New York, that gave him his first start in life. Hoping this will find you well and fit.
"Fatihfully yours,
"John Westwood."
"OSIDGE, LONDON,
"October 21, 1930.
"Mr. J. J. Hickey, Hotel Elton, N. Y. C.
"Dear Mr. Hickey:
"Very many thanks for your letter just to hand and the many important enclosures it contains, among the many statistics from the very fine cabinet that you should be proud of, I am mailing them to you by registered mail for I know how you highly prize them, and I don't blame you for asking they be returned. I thank you for letting me see them.

"I am not quite sure, but I think Sir Thomas will be sailing aboard the *Leviathan* for New York. I will notify you by cable later. This is private.

"Trusting that you are well.

"Faithfully yours,

"JOHN WESTWOOD."

"OSIDGE, LONDON.

"October 10th, 1931.

"Mr. J. J. Hickey, Hotel Elton, N. Y. C.

"Dear Mr. Hickey:

"At the moment I have not yet located the article that you speak of, published in the 'Evening Journal' of July 12th, but will again go through that vast cabinet of news matter sent to Sir Thomas by you, and when found I will run off a copy and send original to you. Sir Thomas and myself are looking forward to our meeting you shortly. Hoping you are well,

"Yours faithfully,

"JOHN WESTWOOD."

The article in question was a mighty interesting one, and like others lost, would have pleased Sir Thomas mighty fine, if given to him first, but no, the "Major Domo" had to read them and lay them one side, forgetting his duty to his employer, that grand old sportsman, but this was not the only one.

I hold all letters and correspondence, even to the letters that passed between my father and good old Nat Langham, who fought and defeated Tom Sayers, an old friend of my dad, away back in the sixties, for in this age of gold-diggers and bad men it is necessary to be very careful and avoid the many gay and other deceivers, old correspondence often is of value, and will save many dollars and loss of night's sleep.

Be advised by one who might have suffered had he not have held on to all correspondence; a word to the wise, never throw anything away in the shape of letter for figures do not lie, for one can never tell what is in the future, and often an old, crumpled up letter will protect you, and one does not need a lawyer to tell the truth. Be your own lawyer. Keep a fellow out of jail and prevent scandal, in all its forms, principally one's character must be protected at all times.

The reasons that I write this stuff here is because Sir Thomas Lipton delighted in "reminiscences" and he, too, delighted in telling his story every time the opportunity permitted, often telling of the night that Jack Dempsey knocked Firpo out of the ring and into the arms of Sir Thomas at the ringside, and other notable incidents; he was always so interesting and ready to tell a story, often saying, "Mr. Hickey, I would sooner stay home with my old friends and talk about the past, than have to dress up and attend the many functions that I am called upon to attend. I am always happier in the company of old friends, 'For kind words will never die.' "

And in conclusion, my friends, please be advised by me in the matter of keeping old letters and what might ever be of use in later years, for if in trouble, and we all get that sometimes, either legally or illegally, but when it presents itself, you may refer to your savings and be your own adviser and if called to court, then you can plead your own case, for one don't need a lawyer when telling the truth.

For in many instances the lawyers are fighting against their clients, as I found it to be in my police case, $500 to put you out of the job, and $1,000 to put you back, for without the aid of correspondence they have you, both coming and going, just as in the case of an ex-judge, when a lawyer about the old Tombs, he would take all the money the prisoner could raise and when the money was all gone, say, "You had better take a plea, for you haven't got a Chinaman's chance. TAKE A PLEA, JOHNNY."

Now, dear readers, in closing this book of books, it might be as well to know our grand old former Chief, always on the alert, to wit:—

One of his many friends wrote him just before the opening race as follows: "Dear Sir Thomas, you must win these coming races for I have sold my home and bet every dollar on *Shamrock V,* and if you don't win I have to go to the poorhouse."

Sir Thomas answered, "Cheer up, old Pal, you had better hire a berth for me also in the poorhouse, but will do our best."

GOOD NIGHT.

HEARTY CONGRATULATIONS, COMMODORE VANDER-BILT. BETTER LUCK NEXT TIME, COMMODORE SOP-WITH.

AUTHOR.

CPSIA information can be obtained
at www.ICGtesting.com
Printed in the USA
BVHW04s1706091018
529699BV00009B/53/P

9 781163 148228